# Foreword



## WHY THIS BOOK?

There are a number of books available on 'International Relations'. However, this is a subject that needs constant updating and revision. The last decade has been one of fundamental transformation that has radically changed the world economic and political order. Some of the factors behind this are:

* Economy becoming as important as military power in national security.
* Globalisation and interdependence leading to cooperation as well as competition and conflict.
* Multi-polarity changing the world economic and political order.
* Trade getting significance in inter-state relations.
* Mounting role of non-state actors in international relations.
* Terrorism increasingly affecting regional stability.
* Overarching reach and impact of Information Technology.
* Spread of media, especially the alternate media, becoming a player in the foreign affairs.
* Climate change becoming a global threat.

While these factors were gradually making the earlier books on International Relations outdated, the Ukraine war that started in 2022, and the Gaza conflict which erupted in 2023, have proved to be so disruptive in world affairs that all the existing books on International Relations have suddenly become totally redundant. These were unexpected events and are still going on with unpredictable outcomes. And hence it has become imperative to make a complete review of international relations in the context of these recent developments, as well as of their inclusion in the book.

Since the book keeps consistent focus on India on all matters, the outcome of these events as well of the general elections of June 2024 have also been included in the book. Hence, this book becomes the most updated among all the others on the subject.

Writing a book on International Relations is a challenging task because of the multilayered nature of the subject. While factual narration of the issues is essential in a book on International Relations, this book is primarily an endeavour to analyse the causes and consequences of the events that shaped our present times. This analysis has been done not only from the political point of view but also from the social and economic aspects, because the three are interrelated. This book also correlates how developments in one part of the world affect the global system as a whole. Hence, international relations have been treated in an integrated manner because with the dawn of the modern age, the planet has turned into one global village.

Another reason for revisiting the subject of International Relations is that with passage of time, the perspective changes. Thus, how we view a historical event undergoes a transformation, and opinions held some years back do not hold good any longer. The characters who shaped the events of history were products of their times. They acted in a particular way in accordance with their views that were shaped by the circumstances of their time. They did not have the benefit of hindsight, but we do have the opportunity to review. And hence, there is a need to take a second look into our past, to analyse why and how things have come to the present stage. Thus, a fresh scrutiny and appreciation of the evolution of international relations has been done in the context of our present times.

The analyses and interpretations presented in the book may appear controversial, politically out of line, and even outrageous. Academicians may not agree with the views expressed by the author. One reason for this can also be that it is uncomfortable to move out of the traditionally held opinions. Nevertheless, differing opinions can always be held and differing views can be argued. All such views may also be correct from their own differing rationale and perspectives. The intention in this book is simply to make the reader to understand, and to think with an open mind, and not to pass any final judgment. Time is its own final judge on events, and hence, the judgements also keep getting revised with the passage of time. It is so because it is the present that decides how we judge the past. Further, we have no inkling as to how the future is going to unfold.

The book makes us aware of our shared past, and of the processes that interconnect them. It serves as a warning as well as inspiration, to know when to stand up for what is good for us, and against what we should know is not. It helps us to better understand the changes that are happening at present and contribute towards changes for a better future. Since the present is always too fast moving, it seems to in an unstable state of constant flux. History of international relations provides us the tools to analyse and decipher the emerging patterns that might otherwise be invisible in the foggy mist of our present times. A fresh interpretation has also become necessary because unless we keep learning the lessons of History, we stand condemned to suffer the consequences of its repetition.

What makes this book unique is that practical suggestions have also been offered

# INTERNATIONAL *Relations*

*India's challenges for the 21st Century*

**AJAY SHUKLA**

S. CHAND
PUBLISHING

**S Chand And Company Limited**

**(ISO 9001 Certified Company)**

# S Chand And Company Limited

**(ISO 9001 Certified Company)**

S. CHAND PUBLISHING

***Head Office:*** D-92, Sector–2, Noida 201301, U.P. (India), Ph. 91-120-4682700

***Registered Office:*** A-27, 2nd Floor, Mohan Co-operative Industrial Estate, New Delhi – 110 044 | Phone: 011-49731800

**www.schandpublishing.com; e-mail: info@schandpublishing.com**

**Marketing Offices:**

| | | |
|---|---|---|
| Chennai | : | Ph: 23632120, chennai@schandpublishing.com |
| Guwahati | : | Ph: 2738811, 2735640 guwahati@schandpublishing.com |
| Hyderabad | : | Ph: 40186018, hyderabad@schandpublishing.com |
| Jalandhar | : | Ph: 4645630, jalandhar@schandpublishing.com |
| Kolkata | : | Ph: 23357458, 23353914, kolkata@schandpublishing.com |
| Lucknow | : | Ph: 4003633, lucknow@schandpublishing.com |
| Mumbai | : | Ph: 25000297, mumbai@schandpublishing.com |
| Patna | : | Ph: 2260011, patna@schandpublishing.com |





***First Edition 2025***

**ISBN:** 978-93-6468-462-0 **Product Code:** H1IRE47PLSC10ENAA25O

PRINTED IN INDIA

By Vikas Publishing House Private Limited, Plot 20/4, Site-IV, Industrial Area Sahibabad, Ghaziabad – 201 010 and Published by S Chand And Company Limited, A-27, 2nd Floor, Mohan Co-operative Industrial Estate, New Delhi – 110 044 on certain problematic issues, especially those that concern India. Whether these see the light of the day or not is another matter. But it does make the reader to think. This book is an attempt in this direction.

## ORGANISATION OF THE TEXT

Composing a coherent book on International Relations is a daunting job because of the complex multidisciplinary nature of the subject. Today, here are about 200 independent nations each having its own history, culture, geo-strategic position, power, economy, social and political structure, etc. Since it is not possible to separate the past from the present, international relations become intrinsically tied with history. However, it is difficult to decide how much historical back ground be given before coming to the current state of affairs. On the other hand, without the historical context, the present cannot be fully understood and appreciated. Hence, a compromise has been made to give the historical backdrop briefly to explain and analyse the present.

Further, many events keep taking place in different parts of the world which have significance to a particular nation or a region. However, all such developments cannot be incorporated in one comprehensive book. Hence, only the issues that truly impact the overall international situation have been taken into account. Nevertheless, as the sub-title of the book suggests, particular attention has consistently been maintained on all issues that concern India.

Another challenge about international relations is that political factors and economic factors often take different, even conflicting roads, and sometimes the two are intertwined. Each nation has its own concerns and interests. There is cooperation as well as competition and conflict and several crosscurrents too, depending on the issue. The whole picture needs to be presented in an integrated manner because it is not possible to segregate each of the various issues into water tight compartments. Hence, effort has been made by way alternating narration, to discuss the themes separately as well as concurrently, while keeping the narration of chronology also in mind. In such an exercise a little bit of repetition has been unavoidable because events of one region often influence the developments in other regions too. Certain repetitions have also been deliberate, as reminders.

There is also the dilemma about the extent to which a theme can be elaborated upon. If one goes too much into the details, then the reader gets confused and loses the big picture, a case of missing the wood for the trees. On the other hand, being too brief leaves many questions unanswered. It was difficult to strike the right balance.

Many of the issues of International Relations are shaped by socio-economic structures and political ideologies like democracy, totalitarianism, liberalism, nationalism, capitalism, socialism, et al. Even though these fall fundamentally in the realm of subjects like Political Science, Economics, or even Sociology, the basic principles of all these ideologies have been discussed at length in the book because these are interrelated and eventually shape the inter-state relations of nations. The actual application of these basically academic concepts has been discussed in the context of our present times, with specific reference to India.

Most of the books on International Relations tend to be excessively West-centric. This to some extent is inescapable because USA and Europe play a vital role in shaping our epoch. Nevertheless, effort has been made in this book to bring about a composite picture of the modern age and important developments of different parts of the world have been discussed. Further, special attention has been given to India and its relations with the world powers as well as with all its neighbours.

## A NOTE FOR THE CIVIL SERVICES' ASPIRANTS

While this book would be fascinating to the general readers who are keen to understand the origin of the current international issues and how these affect us, it also provides the basic reading material for the graduate and post-graduate students of International Relations. The book would be of particular interest and use for those appearing for the higher competitive examinations like the UPSC Civil Services Common Entrance Examination because it covers the entire syllabus of International Relations part of the Political Science & IR Mains paper. Further, the book has addressed all the questions that have been asked in the last ten years. However, the aspirants need to remain in touch with the developments of the current affairs because the situation in international relations takes wild swings from day to day.

The aspirants should keep this in mind that the Civil Services examination is not looking for mere theoretical knowledge about a subject among the candidates. It is not a test of memory because it is expected that the aspirants have already acquired a good knowledge of their optional subject. This examination is to select officers for the highest of the civil services in the country, and those who get selected come to hold most responsible positions. Eventually, as they reach the higher echelons of bureaucracy, they become the policy makers of the country. Thus, it is the ability to critically analyse complex subjects, and above all, to express an independent and logical opinion on the given challenges that becomes decisive in such an examination. Hence, while the book provides the fundamentals of the subject, emphasis has been given to analysis, with special focus on India.

In the Civil Services Examination, candidates are expected to express their own views, and not those of the textbooks. The more original and independent the view the better, because it shows that the aspirant has applied his/her own mind on the subject, formed an opinion, and has the courage to express it, even if it is unconventional and unorthodox, because that is what this examination is looking for in the future officers of the Civil Services. And so, do not be constrained by the traditional views. Aspirants need not agree with the views given in this book either; they can take an independent stand on the issues.

However, while original and unconventional views are appreciated, it must be remembered that whatsoever view is taken, the same must be supported by logic and analyses. Merely expressing an off-beat observation may not cut the ice. When your opinion is asked for, you are not to state just your likes and dislikes. And you certainly should avoid being judgmental about personalities and events. You have to reason out as to how you evaluate an issue. Try to start the answer by giving the gist of your stand in the very first sentence, and then give your reasoning for the same. Or else, start with analysis and end up with the stand taken in the closing sentence.

On many issues two very different views can also be argued, without coming to any final conclusion as to which stand is correct, because both views may be right from different perspectives. If a clear stand cannot be taken for such reasons, then state the same, and give your logic why a final view cannot be taken. That is, you can always state that a conclusive view cannot be taken at the present stage, because of the unpredictable nature of international relations, rather than let the examiner feel that you do not have a view. The examiner must get convinced that the candidate has fully evaluated the issue before expressing the opinion.

It is also to be noted that in such examinations, the candidates are required to answer in a specified number of words, and as such, the answers have to be precise. Hence, do not clutter that space with historical data. Concentrate on the analytical part, and on your interpretation about the facts.

From all these aspects, this book is certain to be the mainstay for the UPSC-CSE aspirants.

**AJAY SHUKLA**

# List of Maps

# Table of Contents

# Chapter I

# International Relations: An overview

International Relations are understandings, adjustments and dealings between governments of nations with each other in bilateral, multilateral and global terms. The study of International Relations is an endeavour to examine and interpret how various factors shape the policies - foreign as well as internal - of nations, and how their interaction with other nations shapes the global order. It helps to analyse how the worldwide system affects a state's behaviour, and conversely, how independent actions of nations in the international sphere affect the common citizens of the nation, as well as the global community as a collective. It helps us to understand the relationship between the governments and the non-government organisations within a state, as well as between international organisations with each other - as autonomous bodies independent of government control - and how this interface influences the foreign as well as domestic policies of a nation, and often determines the same.

## ALLIANCES AND GROUPINGS

While each nation has its own individual and specific needs and concerns, depending upon its national ethos, popular culture, history, political structure, ideology of the ruling regime, economic compulsions, and its geo-strategic position in the regional and global environment, some of these concerns are often shared by other nations. On the basis of the nature of concern, nations establish bilateral relations with other nations. These can be ceremonial - by way of summit meetings of heads of the governments, joint statements of resolutions, cultural exchanges, and agreements on specific issues. These can also be in the form of formal treaties.

On issues of common interest, nations also form groups to join hands and work together for mutual benefit by sharing information and pooling of resources. These groups can be in the form of regimented alliances like NATO; non-binding conceptual associations like QUAD, ideology based non-committal associations like the Non-Alignment Movement (NAM), or may simply be round table platforms - like clubs - to facilitate communication, consensus and cooperation. More than often these groupings are a result of strategic rivalry and are formed more for messaging, positioning, and posturing, rather than for any concrete action.

While security remains the prime concern of each nation, there may be other issues of disquiet as well in the neighbourhood that need resolution by joint effort. On issues of regional character like illegal migration, settlement of refugees, interstate connectivity and mobility of goods and peoples, area specific organisations like the European Union (EU), South Asian Association of Regional Cooperation (SAARC), Association of South East Asian Nations (ASEAN), Organisation of American States (OAS), the Arab League, and the African Union (AU), are formed for harmony and unified action.

Some issues are global in nature, like epidemics, terrorism, drug trafficking and climate change. Inability to tackle such problems on their own forces nations with conflicting interests and ideologies also to come together on open platforms as there is no other way out. These are dealt at forums like the United Nations Organisation and its subsidiary agencies. Some issues are sector specific or thematic, mainly economic, like trade and tariff, customs and taxation, currency exchange, and these are dealt by organisations like OPEC, GECF, WTO, G20, G7, SCO, BRICS, etc. While these are basically economic groupings, there are always political overtones in such groups. There are also contradictions between the political alliances of a nation from its economic alliances.

The Organisation of Islamic Countries (OIC) is unique in the sense that it is based on religion.

Groups are also formed by powerful nations to establish - or at least to exert - their own hegemony at the regional and global level. During the Cold War period USA and USSR formed coalitions like NATO and Warsaw Pact as a measure of security as well as to flex their muscles. As a rebuttal of the concept of a bi-polar world, India sponsored the Non-Alignment Movement (NAM). With the disintegration of the British colonial empire, Britain revitalised the Commonwealth of Nations to retain its own diminishing influence over dominion status nations - which kept the British crown as head of the state (Canada, Australia, New Zealand, etc.) - as also among the newly independent sovereign nations like India. It was mere allegorical exhibitionism, more to satisfy - if at all - the sagging British ego rather than for any good to any member nation.

Besides the security concerns and other benefits, nations join groups also because they do not want to be left behind and get isolated, and even to prevent some rival nation from becoming too powerful by being a member or leader of a group. Thus, during the September 2023 summit of the G20, India played a major role in getting the African Union admitted as the 21st member, not so much to help Africa but more to stress India's role as the leading power of the Global South.

Even as nations share many common concerns, **each nation is guided by its own interests** and conducts relations in multilateral platforms to serve its own ends. This also brings nations into conflict and disagreements with each other on strategic as well as economic issues. Hence there are always splinter groups within the groups, and each nation steers its own course of action because ultimately each nation has to solve its own problems. This has made International Relations stand apart from international politics in the sense that while politics is essentially the pursuit of self interest, international relations is the means to serve the same. It may even be a façade to obfuscate the real intent.

At the international level, nations are also under peer pressure to follow the collective disposition of the group they belong to. This also brings seeming inconsistency between their national policies and their group postures. For example, while most of the Muslim countries today have friendly bi-lateral relations with India - for trade and strategic reasons - they ritually pass resolutions against India whenever they sit together in the meetings of Organisation of Islamic Countries, more as a symbolic gesture of camaraderie rather than as a policy matter. This is because many of these nations are undemocratic and their leaders want to retain the allegiance of the domestic orthodox ulema and the uneducated masses. However, they refrain from criticising China for its repression of Uyghur Muslims because they do not want to annoy China. Similarly, they remain silent about Russian action in Chechnya. Nevertheless, most of these countries keep their relations with India intact and India also does nothing beyond routinely rejecting their joint resolutions.

The **structure and nature of the groups** also keeps changing with time. This may be due to the changes in the domestic politics of the nations and also due to changes in the international environment. The European Union has evolved after going through several incarnations, the process having started around 1923. With time its scope, value, and membership has expanded. At the same time, some groups have lost their significance in the modern era as these are of little benefit to member nations in the current state of affairs. With the disintegration of USSR in 1991, the Warsaw Pact too collapsed. India, the founder of the Non-Alignment Movement, has put the concept of non-alignment into deep freeze and has replaced it with that of 'strategic autonomy', which in simple terms means that India can have dealings with any side where its interests are served, irrespective of ideology. The Commonwealth of Nations too has become merely a ritualistic annual jamboree as there neither is anything common among the nations nor any wealth in the membership.

Often when a nation feels that the group is not serving its interests, it leaves the group. For example, Britain left the EU in 2020 after being a member for decades. (British relations with EU were always tenuous. While many politicians did not want Britain to join the EU, there also were European nations that did not want to admit Britain into the Union. Britain entered the EU half heartedly, and with great effort, and then left it abruptly.) When a nation feels it needs to join a group, it strives for the same. Since the beginning of the Ukraine war, certain European nations are striving to join NATO for security reasons, and Finland and Sweden have recently joined it. On the other hand, Russia has joined hands with China and North Korea giving a serious challenge to NATO. Nations are also expelled from groups when they go against the group policies. Thus, Syria was expelled from the Arab League in 2011. (Syria was re-inducted in 2023.)

There is nothing new about formation of groups and alliances between states to serve common interests. The battle of Mahabharata was fought between two massive coalitions. Alexander's army was another grand coalition of dozens of Greek states. Since Sparta did not join the coalition, Alexander made it a point to be recorded in history in order to depict Sparta as a traitor to the Greek cause. Various wars, including the two world wars, have been fought between coalitions. In the modern age, democracy and economic factors have widened the scope of alliances and made international politics much more complex and multi-layered.

## TRANSFORMATION OF DIPLOMACY

The ancient and medieval ages were periods of autocracy, and economic or social issues were not matters of state concern. National security, territorial expansion, regional hegemony, military supremacy, and loot were the primary factors that shaped the foreign policy. State policy was decided by the despots, basically to secure their own power, prosperity, and position. Diplomacy was the preserve of an aristocratic ruling clique and was conducted in secrecy without involving the common citizen. Hence aggrandisement, glorification of national identity, and strategic security in the neighbourhood remained the pillars of foreign policy. In this scenario, large and powerful nations - the empires - dictated the world order and smaller nations had to play the second fiddle in the role of client states. There was no international order to rein in the aggressor or any rules of the game in international affairs.

However, the two world wars have brought forth the need and importance of an **international order**. At the same time, and partly as a consequence of these wars, **decolonisation** and fragmentation of several multi-racial states during the last century has resulted in emergence of a large number of sovereign states. Today the number of nations is more than twice as compared to a century back. The smaller states may not be powerful but are no more pliant silent spectators in the international arena. They have an **equal voice** in the UNO and in other forums and they can obstruct a powerful nation from taking control of a group. The less developed among them are also a consumer market for the richer nations as well as a fertile ground for neo-colonialism. Many have natural resources like rare earths which the developed countries need. (Chile and Bolivia are the largest sources of copper and lithium.) Hence powerful nations also want these smaller states to stay in the mainstream and remain as partners and protégés within a group. This has changed the international environment and is still constantly changing the same.

While power of the army was the deciding factor for the **strategic security** of nations in earlier times, many other factors have also become equal or even more crucial for the security of nations in the present era. To name a few, oil and food have become critical in the modern times and are also used as tools to conduct the gun-boat diplomacy of power politics. For long, USA and Britain used political power for controlling oil production in the Middle East. To overcome this situation the Gulf nations formed OPEC as an instrument of diplomatic leverage and are still holding the world oil market to ransom.

As an alternate measure, USA and some other nations use economic sanctions instead of military power as a mechanism to brow beat rival nations like Iran and N. Korea. These measures have become most evident during the war in Ukraine and we find that while USA has imposed selective sanctions against Russia, Russia in retaliation is using curbs on export of foodgrains through the Black Sea as its own method of exercising power. Neither side is concerned about the havoc this conflict is creating in the food deficient nations - nations that have nothing to do with the politics of this war.

Another tool of exerting influence in the modern era is the use of **soft power**, and India is among the foremost among the nations to utilise it. Perhaps this is also because India lacks in military and economic heft and uses soft power as a substitute. This is done through cultural exchanges, by aggregating the Indian diaspora, by emphasising common heritage where applicable, and by helping nations - even hostile and/or insignificant ones - in their hour of need. During the Covid crisis 2021-22 India gifted/ exported vaccines to more than 100 countries irrespective of their significance or their disposition towards India. In February 2023 India sent a team of the National Disaster Task Force to Türkiye for rescue and relief after a massive earthquake hit the nation. This was despite the constant anti-India stand of the Turkish President Erdogan. India got no thanks from the arrogant President, but such steps contribute towards image building of the nation. It also points to the limitations of soft power.

Democracy, globalisation of issues, economic interdependence, and the media, has further added to the dynamics of the growing complexity of contacts between nations. It has forced nations to cooperate despite intrinsically being in conflict and has made international relations inter-disciplinary in nature. While international relations remain an exercise of power within the global system, it is no more the exclusive preserve of the governments. Although international relations are still conducted by the governments, these have become too complex to be conducted behind closed doors by a clique of diplomats. Modern means of transportation and communication has also changed the way diplomacy is conducted. The heads of state and foreign ministers travel and personally establish contacts and conduct international relations. Electronic devices also have brought leaders in direct constant contact. There is also behind the scene back channel Track 2 diplomacy conducted between nations.

## DEMOCRACY AND FOREIGN POLICY

In monarchies and dictatorships policy decisions are taken by the state and the non-state actors have a secondary or negligible role in foreign affairs. It is either the ruler (Saudi Arabia), the dictator (N. Korea), the army (Pakistan) or the ruling political party (China) that shapes the foreign policy. However, even despots and dictators have to take care of the domestic mood, or create a domestic mood, to keep control over their subjects. For ages the autocratic rulers exploited religious and racial factors to serve their own vested interests. From the 19th century, racial identity was portrayed as nationalism and the emotive illusion of patriotism was used to gain legitimacy by the monarchs. This also influenced the foreign policies of nations and the First World War was to a large extent driven by the jingoism of public opinion, in democracies as well as in monarchies, by making nationalism and patriotism an obsession by the ruling dispensation.

In democratic nations, the political parties are the principal players in the power structure. Politics is a thriving business in democracy. Party units are politico-corporate entities that function as resource raising and disbursing enterprises. Elected representatives are proprietors of these quasi private limited companies and hence control over the whole business by a family or a coterie becomes crucial. Party workers become employees in the politics of cash flow because elections need money.

Most of the **political parties** are basically intermediaries or brokers and they are either controlled or at least have to cater to the needs of their benefactors - the donators - many of which may have a stake in foreign policy too. At the same time, political parties have to be in line with the popular mood of the voters. The democratic governments have to play a very delicate balancing act of satisfying the needs of specific groups and aligning with the public opinion at the same time. When the two are at cross purposes, political parties try to sell the proposition of the beneficiary to the peoples. If they fail in the endeavour, they have to go by the popular mood because ultimately winning elections is basic to a political party. The party out of power is of no help to its sponsors. While the political parties are primarily concerned with domestic electoral politics, they also shape the foreign policy when in power. Thus conduct of international relations intermingles with the fields of economics and security and the activities of domestic politics like elections.

Domestic electoral politics in democracies also affects international relations in distorted ways. To cite a few examples, certain political parties in the neighbouring countries like Nepal, Bangladesh, Sri Lanka, and Maldives, take a very anti-India stand just to win local popularity. When they win elections, the relations with these governments become tense even though India has generously helped the neighbours. Even in Britain, the Labour Party has started taking an anti-India position to win local Muslim votes. Similarly, the Justin Trudeau government in Canada has been hostile to India simply to win the votes of migrant Sikhs. These nations have no reason to oppose India as there is no conflict of interest. Nevertheless, it happens just because of democracy.

In democratic countries the **parties** in **opposition** also play a role in shaping international relations, especially in economic relations. Corporates - domestic as well as foreign - and foreign governments keep a watch on what the opposition stands for, because the opposition is the ruling regime in the waiting room. Business houses want continuity and consistency of policies and laws. Abrupt changes or the possibility of a sudden reversal of policies and laws is a serious deterrent in investment. One major reason why western nations invested heavily in China and made it a superpower was that the western corporate houses knew that the communist party was firmly in power and there was no possibility of a change in the regime. Hence, they could calculate the long term returns on their investments.

The **opposition parties in India** have recently become very aggressively vocal against the business class. They advocate redistribution of wealth and opportunities on the basis of caste, region, and religion. Due to high level of unemployment, such election-oriented sloganeering has gained considerable traction among many sections of the electorate and even the ruling party is coming under pressure of such demands. Opposition parties also demand many changes in laws that are against the spirit of WTO. In fact, the farmers' agitation has demanded that India should withdraw from the WTO. Such developments in India's domestic politics are being viewed with extreme anxiety by the industrialists as well as by the investors. Even if the ruling government brushes aside such demands, everyone apprehends that today's opposition may be the ruling party in future.

It also needs to be seen how little the persons holding the reins of the governments understand foreign affairs of the modern era in a holistic sense. Elected politicians can be very ignorant of the history, economics, and a myriad of other factors of their own country that shape international relations, what to speak of their knowledge about other countries. Some take their portfolio too casually and instances of faux pas are common. In February 2011, S. M. Krishna, India's foreign minister, started reading out the speech of Portugal in the UNO. In 2009 US President Barrack Obama read out the speech of the Irish Prime Minister! There have been occasions when heads of governments have forgotten the names of their counterpart during meetings. Many cannot even locate a nation in the globe.

Hence, it is always the office of foreign affairs that provides continuity and stability to the policies of a nation. However, since foreign affairs have become multi-faceted, several ministries - besides defence - that deal with matters like commerce, industry, communication, environment, etc., also get involved. This brings in conflict between ministries of the same government. The defence ministry may be hostile to a nation while the commerce ministry may be favourable to the same nation. Hence it is always difficult for a government to coordinate and have a unified approach in international affairs. This makes the role of the head of the government - the President/ Prime Minister - pivotal in the conduct of foreign policy.

**Emotive factors** related to civilisational culture and history also play a vital role in the politics of the society and hence foreign policy is also guided by the social ethos and political ideology of the governments and the political environment of the nations. Some of the conflicts, like those in the Middle East, are so deep rooted in history that the past totally overshadows the present and blackens the future. At the same time, domestic socio-economic compulsions are increasingly making historically emotional and ideological dogmas irrelevant, and diplomacy of external affairs has become a tool to serve internal concerns. Hence, emotive factors are more for local consumption and used as tools to serve material ends. This brings in the elements of hypocrisy, duplicity and ambiguity in the policies of nations.

## ECONOMIC INTERDEPENDENCE

Money has always been the source of power, and kings and warlords could exercise power only if they had the money to muster up an army. Land was the main source of wealth in the earlier times and hence expansion of kingdom was a prime objective of the monarchs. Hence, they used the army to conquer and colonise weaker states, and loot and corner sources of wealth to increase their power. Small but rich trading states which did not have armies of their own hired contingents of mercenaries from outside for their security. This is still the scene and in fact today it is difficult to separate strategic interests from the economic interests. Rather, the leverage of economic muscle has become more powerful than intercontinental nuclear missiles because it can be used universally and on a sustained basis.

While economic power has become a part of the strategic arsenal, land is no more the prime source of wealth. Today, nations become rich by producing valuable goods which need **scientific excellence** and technical expertise. However, modern gadgets have become so complicated that no nation can make all the components of an appliance. One smartphone or a laptop has almost a thousand tiny components. These are manufactured by almost a hundred different companies spread over dozens of countries. The software and the various Apps that make a mobile phone useful are equally spread out. Apple is a unique manufacturer in the sense that it has no factory: It only assembles the phone and provides the software. In fact, no country can today manufacture any sophisticated machine or gadget on its own. This has led to **interdependence of supply chains,** which in turn has changed the character of the very concept of national security.

A tiny country like Taiwan - not recognised as an independent sovereign nation by most of the countries - is the global provider of semiconductors. It produces over 60% of the world's semiconductors and over 90% of the most advanced ones. Rockets, drones, fighter jets, satellites, decryption systems, in fact, all electronics systems require semiconductors. Even cars and refrigerators need chips. Hence China, which does not even recognise Taiwan as a nation, trades with it because the Chinese industry cannot do without Taiwanese technology. Similarly, while USA and China are at loggerheads on all strategic matters, neither can afford to decouple their economies from each other.

**Relations between India and China** have remained tense for decades and there is no solution to the border dispute in sight. Yet they are among the largest trading partners. India is the pharmacy of the world, yet almost 80% of the Active Pharmaceutical Ingredients (API) - the raw material for drugs - comes from China. In fact, India is so dependent on China for various items that if China wants to choke India it need not send its soldiers to the border: It only needs to stop export to India and India will come to a standstill. However, China has a trade surplus of about $100 billion with India per year and any such move would be as destructive for China. Hence, while constantly provoking India on various issues, China cannot afford to go beyond a limit in the mutually destructive hostility. Nor can India. The Indian government may ban certain Chinese apps for public expression of retaliation but the overall trade, as well as the trade deficit, is only increasing.

Take oil for another example. India is among the largest importer of crude oil. At the same time it is also one of the largest exporters of petroleum products because of its surplus refining capacity.

The situation is similar for all nations and none is fully independent. **Advanced technology** is limited to handful of companies in a handful of nations. Development of high-end core technology needs an eco-system of multi-disciplinary scientific research and financial appetite to bear the cost of multiple failures. Hence patents and Intellectual

Property Rights have become vitally important and no one wants to part with this knowledge. Similarly, critical raw materials are also in certain specific countries. While China is the leading manufacturer of batteries (about 80%), a key component of electrical vehicles, it has to depend on Chile, Bolivia, Australia and Argentine for Lithium. There are several other metals that are equally important. Hence, we live in an age where international cooperation is a compulsion because of the interconnected globalised system, and commerce has become politics by other means.

Many nations, especially of the West, have become concerned that **overdependence on China**, particularly in the field of electronics, is not only an economic issue but also a security issue. Chinese gadgets are also tools of patent theft, espionage and surveillance. These can even be used for sabotage by way of cyber attacks. Today, nations do not need a James Bond to steal secrets through microfilm cameras or documents. It can be done simply by hacking into the cyber world sitting at home. Hence cyber security along with data storage and data protection and has become a part of the defence strategy.

Western nations are trying to get out of the Chinese web but it is very complicated. For one thing, developing technology is not easy and also takes time. Secondly, private companies of the western world have invested heavily in China and their products are sold all over the world. Hence, they have deep stakes in China and cannot simply pull out. Since these companies are also donators to the democratic governments of the western nations, the governments too find it difficult to take a radical step. The third problem is the lack of alternative.

At the same time, cutting edge technology is also used by advanced nations as a weapon of dominance. This is also a part of **soft power**. For one reason, much of the technology is in private hands and companies hold patents and Intellectual Property Rights and do not want to share the same for economic reasons. They have invested a lot to develop these and want to maximise their profits. Another reason is that governments also do not want to share or transfer high end technology to other nations, and are very protective about the same. This also leads to theft of technological knowhow. It started with the beginning of the Cold War. USA developed the first atom bomb, and while it shared this knowledge with Britain and France, it did not share the same with USSR. In turn, USSR used communist sympathisers in Britain and USA to act as spies and the nuclear secrets were passed on to USSR. Today, China is the master thief at large in the field of piracy, plagiarism and pick-pocketing of technology.

## DOLLAR AND DEBT DIPLOMACY

Nations adopt various strategies and use different instruments to achieve specific objectives and the whole endeavour constitutes the foreign policy of a nation. The tools and the objectives can be economic, political, and military, and these interact in complex ways. Economic heft can be used to achieve political goals while military power can help achieve economic objectives. While diplomacy through communication is the standard method of establishing international relations between governments, there are other instruments also known as the passive or non-confrontational modes of conducting foreign policy. Helping other nations in their hour of need, developing infrastructure like roads and bridges, protecting valuable national resources, etc., are common tools that achieve both political and economic objectives.

Economic tools can be protectionist or liberal. Protectionist economic tools are embargoes, high tariffs, punitive anti-dumping duties, and quotas. Conversely, liberal policies mean free trade so as to make profit out of foreign markets. During the 17th and 18th century, slaves, spices and textiles were the principal items of trade and these made Portugal, the Dutch republic, and Britain world colonial powers. Britain also thrived in the trade of tea and opium to become a world superpower. Gold and silver were the currencies of international exchange. With the beginning of the 20th century, oil became the most critical commodity while dollar became the world currency of exchange. This made USA a superpower and radically changed the international power equations. USA also loaned huge amounts of money to nations around the world to gain political leverage. It also controlled the World Bank and the International Monetary Fund and thus had a financial influence over a large number of nations. Nations also kept their sovereign reserves in dollars, and this made them dependent on USA.

US dollar is gradually losing ground. This is partly because USA is no more the economic power it once was and partly because nations are cautious about keeping their sovereign reserves at the mercy of USA. When USA imposed sanctions against Iran, it also froze Iran's money in the US banks. Similar action was taken recently against Russia. Hence nations have started reverting back to gold as far as their sovereign reserves are concerned.

On the other hand, China has embarked on a major offensive by giving huge loans to a very large number of smaller countries. China has clout in SCO (Shanghai Cooperation Organisation) and is also using its own money for this new brand of neo-colonialism. It has sponsored the Belt and Road Initiative (BRI) and as a result many small nations are becoming indebted vassals of China. These nations need money and technology to develop infrastructure like roads, ports, etc., and they have no choice. However, this is not sustainable because China's own debt has become huge. On the other hand, peoples of the indebted nations are reacting to this novel form of subservience to China. (There have been many attacks on the Chinese nationals in the debt-ridden Pakistan.)

Even more powerful are **multinational financial institutions** like the World Trade Organisation, the World Bank, the International Monetary Fund, and large international private banks. These are more powerful than smaller nations and often dictate the domestic policies of indebted nations. Rich and powerful nations try to capture these organisations and use them to further their economic and thus strategic interests. US Financial Institutional investors are also powerful entities. They invest in foreign capital markets and can intervene in the economy of a country. [FPI holding in India's capital market is about 20% and their buying/selling seriously impacts the stock market, and hence the entire economic environment.]

These developments in the international economic arena have led to disagreements regarding trade deficit, balance of payments, anti-dumping duties, exchange value of currency, and tariff rates. Today, negotiations on these issues are quite like fighting a war. Container ships have taken the shape of battleships and trade pact discussions are like negotiating a peace treaty. Nations use every ruse to protect their economic interests and use non-tariff barriers - like carbon footprint and use of child labour - as weapons of economic warfare. Hence, national economy is increasingly emphasising the interaction, coordination and cooperation between businesses and the government. Political parties also understand the linkages between economic problems like poverty and unemployment and their political decisiveness in electoral democracy. This is bonding the domestic policy with the foreign policy.

Nothing is permanent in this fast changing global scenario except permanent geo-political interests and economic concerns. Historical legacy has lost much of its meaning except as a reminder and a lesson, but not as a baggage. Hence nations change their stand as per the needs and also remain ambivalent and ambiguous on several issues when necessary. Sailing on two boats and change of horses in midstream is not uncommon in international affairs today.

## NON-STATE ACTORS

In the modern age a large number of non-governmental institutions and individuals - called as the non-state actors - have thus become important and equal stakeholders in the foreign policy of a nation and play an active role in the conduct of international relations. These non-state actors are private sector companies and banks, political and religious leaders, media and business tycoons, writers, powerful collectives like think tanks, non-government organisations called NGOs, amorphous expert groups, and influential individuals. Many have a foothold in several nations and are also called as **transnational actors.**

There are also paid lobbyists and professional agitators who can be hired to mould national policies to suit the vested interests of certain groups. *While these predominantly play a role in the domestic matters, they also influence the policies of the governments on international matters. (It is interesting to note that during the recent farmers' agitation, a section of the activists demanded that India withdraw from the WTO.) In fact, globalisation has blurred the distinction between domestic and global issues. Many of the multinational corporate conglomerates influence the policies of not only the mother nation but also of foreign countries. These factors have altered the traditional dimensions of international relations which concentrated on security and peace.

*There has been a lot of hair splitting by academics to distinguish between **Interest groups** and **Pressure groups**. Members of an interest group have some common interest while Pressure groups are specifically created to address political or policy issues. Thus, while an interest group uses politics to serve its end, a pressure group may be for a political end by itself. Whereas interest groups just want to promote their interest, pressure groups want to compel the government to adopt a policy which may serve the interest of any group they want. Hence, they can be hired to serve the interest of any group or party.

While an interest group may or may not have a strictly formal organisational structure, pressure groups are more formally organised. An interest group uses subtle and manipulative tactics to promote its interest like lobbying, petitions, letters and deputations to ministers and officials. Pressure groups apply coercive strategy for the same. This may include public protest meetings, street demonstrations, advertising, industrial strikes, campaigning for, or opposing, certain candidates at elections, and finally, legal action through courts. Hence, while interest groups can function in democracies as well as autocracies, pressure groups are usually not permitted in autocracies.

While the prime objective of the government may be strategic, and basically international in nature, like balance of power through collective security, the purpose of others may be domestic - economic, political, and even religious. Sometimes the governments and the non-government institutions work in coordination for common purposes and complement each other. Many a times the various non-state actors are guided by different concerns and pursue conflicting goals. This not only creates conflicts among different political parties but also creates divisive cleavages within a political party. Hence, while foreign affairs are officially conducted by the legitimate and recognised governments of the states, these are also driven by a whole gamut of non-state actors.

Here a special mention needs to be made about the so-called **non-profit making NGOs**. While these bodies are ostensibly involved in charitable and humanitarian activities, these are munificently funded by various groups, individuals as well as governments for pursuing different agendas. Some of the evangelical bodies of USA and Europe are richer than MNCs. Many are involved in religious activities that involve conversion as well as subversion and radicalisation. Some also try to influence elections in other countries.

India is a prime victim of such NGOs. (George Soros, an American multi-billionaire, pledged an enormous amount of money to defeat the BJP during the elections of 2024.) When the government tries to check their activities, they are capable of raising international outcry on the pretext of protection of freedom of speech, democracy, and secularism. Many are sponsored by large companies to sabotage economic growth of other nations by stalling projects in the name of protection of environment, bio-diversity and ecology. These are hence often vehicles of foreign intervention through covert and subtle means.

Worldwide communication systems, like mobile phones and Internet connectivity, which includes systems of international payments like SWIFT, are controlled by private entities, mostly of western countries. Corporations like Apple, Microsoft, Google and Twitter (now X) are as powerful as nations. In fact, while oil was the new gold in the 20th century, data is the new oil of 21st century. Whoever controls the **flow of data** also controls power. Most of the Internet connectivity is through inter-continental undersea cable networks. These are laid and maintained by private players. And Internet is a tool no nation can do without. Hence, cutting submarine cables has become a new method of warfare, as Houthis are doing in the Red Sea. They are also targeting ships and the anchors of the sinking ships is scrapping and damaging the cables.

Data storage has also become as important as data protection. The Big Tech companies keep data in their corporate offices and hence are a security concern for other nations. Countries like India want the data of their nation to be stored in their country. Besides the technical problems involved, the companies are reluctant to do this for commercial reasons. Same holds good for encryption technology. Private players have also launched satellites and many nations depend on them for various purposes. Elon Musk refused Ukraine the use of his satellites during the war with Russia while the western nations denied Russia the use of SWIFT for financial transactions. This shows that private actors are as much players in the international arena and can also bring nations into conflict.

There are also a large number of specific purpose international and inter-governmental organizations that act in parallel on their own. Various agencies of the United Nations like the WHO, UNICEF, UNESCO, UNHRC have taken a life of their own and act as autonomous bodies. These are engaged in numerous socio-economic and political activities and influence policies of nations all over the world and seriously undermine the role of governments. There are also humanitarian organisations like the Amnesty International and the Red Cross, climate activist bodies like Greenpeace, religious bodies, cultural organisations, and other sectoral institutions like the International Olympic Association. These non-political bodies are also used for political purposes. Nations regularly use sports as a battleground and boycott of international events and banning of certain countries from participating in games is a common occurrence.

Most of such organisations are controlled by white western nations and have their own biases and hidden agenda. The Press Freedom Index released by Reporters Without Borders in 2023 rated India at 161, nine ranks below Taliban ruled Afghanistan. The World Happiness Index placed India at 126th position, below bankrupt Pakistan, Sri Lanka and Myanmar. Western politicians use these dubious agencies and their coloured reports to attack targeted nations and their governments to serve the economic interests of their sponsors. The white race is yet to come out of colonial mindset of moral superiority and finds it difficult to treat nations of emerging economies like India as equal partners. While posing as champions of democracy and national sovereignty, they do not hesitate to criticise democratically elected political parties of other sovereign nations. Ever since BJP has come to power in India, it is described as a 'Hindu' party many of such groups. (The BBC always calls BJP a Hindu party.) While it makes little difference to India, it puts irritants in the conduct of international relations.

## DIASPORA AND IMMIGRANTS

Many of the nations today have a sizeable number of religious and racial minorities, immigrants, refugees, and asylum seekers. The number has increased substantially in the last century due to globalisation, job opportunities abroad, and displacement due to conflicts. Many of these have become legitimate citizens of the host country, and in some democracies, they also have got voting rights. Others may be transient workers. While they live in these countries, they continue to retain their cultural and ethnic identity and affinity to the country of their origin. Hence their allegiance may not always be in line with the foreign policy of the government of their residing country. Whenever a crisis comes up, they exert their own pressure on the governments to modify its foreign policy.

While they may be small in numbers, they unite very quickly and take to streets to air their protest. This is all too often seen whenever there is a conflict in the Middle East. Europe and America have a substantial Muslim population. They want their governments to side with the Muslim nations irrespective of the issues involved, and despite the overall interest of the host nation. During the recent Gaza conflict, Muslims have held protest marches in Europe and America in support of Hamas. The western nations cannot support a terrorist organisation like Hamas and also cannot ignore the mass demonstrations.

On one hand, this has a political angle. The Labour party in Britain has come out openly in support of the Muslims because it wants their votes. The ruling Conservative party is aware of the political consequences of such a polarisation, but finds it difficult to alter its overall foreign policy. On the other hand, there is also the fear that radicalisation of such minorities may be a security threat to the nation itself. USA and Europe have suffered from several incidents of Islamic terrorism at home. Whether appeasement would calm the situation or dealing it with a firm hand would be better is a dilemma. While some nations have tried to soft pedal on the subject, USA and UK have adopted a two pronged approach: Oppose Hamas terrorism while supporting the Palestinian civilians who actually are the ultimate victims of Hamas terrorism.

**Indians** form perhaps the largest diaspora in the world. Some 30 million persons of Indian origin live abroad. In the Gulf countries, they outnumber the locals. Although they do not have citizenship rights, and Gulf nations are in any case not democratic, yet they provide the workforce without which these nations cannot survive. They also establish people-to-people relationships and help the host nation to have a better and more benign understanding of India. Prime Minister Narendra Modi has effectively used this leverage and always addresses the Indian community abroad whenever he visits a foreign country. This has tremendously helped in improvement of India's relationship with a large number of Middle East nations. The recent release of 8 Indians who had been given death sentence for spying in Qatar is a perfect example of this relationship.

Indians also form the most educated and the most well-off minority in USA and in certain other nations. They are a part of the soft power that India exercises. While they do not matter much in electoral politics, they do matter to the nations in economy. Indians head some of the most powerful multinational companies like Microsoft, Google and IBM. These CEOs interact not only with the top leaders of USA but of other nations as well. As a community, Indians are seen as law abiding and peaceful peoples and have become respected citizens in their host nations. Many have also entered politics and are pulling weight far above their size. The fact that an Indian (Rishi Sunak) became the Prime Minister of Britain, and many Indians are now eying for the presidentship of USA is a pointer of the things to come.

Cricket is gaining popularity in USA because of Indians. In June 2024, the T20 World Cup was held in USA (co-hosted by West Indies) and the US team that shockingly trounced Pakistan had as many as 7 Indians. Deepavali is regularly celebrated in the White House and is also a holiday in many of the US states. All these developments have changed India's image and has helped India manage its international affairs better.

Thus, whether by being valuable or volatile, the immigrants do play the role of non-state actors in international affairs.

## TERRORISM AND REGIONAL INSTABILITY

In the last few decades, terrorist groups have also emerged as powerful non-state actors in many parts of the world. These may be autonomous, like ISIS, Boko Haram, and Taliban, or may be protégés of other nations, or more often, a blend of the two, like Hamas, Hezbollah, and the Houthis etc. These radical Islamic groups want to take over political power in the Muslim nations. These militant groups influence domestic politics as well as international relations and are a major cause of regional instability as terrorism has introduced the element of asymmetric warfare by means of cyber attacks, surrogate operations, and state sponsored terror strikes through proxies.

Iran is a prime sponsor of such groups in the Middle East. The recent attack (on 7th October 2023) by Hamas on Israel has started a war which has the potential of escalating far and wide because Hezbollah and Houthis have also joined forces, all three being funded and supported by Iran. The ruling regimes of the powerful Arab nations like Saudi Arabia, Egypt and UAE are wary of these terrorist groups for domestic reasons but also refrain from opposing them openly as they do not want to appear to be against an Islamic group. Rich Gulf nations are also aware that destabilisation in the region would be economically disastrous for them. Houthis' attacks on shipping in the Persian Gulf have seriously affected the revenue Egypt earns from Suez Canal. But these nations cannot come out openly against Islamic terrorism. Such cross currents have turned the Middle East into a muddle.

Pakistan, being the cradle of world Islamic terrorism, has any number of such state sponsored groups which work to damage India by indirect means. However, terrorism is a monster that cannot be controlled. Hence, there are also several groups that attack the state of Pakistan from within. This has not only made it difficult for India to have friendly relations with Pakistan, it has also turned Pakistan into a failed state. It has tense relations with Afghanistan, itself ruled by a terrorist group (Taliban), and is also creating tension with its mentor China.

Similarly, there are Khalistani subversive groups in Canada, UK, USA and Australia which aim to damage India from abroad. These are primarily funded by Pakistan and China, and by certain religious associations. While they have no following in India, these are able to create tension in India's relations with the concerned countries. Many so-called human rights' group have their own agenda and support such factions, often to attack or undermine the governments of their own countries.

While USA has consistently used CIA, and the erstwhile USSR used KGB, to interfere in the internal affairs of other nations, newer methods of interference have emerged in the last few years. China uses private companies, especially in the field of electronics for surveillance and espionage, and the Chinese diaspora spread around the world is obliged to do the same for the Chinese government. Russia now uses the Wagner group - a private army of mercenaries funded by Russia - to increase its own influence and the group has even staged coups in certain African states, the most recent being that in Niger. There are many other such mercenary groups that are used by nations to not only interfere in other nations but even to topple the legitimate governments and provoke civil strife within nations.

Drug trafficking is another integral part of international terrorism. Be it Afghanistan, Pakistan or Myanmar, drugs and guns go hand in hand, one used to fund the other. In South America, drug cartels have their own private armies and run parallel governments. These factors have led to regional instability in many parts of the world, and as a consequence, are forcing peoples to flee and immigrate to some neighbouring country. As a consequence, immigration - legal as well as illegal - is causing tension between USA and Mexico while immigrants from the Middle East and North Africa have become a crisis for Europe.

This has complicated the conduct of international relations, especially in democratic nations. Hence **public opinion** is playing an increasingly important role in foreign policy. Peoples are actively participating in decision making through lobbying in the social media as well as through street demonstrations.

## MEDIA IN THE MODERN AGE

Blooming of the media in 21st century has changed the way people and the nations interact. It started with the live coverage of Iraq war by CNN in 1991. Today there are thousands of news channels, a TV in every house-hold, a CCTV camera in every nook and corner. Everyone is connected, live, 24x7, on internet, Facebook, WhatsApp, X, Instagram, or some other social-media platform. Everything is being watched, shared and reported. The all pervading media presence has made the world community come closer on an inter-connected, open, free, and democratic stage. This is drawing attention to issues that could easily be covered up earlier, but can no more be ignored. Public pressure is being exercised on political leaders and other stake holders as never before.

In this age of information revolution, everyone has become a stake holder, a claimant as well as a champion of rights and responsibilities. The **common man has become empowered** as never before because of the internet and the social media, also known as the alternate media. The principals are being made accountable, not just to their own peoples, but to the world community through the media. Nations, and their political leaders, cannot afford to remain detached from critical issues, and they do not want to be shamed before the prying eyes of the world community at large while sitting on an international dais.

The media often also offers acceptable options and viable solutions. While it cannot take a direct action on its own, when leaders refuse to heed or respond, the media however has the power to do the worse. It can ridicule the most powerful and put them to embarrassment. A whistle blower like Julian Assange of WikiLeaks can expose a powerful government as that of USA. And those in power do not want to be ridiculed or humiliated, not before the world at large, and particularly not in front of the people they claim to lead. The people whom the leaders represent also do not want their leaders to be ridiculed, and hence demand more responsible behaviour from them.

This is bringing a better sense of accountability among the leaders. Media is also helping interaction even when the leaders want to shut off communication. Even the rogues of first order among the world leaders try to put up the pretence of being a gentleman before the cameras. They smile in front of press photographers, shake hands with their sworn enemies, and even hug each other. They are forced to talk, and release press statements to convince the world that they are sensible and responsible persons who genuinely desire to resolve issues.

Often nations even try to conduct international relations through the media. Like quarrelsome girls who are not on talking terms with each other, leaders post messages on the social media to their counterparts. This is also known as **public diplomacy**. (Whenever there is a change in the government in Pakistan, the new Prime Minister posts a message on X that he wants to improve relations with India - provided the Kashmir issue is resolved. The message is clear that he cannot do anything without the approval of his army.) On the other hand, a single wrong word may be as damaging as a bomb.

In a way, the media is acting like a parallel UNO, trying to effect functions that even UNO often finds difficult to accomplish. It is integrating the world community on one platform. However, media, like any other soft power, has its limits.

It is well said that one who controls the media controls the mind. Napoleon is said to have stated, 'Four hostile newspapers are more to be feared than a thousand bayonets,' and imposed strict press censorship. Most authoritarian states have some sort of censorship. Even democracies put limitations on the freedom of press. [It would be interesting to point out here that the First Amendment of the Constitution in USA gave extensive freedom to the press while the First Amendment of the Constitution of India placed restrictions on press.] However, it is difficult to control the media in the modern age. Thus the information revolution can also be called as **information anarchy** and the media can have immense destructive influence. This is because the new information technology platforms have the muscle power of a street mob.

These computerised tools can be, and actually are being, used to manipulate reality, and thus manipulate the individuals as well as the society as a whole. Much of the social media today works on algorithm based software. Thus, Artificial Intelligence is used to promote consumer goods by guiding the user's choices towards sponsored products. At the same time, it is also used by politicians and radical groups - religious, leftists, as well as rightists - to provoke conspiratorial and alarmist thinking by evoking our baser instincts of insecurity. Emotional issues are turned into moral issues and moral outrage is inflamed through fake news, morphed pictures, misinformation, surrogate advertising, and hate speech, whereby naming and shaming becomes a game, and even a hobby. Artificial Intelligence in the social media can also do much damage without intention or human intervention because it has a half-baked brain of its own.

Media is also being used by governments as well as by non-state actors to intervene into the internal affairs of other nations. It is used to create an alternate narrative, to mould the public opinion and mood. Thus, the Big Tech can, and does, influence elections in democracies. The smaller fries want a level playing field in what is fundamentally an undulating terrain. Hence, the extensive reach of media, especially the television, makes it an ideal weapon in the hands of the owners to push the opponent into a corner by other means. Misreporting, cover ups, ghosting of events, and biased analysis is all too common.

The Media, however, also needs a reality check. Firstly, how much the reporters actually know the truth or understand the issues is questionable. Reporting is one of the last choices among career options but anyone with a smartphone can become a reporter, a YouTuber, and an 'influencer'. Secondly, the media houses decide the policy and have their own predilections and prejudices, often due to vested interests. They sensationalise as well as sanitise news. Hence while the media demands and brings transparency, reality is not that transparent.

Al Jazeera is fully owned by Qatar - a haven for all Islamic terrorist groups - and hence supports these groups. Even the BBC is not independent. Private companies of Islamic nations pay the BBC for advertisements, and in return the BBC never uses the term 'terrorist' for Islamic groups. BBC refused to describe the Hamas attack on Israel of 7th October 2023 in which some 1200 civilians - old women and children included - were killed as a terrorist attack. Pakistan sponsored terrorists in Kashmir are described as 'freedom fighters' and Khalistani separatists as rights' activists by the BBC. The BBC also launched a vicious campaign against the Conservative party so that Rishi Sunak loses the elections of June 2024 in UK just because he is a Hindu. So much about freedom of press, and of the fourth pillar of democracy being neutral! In fact, the fourth estate has become the fifth column against democracy at many places.

The democratic states are particularly vulnerable to media attacks. Media is used to influence elections as well as to provoke agitations and civil discord. While Pakistan, and subversive groups within it, uses media to inflame communal conflicts in India, China and Russia use it as a weapon against the western democracies. At the same time, these nations have put strict restrictions on the use of internet. However, despite all efforts, it is difficult to control the web and we see pictures of human rights violation being perpetrated in China, Russia, Iran and Afghanistan. This creates suspicions and tensions, and thus, in many contrarian ways the media is also influencing international relations.

## THE DARK WORLD

This brief last para of the very first chapter of this book should be taken as a disclaimer, and an admission of ignorance. Much has been written, and would continue to be written, about international affairs all around the world. However, as pointed out in the previous sub-chapter, we know, or believe that we know, is what others - the governments and the organisations - want us to know, or want us to believe, or want to make us believe. This is because in diplomacy, as in all other things of importance, truth is the last in importance. In fact, since the stakes are too high, it is the result and not the truth that matters. So much of all the activities take place in a dark world of which we come to know either much later - when the actions have ceased to have any significance - or perhaps, never. For example, we would never know why US President JF Kennedy was assassinated. For certain events, like the death of Subhas Chandra Bose, maybe no one knows the truth. At least no one can now. Same is about the ultimate fate of Hitler. Did he really commit suicide or escaped to Argentine?

There is of course much of investigative reporting and a plethora of conspiracy theories. But how much of that is the truth and how much is mere fiction for sale, one can never be sure. Diplomacy is the world of Cosa Nostra where silence and opacity are the unbreakable rules. Treaties have secret clauses about which no one ever comes to know. So much is done underground by covert operatives, for equally secret reasons, that we can never really know who did what and why. This is because doing things in open may defeat the very purpose of an action.

A very large number of countries indulge in spying. Spies are a species by themselves. Many of them are double agents, and some work as double agents for their own ends. Spies also do not know the actual motive of their operations: They may be captured by the enemies or may be grilled by the snooping reporters and may reveal secrets. Hence secrets are wrapped in hierarchical layers of agents, handlers, and bosses. The top political leaders also do not disclose much to the secret agencies, and the bosses of the secret agencies do not tell everything to the leaders. That is why all governments have laws to keep secrets and files are categorised as 'classified' that can never be made public. (Official Secrets Acts are more to protect the people involved rather than to keep the secrets.)

So many operations go haywire and no one admits what went wrong and why. We do not even come to know that anything went wrong. Then there are individuals in positions of authority who work on their own idiosyncrasies. Insanity is not confined to lunatic asylums: it very much walks the corridors of power. Sometimes it prevails over the seats of power. How do we explain the decisions of senile despots? Or of rabid radical religious groups like those who govern Iran and Afghanistan who are happy to shoot a woman just because she was not fully draped in a tent like overall? And yet these irrational characters rule nations and matter in international relations.

Then there are individuals who have selfish reasons and their own agenda. To what extent they can go in pursuit of their ends can never gauged. In the 1980 US elections, Ronald Reagan defeated the incumbent president Jimmy Carter because he lost popularity due to the hostage crisis in Iran. It is alleged that Reagan's agents paid money to the Iranians so that the hostages are not released till elections are over so that Carter loses the election. Incidentally, the hostages were released a day after Reagan took office of the President. There are any numbers of such scandals about which we have no idea that played a crucial role in international affairs. Hence, international relations remain in a constant state of anarchical turmoil of the unknown.

At the end of the day, much what of what we surmise about international affairs are guesstimates at best. However, there is no other option but to go along with what we know, or what we believe we know.

❖❖❖❖

Chapter II

# Theories of International Relations

Principles about how a state does, or should, conduct its external policies, and for what purposes, have been discussed from times immemorial. Some of the earliest tenets of International Relations are found in the Mahābhārata. When dispute between the Kauravas and the Pandavas reaches a flash point, Krishna goes to meet Duryodhana and offers to accept extremely humble terms to ensure peace because peace is more desirable than war. However, when Duryodhana rejects even those terms, Krishna then uses every means, fair and foul, to defeat the Kauravas in the war. Both the factions also go out of the way to win allies among other kingdoms. This simply means that there is no point in standing on the high moral ground if you lose in the process. This has been the fundamental principle of international relations from the ancient times. Nevertheless, academicians have formulated various theories of international relations.

## IDEALISM

Idealism and Realism are considered as the two basic schools of thought in International Relations. As both are intrinsic to human disposition, there is nothing new about the either. For ages, these have been adopted by the rulers as well as by ordinary peoples in their life. Idealism is essentially ethical in nature while Realism is worldly by character. While Idealism is about the means as well as the ends, Realism is solely about the ends. Hence this duality is also about the head and the heart. Broadly speaking, while Idealism is an endeavour to solve the problems of the people world over through moral means, Realism seeks to solve the problems of a nation state through whatsoever means required. Thus, while the individual citizen is the centre of attention in Idealism, it is the nation state as a unit that is the prime actor in Realism.

Idealism, as the word suggests, is lofty, vague, hypothetical, and hence difficult to define. There is neither a commonly accepted meaning nor standard principles for the same. In a way, Idealism can also be viewed as synonymous to utopianism. What seems ideal to one may appear as irrational and baneful to the other. Hence, the idealist school of international thought consists of academics who have adopted a certain path to reach a certain set of noble goals. These may be international in nature, like making the world a peaceful place through peaceful methods, or these may intra-national and individual or group specific, to provide justice to all by fair means. Thus issues like suppression of individuals or of certain groups of a society - usually the minorities - eradication of hunger, economic inequality, political tyranny, democracy, freedom of expression, and overall liberty of the citizens become a part of the agenda of Idealism. Consequently, Idealism is often also treated as tantamount to liberalism although there are subtle differences also between the two.

**Idealism sees mankind as one community**. It is based on the assumption that human nature is intrinsically good and peoples of different classes and nations can, and should, join hands to solve common problems and make the world a better place for all to live. It believes that humans have evolved into societies through cooperation and hence nations can set aside, even forgo, their selfish interests to achieve higher goals as a collective by consensus and cooperation. Idealism reposes faith in compromise, non-violence, self-restraint, and compassionate mutual understanding. This would be good for nations as states as well as for the welfare of the individuals of the state. This can be done only by improving relations among nations and by strengthening international institutions and enforcement of international laws to ensure the same. The Idealists stress upon the principles of reciprocity and overall interdependence among nation states. They propose that peace and cooperation can be achieved through formation of international organisations which will help in establishing international cooperation. They emphasise upon international laws based on moral values, rather than on power, as the solution to universal problems. Advancement of human civilisation is not possible without the elimination of war. Peace, prosperity and development go hand in hand, and hence should be a concern of all.

Idealism propounds the view that a country's foreign policy should reflect its political constitution, its internal policies, and the intrinsic values of its society. Hence, if a government upholds liberal democratic values and endeavours to reduce poverty, defend human rights, and promote religious freedom at home because it believes such principles to be morally right, then it should stand for application of the same principles at the international level also. It should do so because these principles cannot be applied on a selective basis. In fact, these would not be able survive in isolation. Only universal application of these values is sustainable because unless the world community stands as one, there can be no real peace, development and happiness. Only liberal and democratic societies can achieve these aims. Idealists believe in actively participating in global affairs to spread the values they hold dear and attempt to shape the policies of other countries in accordance with those values. This approach can entail cooperating with others or going it alone to address what idealists see as the world's problems.

**Immanuel Kant** (1724-1804) was a German philosopher who wrote extensively on a large number of subjects. His basic thoughts were about application of a universal ethical principle, that one should always respect the humanity in others, and that one should only act in accordance with the rules that could hold good for everyone. He argued that moral law is the truth of reason, and all rational creatures are bound by the same moral law. Hence, we should act rationally and in accordance with a universal moral law. He believed in free will of the individual, moral progress of mankind, a rule based civil society, immortality of the soul, and that God has designed the world in accordance with the principles of justice. Although his writings on International Relations are rather meagre - more as a derivative of his overall philosophy - he is considered as one of the earliest proponents of the theory of Idealism because of the universal appeal of his philosophy.

Kant stood for absolute peace. However, peace did not mean mere cessation of hostility: It meant removing not only all the causes that can lead to a war but also the means to perpetrate a war. In other words, if states kept armies and prepare for war, they would inevitably end up waging wars. This was because the feeling of insecurity is basic to human nature. Hence, Kant advocated that standing armies should be abolished because their very existence threatens other states and causes insecurity. This would mean a very major change in the very nature of the political constitution of the states.

Kant held that the state should be republican and that control of the foreign policy should be democratic. He was wary of the role of power in international affairs and recognised that quest and exercise of power is the root cause of conflicts. He held that foreign policy is often guided to protect the interests of a select group within a nation, and hence, the power of the state needs to be controlled by the peoples. Domestic and international issues are interconnected, and as such, if anarchy prevails in the international arena, it will be difficult to achieve domestic political liberty. Individual liberty is possible only if there is peace among nations and a rule based order in domestic politics.

Every philosopher is a creation of his time. Kant justified the goals of the French Revolution 1789, although not the means adopted by the revolutionaries. He was yet to realise the full implications of the revolution, and yet to see that Europe was just about to plunge into a long period of Napoleonic wars. He obviously could not have envisaged the intricacies of a modern industrialised and globalised world. Hence his suggestions should be viewed accordingly. Nevertheless, his basic vision about a free individual in a peaceful world still holds good.

The same can be said of Idealism as a theory. While the aims of Idealism are worthy of being pursued, Idealism fails to provide a universally acceptable and pragmatic roadmap to reach to the goals. This is because the nature and needs of each state is different.

## MARXIST THEORY

While Marxism is not fundamentally about International Relations, it is so wide in scope that it covers international relations as well. While the Realists hold states as the main actor, and the Liberals consider individuals as the main actors, Marx held classes as the principal actor, and economic relationship between classes as the main factor in politics. He believed that society and culture of a state cannot be separated from its economic system. He viewed individuals as members of an economic class, not as citizens of a nation state. He held that workers across the world - the *proletariat* - cutting through the geographical boundaries of nation states formed one universal class who shared similar aspirations and problems. They were being exploited by the capitalist class - the bourgeoisie - in every state as this class controlled the means of production and political power. Since exploitation was the common factor that united all the workers, they were suggested to organise themselves into a politically revolutionary movement to capture political power without which there was no solution to their exploitation.

As a corollary, the proletariat should have nothing to do with the concept of nation state. In fact, the very idea of nationalism was an imagination created to continue the system in which the bourgeoisie held power so that they could exploit the workers. Taking the theory further, Marx held that wars were fought between nations only to serve the vested interests of this ruling class and soldiers were recruited or conscripted from the proletarian class to fight the wars for the bourgeoisie. The victors in the war subjugate the defeated peoples and exploitation only exacerbates in the form of colonialism and imperialism. Hence the workers should have nothing to do with war either. If the workers capture political power, the very concept of nation states would 'wither away', there would be no division of peoples between nations, and there would be no wars, and no colonial exploitation.

Marx believed that world politics can only be understood in totality, not in isolated segmented sectors. Division of social studies into disciplines like History, Sociology, Political Science, Economics, and International Relations obfuscate proper understanding of world politics. Hence, Marxism is also a **structuralist theory** (to be discussed in detail later) in the sense that it holds that world politics takes place in an environment called as the world-system. Marxists believe that the structure of the capitalist world system is determined by who has control over capital and the means of production, and who is deprived of it. They hold that the capital-rich states own the means of production while the capital-poor states are deprived of it. In the capitalist world economy, the proletariat group is reduced to supply cheap labour and raw material to the capital-rich bourgeoisie class and to provide market of finished goods for the bourgeoisie.

Hence Marxism assumes the world system as essentially conflictual. The world system is conflictual because of the incompatible interests of the capital-rich bourgeoisie class and the capital-poor least developed proletariat class. Because of the divergence of interests, both classes vie for control of the capital, technology, natural resources and the market. This competition leads to conflict. Thus Marxist approach uses historical materialism as the method to understand world politics. It believes that the contemporary world order is the result of historical development. Over the period, changing material conditions have shaped and reshaped this process. In the modern era, the Marxist approach explains how unfair terms of trade between the developed and the newly independent states lead to exploitation of the post-colonial states by the developed capitalist states. The powerful states establish and maintain their hegemony - economic as well as political - through a structure called as neo-colonialism.

Marxism has moral appeal as well as logic. The idea of a peaceful world, without wars and without national boundaries, and without exploitation is certainly fascinating. Hence, the Marxist theory is also idealistic in a way, although it cannot be categorised as liberal by any means. It advocates revolution, talks about class-war, and proposes dictatorship of the proletariat as means to achieve the ideal of emancipation called communism. All these concepts are contrary to the principles of liberalism.

As a theory on International Relations, Marxism, as in all other aspects, has its own contradictions. Marxism overemphasises only one aspect of human society - the economic relationship - while ignoring all other features of human psychology. Greed and fear are essential parts of human psyche, an outcome of the basic instinct to survive, even at the cost of other living beings. This lopsided approach has made Marxism utopian and hence impractical. Even communist nations have boundaries and fought wars with each other. China and Vietnam fought a war in 1979. (Much of the time, most of the communist countries were under the Soviet umbrella and hence could not have fought with each other.)

Marxism met its demise with the dissolution of Soviet Union in 1991, and the Marxian theory has also been shelved. Nevertheless, it still provides a point of view which cannot be ignored even today, even if only for analysis and academic interest.

## REALISM

Realism is quite the reverse of Idealism. As the word suggests, is based on grassroots realities and on the crass human nature of brutish survival instinct. Thus, it is all about the brass tacks realpolitik. Self-preservation is the only goal in Realism, and while means do not matter, power is central to the method of achieving the goal: Ends justify the means. While the individual as a unit of the state is central to Idealism, the state is central to Realism and the interests of the individual become subsumed with the interests of the state. This is so because societies need governments and the individual cannot exist isolated from the state in the modern era. This is not the stone age of nomadic life. If the state itself collapses, or is subjugated, the individual would be the worst sufferer. And hence, the fate of the individual is irrevocably intertwined with that of the state, and the state would always take priority over the individual, irrespective of whether the nation is democratic or despotic.

Realism holds that **survival instinct is the most basic trait** of all living beings and this aspect of human nature makes people individualistic and selfish. Even though humans live in cooperative entities like tribes, societies, and nation states, they live only as individuals. They cooperate for selfish reasons of security and sustenance. For survival they resort to immoral and even illegal means. The same stands true for nation states. Since survival depends on managing insecurity, the Realists view international relations basically as a game of power balance and deterrence. While balance of power depends on strategic and flexible alliances, deterrence depends on constant strengthening of muscle power and public exhibition of the same from time to time by way of threats for regional hegemony, and even global dominance. As a corollary, the Realists denounce the Idealists for believing in the abstract concept of global governance and cosmopolitan democracy as it ignores the power of self-interest of the nations and that of the emotional appeal of nationality

While Realism is the predominant practice of international relations today, there is nothing new about it as it has determined the politics of nations through the ages. **Chanakya** (370BC-283BC) was perhaps the first to codify the principles of Realism in his treatise '*Arthashastra*'. He states that the primary goal of the king is to increase the power of the state, to expand the empire, and to destroy the enemy. However, Chanakya held that peace was more desirable than war and basically stood for a welfare state. He wanted the king to be a just ruler, and the state had to be strong for protection and wellbeing of the citizens. He did not approve of a king appropriating power and wealth for his own benefit.

**Tacitus,** the Roman historian (AD56-120), was another ancient exponent of Realism. He says:

*"He that fights and runs away, may turn and fight another day; But he that is in battle slain, will never rise to fight again."*

*"A bad peace is even worse than war."*

**Niccolo Machiavelli** (1469-1527) was the European Chanakya of the medieval age. In his book *"The Prince"* he guides the ruler about the ways he should wield power in order to gain and maintain control over his state. He emphasised how basic human character influences security of the state and held the view that a ruler's main task is the protection of state's interests. To serve that end, the ruler can abjure the principles adopted in life and even make immoral decisions if necessary. He needs to be a lion and a fox at the same time because power and deception are alternate tools for security. Machiavelli stressed that a ruler must be guided by the 'ethics of responsibility' rather than by the principles of morality. He should even use violence, if necessary, to guarantee the survival of the state. War is sometimes justified and rules and customs ought to be interpreted flexibly to suit one's own interests.

**Thomas Hobbes** (1588-1679) in his book '*Leviathan*' elaborated further - to almost a cynical extent - and proposed that there was nothing moral in human beings and that the state of nature was one endless struggle for survival. The condition of man was a '*condition of war of everyone against everyone*' and '*life is nasty, brutish, and short.*' Although Hobbes was not writing primarily about foreign affairs, his views reflect a sense of dystopian realism about the nature of state. (Emmanuel Kant wrote on political issues, including on International Relations, basically as a rebuttal of this philosophy.)

**E.H Carr** is considered as the foremost proponent of Realism in the modern age. This was the period when political thinking - domestic as well as international - had drifted from the clutches of abstract philosophers into the hands of analysts of history. Carr postulated his theory in the book '*The Twenty Years Crisis*' (1939). It was written on the eve of the Second World War and reflects the frustration on failure of the League of Nations to ensure peace through the ideal of collective security. The League was dominated by Britain and was guided by anti-communism. Hence Britain kept pampering Fascism and Nazism which ultimately became the bane of world peace. Carr held that the Idealists were dreamers - 'utopians' as he called them - rather than pragmatic thinkers, and that it was necessary to look at real events and their consequences. [British politicians were not idealists and the British have never been. They were also very much playing for survival. Their fault was that their belief in the value of Nazism as a counterweight to communism was grossly misplaced.]

Carr condemned the idealistic vision as it underestimated the role of power in international equations and glorified the role of law, morality and public opinion. He was critical of the idea that rational negotiation could be an alternate to military power. Power was integral and also the decisive factor in politics. The potential to exercise power brought about changes in favour of those who could wield power. On the other hand, Idealism overemphasises the strength of rational good sense, and refuses to acknowledge power as the key component of international relations, and hence it also fails to fully explain the actions of nations. As such, the book was more by way of criticism of contemporary Idealism rather than a proposition of a new doctrine.

**Hans J. Morgenthau** wrote the book '*Politics among Nations: The Struggle for Power and Peace*' in 1948 which clearly - and cynically to some extent - showed the acceptance of the mistakes that led to the Second World War. Morgenthau believed that international relations had to be based on observed realities. He postulated Realism in the form of six political policy principles:

(i) Politics is driven by objective laws rooted in human nature.

(ii) Interest of the state in terms of power is the key driver in international politics.

(iii) While the form and nature of state power may be contextual, the basic premise of interest remains the same.

(iv) Moral principles do not direct the actions of a state when these are impractical and risky.

(v) Moral principles are specific to a society and not universal.

(vi) Politics has primacy over other factors like economics.

As opposed to the optimism of the idealists who expected international conflicts to be resolved through negotiation and goodwill, Morgenthau emphasised upon power over morality, and held that every political action is directed towards keeping, increasing, or demonstrating power. In fact, morality should be avoided in policymaking as it can lead to weakness and even to the destruction of the state by a rival. Morgenthau distinguished between self-interest and morality in international politics in the sense that pursuit of national interest is 'amoral' and is not subject to the codes of morality.

## SYSTEMS APPROACH

The Systems approach was a method of analysing biological phenomena and was first applied in International Relations by **David Easton** in his book *The Political System* (1953). It proposes that the international system - like a living organism - is an integrated structure of individual units, i.e., the sovereign states, which collectively constitute the system. It held that the system controls the behaviour of the nation-states, and the developments in international relations are consequences of the system as a whole. The Systems approach was thus a departure from the traditional approach that stressed on the domestic factors of nation-states as the decisive element in international relations. The Systems approach looks at the dynamics within a system in totality instead of analysing the developments happening within its units. The four distinguishing features of a system are: elements, interconnections, function or purpose, and a regulating force. Thus, a system is composed of interconnected elements, it has a function or purpose, and it is driven by a regulating force.

**Morton Kaplan** further elaborated on the subject in his book '*System and Process in International Politics*' (1957). It was the period of escalating Cold War and Kaplan saw the international system in the form of a polarised world. In that context, he proposed six types of international systems.

The *Balance of Power System* was the pre-First World War system of a multi-polar world in which nations sought security through diplomatic channels rather than by military means, that is, by entering into alliances. The prime goal of nations was to preserve the system through deterrence, and when one nation became too strong, the other powers formed an alliance against it.

The *Loose Bipolar System* had two large and ideologically rival blocs led by the two superpowers - USA and USSR - and a large number of neutral states. Both the superpowers avoided a direct war due to the threat of mutual nuclear destruction.

The *Tight Bipolar System* comes to be formed if the two superpowers become more confrontational and the non-aligned states as well as the international organisations like the UNO become helpless in stopping a war from erupting.

The *Universal System* comes into existence when the bipolar system ends and organisations such as the UNO become powerful and effective in maintaining world peace. This system is marked by a high level of international cooperation.

The *Hierarchical System* would come into existence when one of the blocs of the bipolar system disintegrates, as it actually happened to USSR in 1991. The international order thereafter gets rearranged in a hierarchy and the surviving superpower tries to spread its domination wherever possible. This system lasted for about two decades after the end of Cold War when USA tried to dominate the world order.

The *Unit Veto System* is one in which all states have the ability to devastate another, but all of them are conscious of its repercussions, that attack will trigger equally devastating retaliation. A multi-polar world deters every nation from attacking another.

While Kaplan's theory is a way of academic analysis, the present state of international relations fails to be classified in any of the above six systems.

## STRUCTURAL REALISM

**Kenneth Waltz** applied the Systems approach to introduce a new way of analysing International Relations called as 'Structural Realism', or simply as Structuralism. This came out in his book titled '*Man, the State, and War: A Theoretical Analysis*' published in 1959. It was a modification of Realism because Waltz believed that conventional theories do not fully explain international relations. Waltz analysed international relations through political and military relations, through political realism, and economic position. He held that a state's actions are not based on human nature but on factors he called as the structure, and the structure is based on the relative power of the states. It is an outcome of human psychology and is rooted in survival instinct. Ego, greed, insecurity and lust for power are offshoots of this trait. He stated that the underlying cause of war was that the international system was competitive, conflictual, and anarchical. There is no organisation that had the authority to control the world order, and none could arbiter and resolve the conflicts between sovereign states. In the absence of a world government which can maintain peace, there is no mechanism to ensure the survival of a state other than its own power. Hence the primary aim of all states is to increase their military strength for self-defence.

## SYSTEMS APPROACH OF WALLERSTEIN

Immanuel Wallerstein developed the 'world systems theory' in 1974 to co-opt the changes that were taking place in international affairs due to the ongoing Cold War. The period saw emergence of new technologies which pointed out the need of an integrated and comprehensive approach to address the complex problems seen during the period. Wallerstein's Systems approach holds that each system in the universe is interconnected and each exerts influence over the other. Hence, we need to study the dynamics of the system - the interactions of its components - as a whole to understand a specific phenomenon instead of analysing the isolated developments happening in nation states.

Wallerstein held that the world is not a random collection of independent states; rather, states are like units of a larger system with specific political relationships, regulated by certain principles. The aim of all states is to ensure their national security, and hence, irrespective of the internal politics, all states behave in the same manner with regard to their foreign policy. Their individual political nature, size or capabilities cannot make any difference in the international system.

Wallerstein stressed upon the increasing globalisation and interdependence in the modern age. Interdependence means reciprocity among countries even in an anarchical international system. However, states are not the only actors in the international system: International institutions and non-state actors are very much part of the system and help cooperation among nations. These can be influential individuals, business corporations and conglomerates, global civil society groups, NGOs, media, etc. While they also exert influence on the states, these have only a limited role. It is always the state, especially in times of crises, which determines the course of action. Hence, the international system is anarchical and interdependent at the same time. Nations have to modify their policies and make domestic laws to conform to the principles of the international organisation of which they are a member, and at the same time also pursue self interest.

This also brought in the distinction between the **Cobweb model** and **Billiard ball model.** The Billiard ball model is state centric - a key tenet of Realism. It holds that states are impermeable, hard-shelled self-contained units, and are the only channel of interaction. States influence each other through external pressure. Since each nation has to depend on itself for survival, nations have to maintain the balance of power, and hence consistently collide with each other like billiard balls. On the other hand, the Cobweb model is society centric and holds that peoples of the world are connected with each other through multiple channels of communication which cut across the national borders. This network of systems looks like a spider's web. Wallerstein's approach was an amalgamation of both the models.

Wallerstein also stressed that inter-state relations depend on their economies. He classified nations into three groups of geographical regions as economic zones. The '**core' group** comprises of highly developed nations of Western Europe, North America and Japan, also called as the 'Global North'. These were technologically advanced democratic states, specialising in the production of the most advanced commodities with high incomes, and high levels of capital intensive investment. The 'core' earns profits from economic activities and has extensive state welfare services.

The '**periphery**', also known as the 'Global South', comprises of the least developed regions in the world which includes several nations of Latin America, Africa, and Asia. These states produce labour intensive and technologically low-end primary goods and hence earn relatively little. These are largely quasi-democratic states, with subsistence level incomes, and poor public welfare services. The 'semi-peripheral' states are between the two extremes.

According to Wallerstein, the modern world-system is capitalist and under this system economic power rests in the hands of those who own the means of production. The regulating force in the modern world is the global capital, and through international organisations like IMF, the global capital is able to challenge the sovereignty of the peripheral states. If a nation keeps away from such institutions, it becomes an international pariah. Hence, the modern capitalist world-system is inherently exploitative. The capitalist core exploits the peripheral states, thereby leading to extreme economic inequalities in the world economy, and hence to conflicts.

## NEO-REALISM

Neo-Realism was further elaboration of Structural Realism proposed by Kenneth Waltz. It was put forth in his book '*Theory of International Politics*' which was published in

1979 when the Cold War was at a peak. It was a sombre recognition of the realities of the situation of confrontational competitiveness in a bi-polar world.

Waltz reiterated that the international system is composed of interacting units, i.e., nation-states. The structure of the international system regulates the behaviour of nation-states and not the other way round. This is done through the distribution of material capabilities among the states. Material capabilities are weapons, military manpower, and economic resources to support the military infrastructure. When one nation augments its capabilities, its potential rivals are also compelled to increase their military strength and make alliances with more powerful states. Disproportionate distribution of capabilities may even lead to conflict. However, states being rational actors are aware of its consequences also and hence take sober decisions.

Neo-Realism holds that international politics is basically anarchical in nature. Sovereignty is the distinguishing feature of the state and the state is the main player in international politics. The **state is a rational unitary actor** which operates for its own national interest, that national security and survival are the primary goals of the state, and national power and capabilities determine relations among the states. States are rational actors in the sense that they know that they are on their own for survival and hence act for their own interests. The states are also apprehensive about other states and have to be prepared for eventualities and cannot let off the guard. Hence, it is reasonable for the states to assume that the more power they have, the more they are likely to determine international arrangements in their favour. The decision makers are rational because making the state weak or vulnerable would not be sane.

While there are laws within a state, and agencies to enforce the same, there is no such body in the international arena to control world order. International laws exist but international organisations can only monitor and arbiter. They have no enforcing power and their authority rests solely on being accepted by the involved states. It is a cold blooded recognition of the reality that each state has to safeguard its own interests, and this is possible only by having the capability to exert power. Insecurity is a permanent feature in the international sphere and every state competes with other states by increasing its power. This endless pursuit of the national interest may also lead to an aggressive quest and lust for regional, even for global hegemony. Selfishness and inability to trust others has made wars the most common feature of human history.

Waltz made a clear distinction between national politics and international politics. He termed domestic issues as '**low politics**', and issues related to international politics such as war, defence, national security, and foreign policy as '**high politics**'. Low politics cannot affect international politics. The nature of political systems, like democracy or ideological totalitarianism, cannot make any difference in their role in the international system. The issues of high politics are determined by the international system. The function of all nation-states is to ensure their security. Hence, irrespective of their domestic political nature, all nation-states behave in the same manner in international politics.

## ANALYSIS OF REALISM

Realism emphasises upon the absence of any authority that governs the international system, and that there can be none because the states are sovereign. In this anarchical environment, survival and preservation are primary and power is the only means for the same. In fact, international organisations like the United Nations are the medium through which states exert power over other states rather than the organisation controlling the nations. Conflict, and not cooperation, is the norm in a real world. Power can be exerted through various different tools - military, economy, technology, and coalition. Realism does not deny the principles of human rights or democratic governance. It only puts survival in the higher order of priority.

Realism is criticised for professing an ideology that only encourages apprehensions which lead to confrontation. By asserting the uncooperative and selfish nature of human beings and the absence of a world order, Realism drives leaders to act in ways based on distrust and power. Realism can thus be seen as an excessively pessimistic self-fulfilling prophecy. However, for the realists, facing the reality is prudence, and not pessimism, and to deny the stark reality for an idealistic outcome would be sheer folly. While it would be incorrect to treat Realism as a warmongering theory, it does rationalise use of power as a necessary tool of statecraft in an imperfect world where survival of the state is paramount. All other goals become irrelevant if state's existence itself is threatened. This quest for power can even turn into an obsessive lust for power.

Neo-Realism holds that states are **rational players** and that their decisions are based on prudence. However, history shows otherwise, because ultimately, decisions are taken by individuals - be it a dictatorship or democracy. Napoleon was one of the most intelligent leaders, yet his decision to invade Spain, and then Russia, was based on pride and self glorification, and not on rationality. Waging wars all over Europe led to his disastrous end. Similarly, Hitler's decisions to declare war on Soviet Union and USA were acts of madness. The.se led to decimation of Germany instead of supremacy of the Third Reich. Similarly, were the decisions of USA to entangle into wars in Korea, Vietnam, Iraq, Afghanistan, and at many other places, based on rationality? These were motivated decisions - to serve the domestic war industry - with catastrophic consequences for American citizens as well as for USA as a nation.

The idea of ensuring survival through the model of **'balance of power'** has also come into much criticism. Firstly, the very concept is highly subjective and depends on the threat perception of leaders. Hence, there can never be a stable state of balance.

While realists describe balance of power as a prudent strategy in an insecure world, critics see it as a way of legitimising war and aggression. Secondly, as history has shown, balancing power through alliances is more likely to lead to larger wars rather than to lasting peace, which is critical for survival. The system of alliances turned a minor conflict into the First World War which shattered the established empires of Germany, Russia, Austria and the Ottomans. At the same time, no single state can keep the world order under its direct command. Overpowering of one state - Nazi Germany - led to the Second World War. Thus, the very concept that was meant to ensure survival led to its destruction and demise.

There is also a contradiction between the **hegemonic approach** and the concept of balance of power. The idea of hegemony holds that states should pursue domination over the international environment. On the other hand, balance of power means that pursuit of hegemony would lead to distrust and conflict which may not be in the interest of the state. Hence, states should seek stability through mutual assurance of power equilibrium in the world order. And hence, the two approaches cannot go together.

Further, there is no permanence in power equilibrium through alliances because alliances are transactional and nations keep their stand flexible and switch sides at will. Italy was an ally of Germany before the First World War but later joined hands with Britain. Many states are only fair-weather friends and do not come for help in times of need, because no state wants to entangle itself in a conflict with the strong for the sake of helping a weak friend. Even less for a moral cause! There is also the concept of 'enemy of my enemy is my friend'. Hence, as soon as Nazi Germany attacked USSR in June 1941, Britain, and later USA, became allies of their sworn enemy - the communist Soviet Union. However, the Second World War had hardly ended and the Cold War started between USSR and the western bloc. This only proves that there are no permanent friends in international politics, only perceived immediate interests.

Coming to democracies, it must be said that democracies can be as hypocritical as any dictatorship and values of idealism are used as tools and pretext to serve the vested interests of non-state actors. In fact, the non-state actors determine the character of the state itself in democracies, and hence dictate its international policies for their own ends. This feature contradicts the tenet of Realism that only the state - the government - decides the foreign policy in a rational manner. The government may be the front, the façade, but the real power rests behind. This brings in the question, what really is the state?

As such, the idealism expressed by the Western nations is simply pseudo-idealism, a farce. They pose as champions of values like democracy, free speech, and racial equality but these are selectively used for the ultimate purpose of realistic self interest. USA is the oldest and the strongest democracy and has waged wars in the name of democracy and human rights while joining hands with monarchies of most dubious reputation about human rights. Again, were the decisions to enter into regional wars in Korea, Vietnam, Iraq, Afghanistan, and at many other places, based on morality? US invasion of Iraq in March 2003 is the most glaring example of hoax. US accused Iraq of having weapons of mass destruction and invaded Iraq. No such weapons were ever found but over 300000 Iraqi citizens were killed. The other wars also caused havoc in the concerned regions and affected the common citizens the most, not to speak of the death of thousands of US soldiers and wastage of US tax payers' money. Hence, many realists believe that democracy does not ensure peace as democratic countries also go to war, even against each other.

In the final analysis, while Realism does truly depict the picture of certain aspects of the actual state of affairs, it has no clear solution to offer. Maybe, it believes that there is none, and that the state of affairs will continue to be anarchical till eternity. This belief is not only cynical but also not entirely true as proved by peace prevailing for long durations in many parts of the world. Further, most of the people do not want wars because no one wants to die, and most of the people genuinely work for peace and prosperity.

## NEO-LIBERALISM

The year 1991 saw the collapse of Soviet Union, of the East European Soviet bloc, and thus the end of the Cold War. It happened because the ordinary citizens of these nations rebelled against the state power as communism provided neither material prosperity nor personal freedoms. On the other hand, the states had become so weak - because of their socialist structures - that they were in no position to control the rebellion. This gave a jolt to the theory of Realism as it had not provided any room for the power of the average citizen. Thus, the doctrine of neo-liberalism emerged to overcome the criticism that Realism has failed to acknowledge the importance of economics in politics, and of the role of non-state actors in international relations. The decades that have followed the end of the Cold War have shown radical revision in the theories of international politics.

Neo-liberalism was developed as a Systems approach by **Robert O. Keohane and Joseph S. Nye**. It states that the modern age is an era of interdependence due to global communication and trade. Interdependence means complex reciprocity among countries. This needs cooperation among nations and the international institutions facilitate mutual interdependence and regulate the behaviour of states. The function of international institutions and international organisations is to strengthen interdependence. International institutions like UNO, IMF, WTO, etc., set the rules and principles of interstate relations including that of trade. These regulations often need changes in domestic laws. For instance, many nations had to amend their patent laws to conform to the WTO's guidelines on intellectual property rights. The role of institutions is increasing in this era of complex interdependence. The non-state actors and civil society groups can gain public support on issues like environment and influence the governments to change policies and amend laws.

While Waltz held a pessimistic view about international anarchy, Keohane and Nye are optimistic that the ill-effects of the anarchy can be mitigated through institutions. While Waltz gave primacy to nation states, Keohane and Nye held that states are not the only actors in the international system. The international system also incorporates **international institutions**, non-state actors and civil society groups. While Keohane and Nye share the Neo-realist belief that the international system is anarchical by nature, they hold that interdependence also is a structural feature of the international system. The international system is anarchical and interdependent at the same time. While agreeing with the Neo-realists that there are conflicts among states, they repose faith in interdependence to bring cooperation among the states. The international institutions can function as the regulating force for the same and thus control the behaviour of states. This can change the model of international politics.

Realism on the other hand belittles the role of international organisations. The proposition that nations shirk the moral obligation to alleviate suffering of the common man around the world by focusing on self interest is also not accurate. While some neo-liberals agree that the international system is anarchic, they contend that the risks of anarchy can be mitigated through institutions. Institutions like the WTO and the IMF help states to negotiate and enter into mutually beneficial agreements. These facilitate liberal trading and prompt states to open their markets for international trade. There are also institutions to govern global climate change and proliferation of nuclear weapons. The number of such formal international organisations had risen exponentially in the last few decades.

**Economics** is not only supplanting diplomatic politics but has become a part of overall politics and an essential feature of national security. Today, balance of power means not mere leveling of armed power but squaring of money power. While it has opened more areas of competition between states, it has also opened, often out of compulsion, room for opportunities of cooperation. This transformation is suggesting emergence of a positive vision of world order and hardcore Realism is being regarded as an obsolete theory. It is so because Realism focused more on strategic foreign policy and less on the domestic economic policies of nations, ignoring the strong relationship between the two in the modern era. Realism is criticised for giving disproportionate attention to the state (government) while ignoring non-state forces within the state, and also for overlooking issues not directly related to the survival of the state.

Many rich nations contribute financially as well as by logistic support for several humanitarian causes that serve no national interest. USA joins hands with non-democratic states for its own interests as well as to address various global issues including climate change, refugee crises, and pandemics. It can be argued that serving humanitarian causes also serve the national interest in the long term, but then, such a contention dissolves the division between Realism and Idealism.

Neo-liberalism stresses that major powers have a deeply interconnected economic relationship. Problems in one country affect the other, and hence, the states have a rational interest in cooperation. They recognise that cooperation can bring positive sum games that benefit both the partners. Individuals, international organisations, and multinational corporations play an important role in shaping the global order, not just the governments. The neo-liberals emphasise the importance of universal bodies such as the UNO for creating world public opinion. While the states have competing interests, they are also interconnected to each other in such a way that reliance and partnership is more the norm than autonomy and isolation.

The neo-liberals believe that the spread of **education and democracy**, and increasing democratic control over foreign policy, would empower public opinion, and make it a force that no government can defy. They view war as a scourge of the global order that serves the interests of only a few, not of the common citizens. They attack unrepresentative governments who in cahoots with the arms industries, corrupt bureaucrats, and financial institutions, are perceived to pursue aggressive policies. In this endeavour, the left-internationalists join hands with the liberals. (The leftists favour international organisations only when it suits them.) They hold that by such methods it is possible to reduce the role of brute power in international arena and replace armed strength by rational negotiation. The neo-liberals believe that over and above the seemingly conflicting interests of their governments, there exists a commonality of concerns among the peoples, because despite all the differences, human beings belong to the same race. They share the same desires, the same problems and the same moral values.

Similarly, there is no zero sum game between nationalism and internationalism and each nation can contribute for universal welfare of humanity. If all nations understand and adopt this spirit, international peace would prevail. With this belief, the neo-liberals seek to check the power of nations by collective action through international organisations because lack of international order leads to devastating wars. Collective security, compulsory adjudication of disputes, national disarmament, open diplomacy and international accountability are the basic pillars of neo-liberalism. It also claims that exercising economic power over military power has proven more effective, and that the consequences of use of military power outweigh the benefits of power, and that international cooperation is in the interest of every state, and every citizen.

Thus, while Neo-liberalism has much in common with theory of Idealism as far as the aims are concerned, it is more pragmatic in outlook and provides a basic framework for achieving its aims. Whether states accept this framework or not is another matter.

## FUNCTIONALIST APPROACH

Functionalism is an academic approach to the study of International Relations that focuses on the way in which international organisations and governments facilitate cooperation and collaboration among nations. According to this theory, states are more likely to work together when they have common interests and institutions to make way for cooperation. It holds that states have a vested interest in maintaining the stability of the international system. Hence, they can reduce to role of power politics and play a key role in resolving conflicts. In this sense, Functionalism is opposed to Realism which stresses upon the role of power and self-interest in shaping international relations and holds that the international system is inherently competitive and conflictual. Hence, while Realism appears to be sceptical - even cynical - in outlook, functionalism tends to be more optimistic about the potential for international cooperation.

Functionalism gives **importance to specific issues** or problems, mainly technical in nature, in prompting the need for cooperation among nations for addressing common challenges. It proposes that collaboration between specialists in certain functional fields will create international institutions that will drive nations to cooperate rather than compete and reduce the potential for conflict. Cooperation in one sector will build trust and help similar collaboration in other fields as well such as trade, public health, and environment protection. This would bring together different interest groups, and eventually the political parties also for common causes. This would lead to further multilateral cooperation which would help in development of even more international organisations that can work for global peace and order.

The basic proposition of this approach is that cooperation amongst nations should begin by dealing with certain specific transnational problems. Success in one field would increase the scope of cooperation. The integration of Western Europe after the Second World War is a good example of this approach. In 1952 the European Coal and steel community was founded. It evolved into the European Economic Community in 1957. Eventually, the European Union was formed in 1993.

Functionalism believes in the establishment of international organizations like the UNO and its specialised agencies that work for global issues. These organisations provide a platform for communication, negotiation, and conflict resolution. Economic cooperation leads to interdependence between nations. When nations have economic relations, they work for mutual benefit and avoid conflicts. By working on shared interests and common goals, nations move from confrontation to collaboration. Thus conflicts are replaced by cooperative relationship. To cite a different example, cultural events like the Olympic Games create a constituency for cooperation and peace.

While Functionalism seems a positive approach for promoting peace, it also suffers from oversimplification of the world order. It expects too much of cooperation while neglecting the fact that there is always the element of competition within cooperation, and hence of conflict. There are also ever present the factors of power politics and security concerns. In fact, it is not possible to separate technical from political issues, largely because the governments would not hand over power and responsibilities to institutional structures. International organisations are also incapable of acquiring popular legitimacy of the state.

Functionalism also has often failed the test of time. The European Union has internal disputes on many issues and Britain has already left the EU. The UNO is neither able to prevent wars nor maintain peace. Nations are also abdicating their responsibilities in the various agencies of the UNO. Hence, while the functionalist approach provides a valuable perspective in understanding international relations, its practical implementation is limited due to the challenges of the multi-layered nature of the global order in the modern era.

The **Structural functional approach** is a blend of the two approaches and describes the relationship of political life with other aspects of social life. Gabriel Almond was the chief promoter of this approach and held that a political system operates within the social environment and the society is a single inter-related system where each part of the system has a definite and distinct role to play. Consequently, it is not possible to analyse political events in isolation from other aspects of the society because influences from the society shape the political processes of nations.

He depicted political system as an arrangement of interaction that exists in all societies to carry out certain functions. According to him, the salient features of a political system are comprehensiveness, inter-dependence and existence of boundaries. The functions of a political system are categorised as input and output functions. The environment produces demands from different parts of the society. The political system receives these demands and the government takes actions by way of laws and policies and by their implementation. Through this conversion process, the inputs are converted into 'outputs' by the government. The 'outputs' revert back into the environment through a response mechanism, giving rise to fresh demands.

## FEMINIST APPROACH IN IR

'*Women of the world talk in the same language – the language of silence*'. This is not just an emotional piece of poetry but a prosaic statement of truth. Women are an equal part - and partners - of the global human community, but they are also different. Yet they are invisible in the critical arena of global politics. This is the crux of the Feminist approach to International Relations, that the voice of women is not even heard in this vital area although they suffer equally or perhaps even more than the men out of the consequences of accidents of international politics.

The Feminist approach acknowledges the commonality of women's struggles globally and the need for collective action to address common challenges. It emphasises upon the need for transnational solidarity and cooperative action by women for promoting justice to mankind as a whole. Thus, the Feminist approach is not a separate theory by itself. It is a fresh form of narrative from a different viewpoint. It is a clarion call to share the experiences of women and to analyse IR from the women's perspective. It holds that the traditional IR theories are not gender-neutral but rather gender-blind.

The Feminist approach is not just another feminist movement that struggles for gender equality at work places, or for women's rights on issues like abortion, pay-parity, overall subordination in a patriarchal society, etc., - issues that are exclusive to women. The Feminist approach seeks **inclusion of women** in the matters of power politics because their problems are simply ignored by men who totally control this domain. It is not simply another chapter of liberalism or idealism that talks about women's emancipation in the domestic social sphere. It is a cry to acknowledge that women's problems are not only different but also very real. Hence, this approach has the element of realism in highlighting the existence of female world as well as the element of liberalism and idealism in offering solutions.

The Realists have been concerned primarily with state security in the international arena and neglected security inside the state and hold that the state is the best instrument for ensuring the security of the individual. Feminists however show the relationship between power and gender consideration in international politics. **Gender identities**, which are produced socially and politically, are imbued with power and define distribution of power that influences the place of women in world politics. The traditional gender identities perpetuate assumptions about who should do what and why.

Masculinity has traditionally been associated with power while femininity with domesticity and the need for protection. These gender identities shape global politics. Hence, power politics has been - by and large - an exclusively masculine subject for ages. Men have run the governments as well as the military machine. Men talk about war in the binary of death and victory. Men go to the warfront and die. (Men as well as women die when bombing of civilian areas is done.) However, women continue to live and suffer and are in fact the worst victims of war. They are subjected to violence during and even after the conflict, rape being the most common. They become pregnant and often are burdened with illegitimate children. They have to take care of the wounded, face widowhood, have to take care of their fatherless children, and often driven to prostitution for livelihood. They face displacement and have to live in refugee camps on charity for years on end. Nevertheless, this is considered as an unfortunate but unavoidable by-product - collateral damage - of war and hence is simply ignored.

The Feminist analysis suggests that war's origins and consequences should be viewed in a new light, focusing on the human costs of militarism rather than merely as an interstate conflict. The Feminist approach decries the marginalisation of women's experiences in war, conflict, and diplomacy in a male-centric generalisation. While women are not a part of discussions and processes of war, they are also excluded from peace negotiations. Hence, **peacekeeping after the conflict** is also central to the Feminist approach. The prevalent norms of keeping peace ignore the women specific issues as these are considered as less important. The Feminists decry that traditional peacekeeping is shaped by the masculine notions of security which is limited to policing. Women's security as women is not central to it. Hence, the Feminists re-evaluate the very concept of security.

While the Feminist approach has certainly presented a fresh narrative, and has also suggested options for solution, or at least mitigation, the elephant in the room is the moot question that does the average woman considers herself as a woman first? Do women really care for the women on the other side of the fence? Is gender identity stronger than the emotive identity of nationalism, regionalism, religion, (or caste in case of India) or of belonging to a linguistic group or an economic class? Is a Muslim woman a woman first or a Muslim first? Women contenders like Hillary Clinton and Nikki Halley would not have lost elections to an avowed misogynist like Donald Trump had women voted for them in overwhelming numbers. So much about women's liberation in USA!

The Feminists demand greater female participation in high-level politics and in decision-making bodies. They contend that the presence of more women - in domestic political structure as well as in global institutions - would lead to more peaceful and more humane policies. However, is inclusion in power politics a panacea? Queens - from Cleopatra to Catherine of Russia - have ruled nations and many of them were as fanatic warmongers as men. And what about the women of Nazi party in Germany? They fully participated in the genocide of Jews which included women and children - in fact, more women and children than men because men were used as slave labour. But the German women cheered Hitler all the way down till he reduced Germany into grand rubble.

Similarly, when the Hamas terrorists attacked Israel on 7th October 2023, they tortured, raped and kidnapped women. While perpetrating this crime some of the young terrorists kept informing their parents on phone of what they were doing. As recordings have proved, their mothers cried in joy what a noble task their sons were doing in killing Jews and encouraged them to do more in the name of Allah. Such instances make the claim that women are more humane and peaceful sound hollow and hypocritical.

The feminist approach also ignores the fact that there are over 40 Islamic nations in the world where women have no voice. Many of these regimes care two hoots for gender justice and women are not even allowed to come out of their homes without a male relative, and without wearing a hijab. In September 2022, the late President of Iran Ebrahim Raisi refused to be interviewed by CNN's anchor Christiane Amanpour as she was not wearing the hijab. There were some anti-hijab demonstrations in Iran but they were soon smothered. While Muslim women have come out in street demonstrations in Europe and America protesting against Israeli action in Gaza, there has been no such show of solidarity for the repression of women in Islamic nations like Iran and Afghanistan.

Nevertheless, the Feminist approach has merits as it recognises that women are important and indispensable actors in all political, economic and social processes and points out the value of taking women's experiences and contribution in global affairs more seriously. It is an ideal acknowledgment of the reality.

## INSTITUTIONALISM

Institutionalism is a blend of realism and liberalism, and in many ways akin to Functionalism. The Institutional approach deals with the study of the formal political structures like the legislature, the executive, and the judiciary. It focuses on the rules of the political system, the powers of the various institutions, the legislative bodies, and how the constitution works. While it shares the basic assumptions of realism, that states are driven by rational self-interest, and that the world order is lawless, it also believes that cooperation through international institutions is still possible. This cooperation is possible not because people are basically good and cooperative by nature but simply because cooperation is mutually beneficial. Hence, cooperation is a rational response for self-interest. This cooperation can best be ensured by international institutions.

Institutions can provide the platform as well as framework for cooperation by laying down the norms, rules, and procedures of international interaction. They can make it easier for state actors to identify and seek the benefits of cooperation and overcome the anarchic preconditions that lead to a conflict. This relationship can also be described as reluctant cooperation with a healthy mutual distrust.

Institutionalism also points to the similarities between realism and liberalism in the sense that both affirm the rationality of actors in the global arena. State action is a product of unique national characteristics of the states and does not project a unified set of interests. Hence, all states are not going to act in the same way in any international situation. The non-state actors are as fundamental to global politics as the governments. In fact, states are merely a collective of dominant individuals and groups that form the state. The individuals can cooperate, and do cooperate for collective good provided there are international institutes to facilitate the same.

However, the major problem with this approach is that it overemphasises the formal structures and agencies of government and treats institutions as independent bodies. It includes political parties, constitutions, bureaucracies, interest groups and other institutions. It overlooks the informal factors of politics like the individual's will, cultural values, and group attitudes, that constitute the substructure of a political system.

The Realist and Liberal theories may simply be a matter of perception. States may see the world order as filled with threats, or may also see the global environment as one in which cooperation is possible and mutually beneficial. Successful partnership through institutes may strengthen this perception of cooperation, facilitating positive reinforcement of cooperation among the state actors.

Like all other theories and approaches, Institutionalism also has its own limitations. There is no doubt that international institutions have grown in number and have provided a platform for cooperation. Nations do not want to be left out and join such groups. However, cooperation among nations is basically for self interest - often out of strategic and economic compulsion - rather than out of any intrinsic desire for peace. When there is a conflict of interest, the institutions become impotent, often defunct. Nations flagrantly defy the rules of the institutions and pursue their own course of action. Rogue states like North Korea, China, Iran and Afghanistan care two hoots for the institutions. Yet they are a part of the international order.

## SITUATIONALISM

Having discussed the various theories and approaches of International Relations, to what conclusion do we come to? Perhaps none! It is so because academics try to portray politics as a science which it is certainly not. Theories can neither predict nor control state behaviour. These also have no explanation about actions of non-state actors which can, and do, seriously jeopardise stability in a region, or even in the entire international arena. The recent assault of Hamas on Israel (7th October 2023) is one such example. Further, there are individuals in position of power who are bent upon destabilising the world system for their own personal power. The recent attack on Ukraine by Russia is Putin's personal war for his own power. North Korean dictator Kim Jong Un also keeps the world on tenterhooks by test firing missiles for no apparent reason.

At the end of the day, academic theories mean nothing in the real modern world. International Relations are fundamentally transactional. Every situation and every event are unique and multilayered, and with unpredictable outcomes. Hence every nation, and every leader, takes decisions as per his understanding of the existing situation and its capability to take any action. Nations also keep changing positions on the same issue from time to time because the situation keeps changing. Every day is a new day and a night is a long time in international relations. It is inevitable because of the dynamics of international events. This has been most evident during the current Ukraine war and we find nations shifting stand all too often as they are not sure what position to take. This acrobatic balancing - or rather dancing - act between the forces of needs, compulsions, limitations, expectations and apprehensions, and capabilities, can best be described as situationalism. One never knows, one day it can become another elaborate theory of International Relations.

❖❖❖❖

# Chapter III

# Comparative Politics

There are different types of political systems in the world depending on ideology, religion, culture, history, geography, economic conditions, strategic compulsions, etc. Comparative politics is a methodology in Political Science of comparing the diverse political systems of different states. It is also the study of the effects of the various factors that lead to the formation of the political system of a state and identifies their strengths and weaknesses. It examines the role of institutions, the response of peoples, and how developmental changes evolved in different states. It examines the causes and effects of the similarities and differences, and looks for trends, processes, and patterns among the divergent political systems in order to develop a general hypothesis to explain these trends.

Evaluation of the political system of a state helps in understanding the behaviour of the state in domestic as well as in the international affairs. Hence, Comparative Politics also tracks the domestic origins of foreign policy and its influence on the international system. This methodology thus becomes common to Political Science as well as to International Relations. Traditionally, International Relations dealt with inter-state relations while Comparative Politics examined the structure and functioning of the state from within. However, factors like democracy, media, economic globalisation and consequent interdependence, etc., have expanded the scope of political interaction and the two fields overlap much more in the modern era.

There are many ways of analysis in Comparative Politics. The **Traditional approach** was limited to the study of the formal structures of the government, laws, rules and regulations, and constitutions of the western world. There was much similarity among these states in terms of societal norms and economic development, and hence there were certain common parameters of comparison of politics. Much of Asia and Africa was under colonial rule and had no independent political systems. Hence, this approach was only about the forms of governments and it was more a study of **'comparative governments'** rather than of comparative politics. It was parochial and static and confined to the legal powers of the political institutions existing within the states. It ignored the role of individuals who control the structure and functions of the state and shape the nature of domestic as well as international politics. Exclusion of the non-western political systems was also a flaw as it made it too Eurocentric. Truly speaking, politics is a constantly evolving process that encompasses subjects beyond constitutions and laws.

The **Historical approach** held that since politics and history are interwoven, political systems can be understood only by taking history into consideration. History links the past with the present and without the context of the past political events, analysis of the present cannot be understood in perspective. History tells us how the governments and the non-government institutions worked, and evolved out of their successes and failures. These gave lessons which determined the future course of action. However, the Historical approach does not explain the occurrences of the unexpected and serendipitous events of the past, nor can it predict those for the future. So much depends on the human mind, and consequently on the common imagination, that the Historical approach cannot present a comprehensive political picture.

**Modern comparative politics** emerged primarily after the end of the Second World War. This was the period of decolonisation and independence of 'Third World' countries. These states were too diverse to be classified by a single set of parameters. This dissimilarity enlarged the scope of comparative politics. The Modern Approach goes beyond the study of political structures and history and believes in inter-disciplinary analysis. Newer methods of analysis have also come up that include Social Psychology, Transactional Analysis, and Behavioural Science. It includes democracies and dictatorships, of developed and the Third World nations. It comprises of the study of extra constitutional agencies along with that of the formal governmental organs. Hence, issues like human rights, outcry for regional autonomy, ethnic conflicts, political violence, demand for welfare services, etc., also become subjects of relevance.

Functionalism, Institutionalism, Structuralism, and the Systems approach are also a part of Modern Comparative Politics and have already been discussed in the previous chapter.

The **Legal approach** treats the state as the central organisation for the creation and enforcement of laws. In this approach, the study of politics is mixed with legal processes and institutions like the judiciary, and the state is seen as the trustee and executor of an effective and equitable system of law and order. However, the Legal Approach looks at only one aspect of people's life and does not cover the conduct of political actions in its entirety.

**Political Economy** is the study of the interface between politics and economics. Kautilya's *Arthashastra* is the ancient treatise on Political Economy. Kautilya held that the most important duty of the state is to ensure material well-being of its people. In the modern era, Karl Marx was among the first who proposed that economics and politics have a very close relationship. The Political-Economic approach deals with the impact of economic policies on the political environment of a state. It examines the economic policies of the state, the role of political factors on the economic policies, and their fallout on the peoples. It also includes the trade policies of a country and the role of international financial institutions on nations.

**Political Sociology** is the study of the interface between politics and the society. It is a study to understand the interaction between the decision making authorities and the conflictual social forces. Since similar political institutions function in dissimilar ways in different societies, it is necessary to understand the socio-cultural environment of a state in order to comprehend the political system in totality. Aristotle, who is considered as the father of Political Science, was also the originator of Political Sociology. His hypothesis, that social factors like rising inequality can cause a revolution, is regarded as an illustration of Political Sociology. Machiavelli too held that the structure of a government depends on the nature of the society and the ruler must govern accordingly. Karl Marx played a major role in the development of modern Political Sociology. He held that we have to understand the basic structure of the society in order to understand the political structure of the state: Politics could not be studied separately.

Political Sociology examines the formation of a modern state, how social inequality between different groups influences politics, how public opinion, ideologies, and non-formal political institutions like political parties and pressure groups affect politics, and the power relationship within and amongst the social groups. However, Political Sociology undermines the role of institutions in politics and gives too much emphasis on the society. It ignores the fact that society itself is a product of multiple factors and composed of different individuals, and hence cannot be generalised as one entity.

The **Behavioural approach** focuses on the individual as a voter, party member, or leader. The individual's political behaviour influences the political system of the state because the state is composed of individuals. Traditional Political Science did not recognise human behaviour as a factor in politics. Behavioural approach takes into account the role of the individual's emotions as an important feature in shaping the political environment of the state. Hence, exponents of this approach hold that Political Science is not insulated from other social sciences such as History, Sociology and Economics. However, this approach has been criticised for its generalisations. Human beings do not always behave in similar ways in similar circumstances. Moreover, it is a difficult to predict human behaviour and there is no scientific tool to study it. Further, human behaviour itself is also a product of the very environment it has created.

Such aspects mark the limitations of Comparative Politics. The factors that affect politics include history, geography, economy, culture, climate, technological resources et al. They are in a very intricate and complex matrix and it is difficult to observe, identify and quantify all the factors in a comprehensive and holistic manner. They also vary from time to time at varying levels of significance in different states. Comparison also becomes difficult because of lack of sufficient and reliable/verifiable data. It is even more so in states that control or manipulate information. Totalitarian states do not release any information at all.

Objective analysis also needs detachment, which is always a problem. Further, cultural values and norms vary so much from state to state that it is well nigh impossible for a foreigner to make an unbiased comparison of other states. The priority of these norms also keeps changing with the situations. Hence, subjectivity comes in right from the beginning. We can compare apples only with apples and not with oranges.

## CHANGING NATURE OF STATES

As humans shifted from the nomadic hunter-scavenger way of life to agriculture based settlements, the concept of state came up. The prime functions of the state were to defend the settlement from external aggression, maintain domestic peace and thus protect the lives of the citizens, enact laws to resolve disputes among the citizens and provide justice, and protect the property rights. To discharge these functions, collection of taxes became an essential feature of the state. To ensure collection of taxes, the states exercised authority. The ability to exercise authority, and acceptance of the same by the peoples, made the states interventionist and authoritarian. To maintain continuity and stability of the system, most of the states turned into monarchies. The monarchies could be benevolent at places but remained despotic all the time.

Power of the state depended on the geography of the region where the nomads had settled. Those who reached large fertile plains established larger and more populous states with greater cultural and racial homogeneity. Commonality of racial identity thus became a prime factor in the formation of nation states.

Monarchical authoritarianism had also brought in the element of lust for power and many states became expansionist and imperialistic. In fact, colonialism is not a phenomenon of the medieval age: Subjugation, annexation, and colonisation of the weaker states by the stronger ones had started from the prehistoric times, with the formation of state itself.

Colonialism became increasingly global from the 16th century onwards, and by the end the 19th century, much of Africa and Asia had come under European rule. Britain, France, Spain, Portugal, and the Dutch Republic were the major colonial powers. Colonial rule obliterated the indigenous nature of the native states. While liberal values had started emerging in Europe during the period of Renaissance - also known as the Age of Reason - the colonial powers were predominantly tyrannical for the subjugated peoples. While they imposed European administrative structures in the colonies, they adopted policies specifically designed for exploitation. It showed that the nature of state is not the same at all places and that the state applies **different laws for different peoples**.

At the dawn of the 18th century, the states were mostly agrarian, region or culture/ religion centric, feudal and monarchical police states. During the period, Russia and Turkey (the Ottoman Empire) had also expanded landwards and became multiethnic states.

From the later part of the 18th century onwards, the monarchies started facing domestic problems. There were demands for civil liberties, self-determination, public sovereignty, constitutional governance, and the separation of church from the state. The states' power to impose taxes without people's representation or consent was particularly resented in certain regions. These issues led to the American war of Independence and the **French revolution**. These two events triggered the beginning of major changes in the nature of the states and were to transform the police states into citizen oriented administrative units.

Another phenomenon that happened during the early 19th century was the **Industrial Revolution**. It started from Britain and spread to Europe and America. It brought development and created a system of wealth creation through private enterprise known as capitalism. Capitalism created a class of industrial-businessmen, who along with related commercial services sector led to the formation of a strong middle class. It broke the traditional power of the feudal aristocracy, compelled enlargement of franchise, and thus paved the way for democracy. At the same time, the increase of industrial workers led to strengthening of the ideals of socialism. As an antidote to the rise of revolutionary socialism, states began to adopt policies of state welfare.

The two world wars led to the end of colonialism and fragmentation of multinational empires, and consequent emergence of a very large number of small culture-cum-ethnocentric states. The beginning of the Cold War politically divided the planet into the communist/socialist and capitalist groups, as well as between totalitarian and liberal democratic groups. Further, with the independence of a very large number of countries in Asia and Africa, the planet was also economically divided into developed and developing/underdeveloped groups.

Thus, watershed events like political revolutions, wars, and economic crises, and the compulsions of the consequent changes in the world eco-political order, have remarkably changed the nature of states in the last two centuries. Nothing is static in this universe and the nature of the state keeps evolving to adapt with the changing situation. Where the state accepts the necessity to adjust with the situation, the process of change is constant, gradual and invisible. Where the state decides not to change, the outcome becomes unpredictable. It may be lead to anarchy, revolution, or even disintegration of the state.

In the common parlance of today, a state is usually defined as liberal/democratic or totalitarian, socialistic or capitalistic, agricultural or industrial, and developed or developing. While such characterisation pertains to the domestic eco-political structure of the society and the state, the nature of the structure may also have an impact on the foreign policies of the government. Hence the study of the nature of a state becomes a subject of Political Science as well as of International Relations.

However, such pigeonholing of states into watertight compartments suffers from the problems of simplistic generalisations, and is more of hair splitting by armchair theoreticians who search for some pattern to propound a theory. As we shall observe subsequently, the fact is that the issue is much more complex and multilayered in the modern era, with several crosscurrents running concurrently. While there are stark differences in the nature of different states, there are also certain commonalities and much overlapping of character. Instead of rambling about on mere theory, or going too much into history, let us examine the issue on the reality of the contemporary position.

## CAPITALIST STATES

The basic tenets of capitalism evolved in Europe from the late 18th century, most emphatically put by Adam Smith, and were centred on the concept of laissez faire. It held that people should be free of state control in economic affairs and that free enterprise and free markets would bring prosperity to all. As a moral concept, it also held that such freedom constituted the natural system of individual's liberty. Hence, in theory, a capitalist state ought to be one where production and distribution is in private hands and the economic policies are market driven. By implication, a capitalistic state should be also liberal and democratic. However, there are contradictions amongst the ideals of capitalism, liberalism, and democracy.

**Democracy** means sovereignty of the peoples, that is, the government should be chosen by the citizens through open and periodical elections and its policies should reflect the will of the people. The state should also have a constitution which frames the rules of the political game. Thus, in democratic states the government has to take care of the individual voters. While the people want protection of individual liberties, they also want the government to provide them certain public services and civic amenities. Although the state is regarded as inefficient and unproductive for economic activities, the public services cannot be left in private hands. In many sectors, like education and affordable health services, the government has to make good the deficiency of the private sector. The government needs money to provide these services and hence imposes taxes, which may not be to the liking of the rich.

In the field of conducting business, while certain corporate houses may like the market forces to have a free hand, there are also pressure groups that demand a level playing field for fair competition. However, the question is, how does the state create a level playing field in what is basically an undulating terrain? And what good would be a level playing field when the race is between a sprinter and a cripple? And what is a fair competition between a goliath and a dwarf? Thus, the government again intervenes, and acts more like a regulator than a facilitator. Such issues go to the courts and there are no agreed parameters for a solution.

The state has also to intervene to handle any economic crisis created by the domestic or international market. Further, the democratic government has to take care of issues like unemployment, economic inequality, labour protection, environment, etc. For every problem or need of assistance/relief, the public looks at the government to intervene. For every solution, the governments in democracies look at the forthcoming elections and decide the level of intervention. And it is always problematic to strike the right balance between freedom and control in capitalism.

Hence, the one factor that has become common to all states - capitalistic as well as socialistic - is the rise of state intervention and control. While **state control** is the basis of formation of socialist/communist states, it has risen in capitalistic democracies too because the peoples on their own are not in a position to deal with the complex problems arising out of development without state intervention. The democratic capitalist states also do not want socialism to rise and create domestic problems. This led to the universalisation of franchise and increase of state welfarism in the 20th century. As the capitalist states developed, the needs of the people increased and the democratic states had to change in nature and scope of intervention. During the periods of each economic crisis, state intervention and control in every sphere of life increased further.

With the ideal of **Welfare State** becoming central to all democracies, the functions of the state have been increasing constantly and today there is hardly any field of activity which is beyond the purview of the government. State interventions are accepted by the peoples in democratic states because they need the state for various functions and demand the governments to own greater responsibilities.

## LIBERALISM AND THE STATE

A capitalist democratic state is also supposed to be a **liberal state**, one which tolerates divergent views and does not interfere. It provides equitable justice to all and upholds democratic civic and political freedoms like fair elections, free speech and freedom of religion. It promotes free enterprise and facilitates the individual's endeavour for wealth creation, and hence is capitalistic in economic nature. This makes the peoples and the nation prosperous. Many of the western nations come into this category. However, by definition, a liberal capitalistic state should also be the one that exercises minimum control and does not intervene much in the personal life of the citizens. And here comes the problem.

Belgium, Finland, Sweden, Japan, Denmark, Austria, Netherlands, Norway, Luxemburg, Germany, and Singapore are among the richest nations of the world. These are highly developed, industrially advanced, democratic nations, with capitalistic economy and adopt open and progressive policies. But at the same time, the state controls the various aspects of the economy. While being proponents of free trade, the governments control the export/import duties as well as quota of quantities. They make free trade agreements with other nations in a very selective manner.

These states have the highest personal income tax rates in the world - mostly above 50%. However, these are also welfare states and the money is spent on the society, on public services like health and education, general utilities like transportation, civic amenities like water and sanitation, etc. While communist nations do not have elections, most of the capitalistic nations today adopt the same public welfare measures as the socialist countries do. Hence these states blend capitalism with socialism called as redistributive justice. Capitalistic in earning and socialistic in expenditure!

Domestically, while these are extremely liberal states on certain matters, the governments of these states are also **extremely interventionist** as well as strict on certain other matters. While promiscuity, prostitution, gambling, and nude shows are non-issues for the state, the social service workers can barge into anyone's home and check if parents are regularly changing the diapers of their baby. A child after a certain age is not permitted to sleep with the parents. If it is found that parents are not up to their standards in taking care of the baby, they can forcibly snatch the child away and hand it over to foster care. Many immigrants get into major problems for not adhering to such laws simply because they are unable to comprehend something that is totally alien to their own cultural norms.

The state thus draws deep red lines on many such issues which the citizens would not be permitted to cross and hence the level of crime is low. The police would generally not be visible in public but very swift and firm in action. Laws are formed democratically, after intense debate and deliberation, but enforced with a heavy hand. If the grass in someone's front lawn is not regularly mowed, the owner may be fined. In this complexity, it becomes difficult to classify these states as liberal or totalitarian because they are both, depending on the issue.

As regards their foreign policy is concerned, all of them need security. Not because they are peaceful by nature being liberal and democratic. In fact, Germany, Japan and Sweden were among the most war mongering nations in the past. However, today they need peace simply because they are weak and depend on USA for protection. Hence, while the state is strong in domestic matters, it is weak in the international stadium.

USA also has almost the same characteristics as the aforementioned nations but is always ready, even eager, for war. This is because it has the power. This brings in the conclusion that **exercise of power is the product of military strength** of a state and does not depend on the nature of the state. One who has the power uses it. At the same time, USA is ever ready to enter into war, not because the people want it, but because its arms industry needs constant demand of weapons. This also shows that capitalism or socialism has no bearing as far as exercise of military power is concerned.

There are also many democratic states around the world that legally fall in the category of being liberal. But it may not always mean that these are liberal by choice or nature. A weak state may be liberal simply because the state machinery is not effective enough to control things, even dissidence and subversion. This often paves the way to anarchy. Since people, especially the middle class is afraid of losing life and property to an anarchical mob, it willingly surrenders personal liberty to a strong leader and the liberal state turns into a totalitarian one. Putin's rise to power in Russia is a perfect example of this. The rise of Fascism and Nazism were also largely outcomes of weak though liberal states being unable to provide either wellbeing of the peoples or to control the law and order. As such, people chose totalitarianism over liberalism. It must be remembered that Hitler and Mussolini came to power by popular support, and remained powerful because of popularity, till they brought their own nations to ruin. Hence popular support, which is the foundation of democracy, does not necessarily lead to a liberal regime.

## SOCIALIST STATES

Marx predicted that socialism was the inevitable natural fruition of class struggle. However, there has been no Marxian socialist revolution in history. The communist revolution of 1917 in **Russia** was not a socialist revolution against capitalism as predicted by Karl Marx. In fact, two revolutions took place in 1917. The March revolution was against a decaying autocracy which had failed to conduct the war. This brought in a brief period of democratic anarchy. In November the same year, another revolution took place against the democratic government which had failed to govern and also failed at the war front. This so called revolution which brought the Bolsheviks to power was basically a coup engineered by a militant group which had to take the help of armed forces to capture power. Nevertheless, the Bolsheviks had long professed to be socialists and they began implementing socialism by force after they had taken over political power. [The emergence of socialist states in Eastern Europe after the Second World War was sheer military expansion of USSR.]

As per classical Marxism, a socialist state is one in which the government owns or controls the means of production and the system of distribution. For exercising this control, the state has to be powerful and the Soviet regime was primarily concerned about retention of power. Hence, instead of attaining the Marxian ideal of 'withering away of the state', and the 'dictatorship of the proletariat' being an interregnum for transition from capitalism to socialism, the nature of the state became a ruthless dictatorship of the communist party, dictatorship of a clique over the communist party, and dictatorship of an individual over the entire nation. The ideology of socialism became merely a façade to exercise this control.

During the communist rule, Soviet Union became a highly advanced industrial nation with most modern technology that matched USA. This shows that development is not necessarily related with democracy or capitalism. Further, a socialist state can be a welfare state as well as totalitarian at the same time: Dictatorial in political matters while taking care of the economic wellbeing of the peoples. Hence the state provided employment and basic necessities. However, while the state ensured distributive welfarism, it was more a distribution of poverty because the socialistic mode of development was extremely inefficient. By the 1980s, the fallacy of socialist economy became too evident to control. Socialism met its doom with the disintegration of the Soviet bloc, and of the USSR itself, during 1989-91. It showed that while socialism may bring industrial advancement, it may not bring economic prosperity to the citizens or to the nation.

Today, USSR has been reduced to Russia. Although it is no more communist, it is a strange mix of capitalism with totalitarian democracy. It continues to be an advanced industrial nation and is much more prosperous as compared to its socialist days.

In **China**, the Maoist capture of power in 1949 was again not a socialist revolution but a victory of the Red Army in a civil war against a corrupt and unpopular but equally undemocratic regime that had lost legitimacy during the Japanese aggression in China and failed to govern after the end of the Second World War. Mao Zedong implemented his own brand of socialism which brought famines and caused death of millions of citizens. It showed that because of its totalitarian nature, socialism is also no guarantee for the welfare of the citizens.

After the death of Mao Zedong, China began a process of supervised capitalism. While the communist party gave no political freedoms, it liberalised the economy considerably. Private investment - foreign as well as domestic - was encouraged and within two decades, China turned from a backward insular nation to a developed one. Today, China is a totalitarian state but the economy is more in line with a fascist state than a socialist state. It is also a highly advanced industrial nation with most modern technology that challenges USA in every field. It is also much more prosperous than what it was under Mao. This again shows that development is not necessarily related with democracy but capitalism does bring overall prosperity while socialism can only distribute poverty.

The communist nations - the erstwhile USSR and China - when these were communist states, built powerful armies, not because these were socialist but because these were historically large and totalitarian empires and always had powerful armies. They followed aggressive foreign policies partly because of the Cold War rivalry, which again was not because of ideology, but largely because Russia and China have traditionally been hegemonistic empires. Both nations still follow the same policies as they did when these were communist states. Hence, foreign policy does not depend on the eco-political nature of the state but rather on its culture, geo-strategic position, and the capability to exercise power.

## TOTALITARIAN STATES

A totalitarian state is one in which a ruling regime controls all aspects of the life of the citizens. It is restrictive in nature and does not provide political freedoms. There are different types of totalitarian states: These can be monarchies, single party dictatorships, military establishment dictatorships, and one person dictatorships. While the ruling regime may draw legitimacy through tradition and lineage, as it happens in monarchies, or through adherence to an ideology, all basically rely on the power of the army, the police, and an elite bureaucracy that stands to gain from the authority of the regime. However, totalitarianism is no bar to development, prosperity and public welfare. These are not mutually exclusive.

Take the example of the **Gulf States**. Saudi Arabia, Oman, Kuwait, Bahrain, and Qatar are extremely rich nations but have some of the lowest tax rates. It is so because these are monarchies and the extended ruling families control wealth, not the peoples. These have no advanced industry - crude oil extraction being done by crude methods of drilling - but they are diversifying their economy into the services and realty sectors. So they are developed nations without having advanced industry. These are totalitarian but progressive states, and the ruling regime takes care of the peoples although treats them as subjects. Hence, these states cannot be put into any category.

These are liberal in foreign policy but ruthlessly authoritarian in domestic affairs. They also treat the migrants, who are often more in number than the natives, by different sets of rules. This shows that the same regime can be one thing for one group of peoples and very different for the other, and generalisation does not hold well.

In foreign policy, they seek peace because they are weak and scared of regional instability. But at the same time, these states have the capacity to put the international order in total disarray because of their geo-strategic position and oil wealth. Hence, they have **power in international politics without having military power**.

North Korea is a strange example of a totalitarian state. The ruling dictator Kim Jong Un is the third generation ruler of the dynasty and the state has become a monarchy although it is supposed to be a socialist state. Thus, it has become a communist kingdom! It is highly advanced in weapons' technology (largely provided by China) but is poor and the regime is least concerned about the welfare of the peoples.

There are also totalitarian regimes which are poor, underdeveloped and have no welfare policies. Myanmar is the right example of such a state.

## THE GLOBAL SOUTH

The Global South includes the developing and underdeveloped countries, primarily post colonial states of Africa and Asia, and others in Latin America. These nations have high levels of poverty, income disparity, difficult living conditions, and domestic political problems. These can be progressive as well as stagnant, or even deteriorating. These can be liberal democratic or dictatorial. Hence, we find the following combinations.

* Progressive democratic
* Progressive non-democratic
* Non-progressive democratic
* Non-progressive non-democratic

In the **progressive democratic** states, the people are educated and conscious of social and economic issues. The political parties also are democratic and have to come to the expectations of the voters. Although these states allow liberal democratic freedoms, the governments are strong, and focused on development. They are selectively absorbing the best of capitalism, liberalisation, privatisation and globalisation. While these may be in a developing stage, the people are aspirational and want to become a developed nation. In foreign affairs, such liberal states have no policy and work on situation-cum-opportunity basis.

In the **non-progressive democratic** states, the people are less educated and less conscious of the economic issues. The political parties are family or clique controlled (internally undemocratic) and stress upon emotive factors rather than on economic issues. Elections become an arithmetical jugglery of numbers. Muscle and money power is also used to win elections. While supporting the rich get to get funds, they lure the voters by offering freebies. Politicians use slogans to garner votes and keep changing policies in tune with the momentary popular mood. The governments lack long time policies, remain inconsistent and the state remains less developed. A liberal but poor state may also not necessarily be a welfare state because it has no money for public good. At places, laissez faire may simply mean abdication of basic state responsibilities. Those who benefit in such a system - the elites and the oligarchs - support such a state while those who are deprived go against such a regime.

The **progressive non-democratic** are the ones where the regime does not believe in liberal democracy but adopts progressive policies for its own good, to retain power.

The **non-progressive non-democratic** states are the ones where the regime does not care for the peoples and keeps them under control by sheer policing measures and the army. Increasing globalisation has also led to job losses and unemployment in these countries. When capitalism comes into a crisis, there is a rise of leftism as seen in certain Third World nations. These nations are in a state of transition. Many of these states adopted democracy but it failed to deliver and was replaced by authoritarian regimes. These are struggling for their existence.

**Politics of Representation**

Democracy was not uncommon in ancient times. Republics, known as the *janapadas*, flourished in India around 400 BC. Scriptures also laid out the tenets of consensual governance for a king to rule. With the advent of the medieval age, despotism became the normal form of governance all around the world. While army was used everywhere to maintain absolutism, religion was also used to justify despotism in the Muslim world. However, despotism began to be challenged during the 17th century in England and became a major issue during the American and the French revolutions. Almost the entire 19th century saw agitations demanding democracy and constitutionalism in Europe. Today, more than half of the world's population lives under democratic rule.

Democracy is based on the lofty assumption that an elected government represents the will of the people, that people know what is good for them, and that they can participate in the political process for common good and collectively establish a government that works for their betterment. However, there is a perceptible despondency also about how democracy works on many of these parameters.

Elections are considered as the foundation of a modern democracy. However, the very concept is not based on consensus but on dividing the society between the majority and the minority, between the winners and the losers. Thus, how far an elected government truly represents the collective will of the society as a whole becomes debatable. In truth, elected democracy is simply the rule of the majority and not a reflection of social consensus.

The **systems of elections** also differ from nation to nation. The ridiculous system of Electoral College for the presidential elections in USA sometimes leads to a situation that a person gets elected even when he gets lesser popular votes than his rival, as it happened in 2000 and 2016. On the other hand, the system of proportional representation as followed in Europe leads to no party getting a majority. Hence, fragile and unstable coalition governments are formed that make endless compromises to stay in power.

The multi-party and multi cornered contests based on the British principle of first-past-the-post-winner leads to a situation that a party with a slight edge over the others wins a disproportionate number of seats. In the elections of 2019 **in India**, the BJP got 37.36% of the polled votes but won 55.8% of the seats while Congress with 19.5% of the total votes got only 9.5% of the seats. As compared to 2019, in the elections of 2024, the BJP got 36.6% of the votes, only 0.7% less, but its seats plummeted from 303 to 240. On the other hand, the Congress vote share was 21.2%, an increase of mere 1.7%, but it won 99 seats, almost double that of 2019. Thus elections do not indicate popularity but only the ability to manipulate electoral arithmetic.

One factor often overlooked by the psephologists is that often the winning margins are so thin that it seems that it was not the voters but the **non-voters who decided** the fate of the candidates, and in turn that of the nation! Rather, their own fate.

Further, it needs to be debated that since the overall voting was around 66% in both the elections, the absolute winner had the active consent of less than a fourth of the enfranchised populace. Hence, to what extent the winning party really represents the will of the people at large becomes questionable. And what about the extremely poor representation of women in the legislatures when their voting percentage is almost the same as that of men?

In India, almost a fourth of the seats are reserved for certain castes and the electorate has no option but to vote for candidates belonging to that specific group. Thus, a cluster of certain castes have legally ensured their perpetual political dominance in the name of social justice. Is this restriction of freedom of choice democracy?

People are also disenchanted that other than casting their vote, they are not a part of the process of governance, that their elected representatives are cut off from the electorate and do not share public concerns. A member of Lok Sabha in India represents about 26 lakh citizens on an average. An MLA represents over 4 lakh citizens. There is no way the representative can remain in touch with the constituents, nor can the common man reach to his representative.

The size of the municipal constituencies is much smaller, but elected municipalities cover only a very small part of the country, most of these have neither the powers nor the funds to do any good, and people hardly go for voting or even know the name of their corporator. The average voting for municipalities is below 50% showing public apathy of the urban voters towards what should be the primary units of democracy. In rural areas, the panchayats are the primary units of democracy but the less said about the panchayats, the better.

The urban middle class finds itself as a dispensable minority. While there is a rise in voting percentage in rural areas, and in the slum clusters of cities, there is a decline in urban middle class localities. This does not augur well.

## POLITICAL PARTIES AND PRESSURE GROUPS

In any case, the party system has made the elected representative helpless and a rubber stamp of the party leadership. The legislators have to abide by the diktats of the party whip whether they like it or not. Most of the political parties in India are family owned corporations with a top down approach. It is the hereditary leadership that decides the policy as well as the process. There is no inner party democracy in any party. Of course, a phoney internal election is held from time to time to satisfy certain statutory requirements, but it beguiles no one.

A person can contest the election from any part of the country whether he belongs to that region or not, whether he can even speak the language of his constituents or not. After getting elected, many do not even visit their constituency and hardly know the people they are supposed to represent. The elected representatives thus represent the party leadership to the people and not the other way round. Sometimes, they do not even represent the party leadership and switch sides leaving their voters confused about which party they had voted for. Hence, people feel excluded from the instrument of governance, frustrated with the politicians, and disappointed with the entire electoral process which is the cornerstone of a democracy.

**India is a vibrant democracy** in the sense that regular elections are held as per the Constitution, the elections are largely free, fair, transparent and verifiable, and transfer of power keeps taking place without much problem. But do the issues of common man even get a mention during the elections? Elections are won by caste and communal arithmetic, regional and linguistic identity emotions, while issues like civil infrastructure, education, pendency of court cases, healthcare, et al, are not even mentioned. In order to bury material problems under the carpet, populist leaders talk about emotive and polarising issues like reservation and religion. Hence, people question the value of the popular vote when it leads to election of manipulators and demagogues.

Media is used to launch propaganda to malign the rivals. Caste and community leaders, in connivance with political parties, or at their behest, turn the ignorant communities into emotionally committed vote banks and herd their groups to the polling booths while the discerning voter feels himself in a hopeless minority and often prefers to stay at home rather waste his time. This is the 'tyranny of the majority' about which the French philosopher Tocqueville warned long back.

**Majority rule can also make a democracy illiberal** even while elections keep taking place. While a democracy is supposed to be governance by general consensus, overpowering of the state leads to intimidation by the state and thus makes elections irrelevant to personal freedoms. Leaders use the brute power of democratic majority to do things that despots used the army to do earlier. The state is supposed to be governed by the Constitution, and not be subject to popular vote, but the governments can, and do, change the Constitution itself. When such acts are done in the name of 'social justice', the political parties also acquire a moral stance. And India has the dubious distinction of having the most amended Constitution in the world! Britain has a smooth democracy without having a written Constitution. On the other hand, India has the most voluminous Constitution in the world, while some hundreds of constitutional cases are pending in the Supreme Court to decide what the Constitution of India actually says.

Political parties also go about offering freebies - free electricity, water, rations, cooking gas, laptop, mobile, scooter, waiver of loans, etc., without explaining or bothering where the money is going to come from. How many of the voters know anything about deficit financing or care about the long term implications of excessive and unproductive government borrowing? People are hardly conscious that it is their own next generation who will have to pay for it. Parties are only stealing from the piggy bank of the voter's child to gift him something today. Democracy has degenerated into illiberal populism depriving the future for satisfying the present.

People are hardly bothered because only about 1% of them pay any income tax and seem to have no stake on the issue. Thus, we have a situation where a miniscule minority bears much of the financial burden while the ignorant majority governs the country and makes laws. The situation becomes worse when socialism is mixed with democracy, which in effect it is only parasitism - to tax a few and dole it out to a poor majority to get votes. However, the majority has also to bear the consequences in many other ways. While they have to pay the indirect taxes, they also suffer from deficiencies in public services and infrastructure, which in the long term affects employment opportunities and purchasing power by way of low per capita income.

People also see **politicians as corrupt**. Politicians as a class have seen the highest rate of incremental rise in wealth as compared to any other class. Those who have not done a dime's worth of work in life except playing politics own extensive properties. They also get abundant powers, perks and privileges. Hence, crores are spent in each election. This has brought criminals also into the electoral politics and almost a third of the elected legislators, MPs as well as MLAs, cutting across party lines, have pending criminal cases in various courts for committing heinous crimes like murder, dacoity, rape and abduction. While a convict on bail can vote, an undertrial in prison cannot. But he can contest an election, and criminals facing court cases contest and also win elections even while lodged in jails. There are also cases where a minister is sent to jail but continues to hold the office of minister. [In the Delhi state, the Chief Minister was jailed on corruption charges. Another inmate was also the minister for prisons. They continued to be ministers for months while still being in a jail that was legally under their own charge!]

**But what choices does the ordinary voter have**? He can choose; choose the robber whom he wants to be robbed by. Such thinking generates pessimism about democracy in public mood. The situation varies from country to country, but democracy faces roughly similar challenges everywhere. Many believe that elections bring about little change. People watch autocracies like China and Russia rising in power and prosperity with envy. Leaders of such nations also debunk what they call 'western type of democracy'. The idea that autocracy and economic success cannot go together has been rejected by the success of China which has attained both military status and economic power, while restricting personal freedoms of the peoples.

Aggressive **agitations by pressure groups** leading to disruption of normal life of citizens are increasing in most of the democracies. Professional activists use the freedoms given by democracy to challenge and undermine the democratically elected governments. During the Kisan agitation in India 2020-21, the protesters paralysed the movement of road and rail traffic in certain areas for months demanding repeal of laws passed by the Parliament. Ultimately, the government succumbed and the laws were rescinded. If laws are to be made and unmade on the streets by unruly mobs, then what is the role of the legislatures? This makes people pessimistic about the future of democracy. Does it mean that democracy has failed, or is unlikely to survive long?

At the end of the Cold War, it looked as if totalitarianism has been finally defeated. The generation in Europe which survived through the oppression of fascism and the brutality of Nazism is no more. Indians who lived under the infamous period of 'Emergency' are phasing out. We do not even know the reality about today's China. People need to be reminded that it is only because of the freedoms that democracy has provided that people know about the facts and can also openly discuss about the same. People also need to know that undemocratic regimes are not only detrimental to domestic liberty; they are a threat to world peace as well. Autocrats are prone to ignore international laws and treaties. Whether people care about these factors or not, is another matter. Ultimately, any system is only as good as the people using the system.

The optimistic view is that nations cannot survive without economic development, which can take place only with expanding levels of education and uninterrupted information. An open environment makes people to think for themselves rather than accept the diktats of the ruling regime. Hence, there is a fundamental contradiction between authoritarian systems of governance and the human desire for personal freedom and the opportunity to rise. With each passing generation, there is a cultural shift in society that favours values that provide a foundation for liberal democracy. As older generations, who grew and lived under more hierarchical and deferential environment are replaced by newer generations, there is an ever greater inclination for liberal values. Swings in public mood about the perception of democracy would recur in regular cycles, but as a general trend, modernisation, more knowledge, information, and greater awareness would strengthen democratic values.

Yet nothing is fail-safe or predictable in politics. The question is what is the alternative? The answer is that there is no perfect solution. Voltaire said that perfect is the enemy of good. Churchill said that "*democracy is the worst form of government - except for all the others that have been tried.*" Plato's '*Republic*' rejects democracy and proposes the idea of rule by 'Philosopher Kings'. But who will install a philosopher as a king, and what good will he do, remains a moot point.

In the end, people get the government they deserve.

## SOCIAL MOVEMENTS

Social movements are peoples' expressions of frustration, despair, and dissent for causes that demand corrective measures. These may be initiated by a group as well as by a single individual. There is nothing new about social movements and foundation of organised religions was an outcome of social movements. The various revolutions were also basically social movements that took a political colour. In fact, it is difficult to distinguish between social and political movements because the change that the social movements seek can be brought about only by political, administrative, and judicial intervention and action. To cite an example, law and order is a social issue but needs state action.

In the **totalitarian states** there is little room for the citizens to express any type of dissent and hence social movements are hardly visible. Nevertheless, when repression becomes too unbearable, people do come out in protest as seen during the anti-hijab demonstrations 2022-23 in Iran against the moral policing of the theocratic state.

Similar was the pro-democracy 'Umbrella Movement' of Hong Kong in 2019. However, the totalitarian regimes like that of Iran and China hardly care for human rights and have no hesitation in brutally suppressing such movements. They also care little for world public opinion and the world community also reconciles to the fact that it can do little about it. In fact, totalitarian regimes get support of other totalitarian regimes in suppressing domestic popular unrest. Hence, Myanmar gets the support of China for all its repressive actions.

Social movements are an unavoidable feature of a healthy democracy. It is also easy for people to form groups and come out on streets to stage a demonstration. In the **democratic developing nations**, social movements are more political in nature and are mostly on economic and livelihood related issues. While the democratic governments have to accept dissent and peaceful protest, they also try to measure the strength of the movement. If the protest is not supported by the masses, the government tries to diffuse, deviate, and dilute the movement. If the movement crosses the red lines, even a democratic government resorts to strong measures. The argument is that people should express their dissent through the ballot box rather than by putting the daily life of the common man out of gear. However, if the movement is truly popular, the government has to address the issue or run for cover. For example, the collapse of economy in Sri Lanka led to unprecedented protests against the democratically elected government. President Gotabaya Rajapaksha had to flee the country in July 2022 and people occupied his official residence.

In **India**, true social movements have been few, local and sporadic. Most are eco-political in nature and the ruling government looks at the electoral fallout of the movements rather than at the root cause of the agitation. There are professional activists who can be hired for any cause or raise a non-issue and turn it into a political movement. It is also no problem to mobilise a hundred thousand people in India. Politicians also look for an issue to put the government into a corner. The leftists are the foremost in this field. Having failed at armed rebellions, popular revolution, as well as in elections, they rally behind any agitation. The maximum numbers of agitations that have taken place in the last few years in India have been regarding demands for caste based reservations. Although these are given the colour of social movement, these are basically political agitations for group benefits through electoral vote-bank blackmailing.

In the **democratic developed nations**, social movements are truly social in nature and raise concerns of the society as a whole. The 'MeToo' hashtag movement of 2017 aimed to expose the perpetrators of sexual assault and harassment of women by ending the silence of the victims. It was to show the true picture of the extent of the problem through empathy and the strength of numbers. The # MeToo movement started from the western countries and reached the far corners of the world with women daring to come out and sharing their own gory experiences to show solidarity with other women. The movement led to many high profile convictions and jail terms.

The 'Black Lives Matter' movement was against racial discrimination. It started in 2020 in USA and became a global human rights' movement. Similarly, there are movements related to environment and climate change, rights of indigenous peoples, and gender justice. These are global issues and no longer limited to the western developed world.

In the western societies certain social movements are often called as the '**New Social Movements**'. Their goal is to reclaim people's control over their own lives from the state that intrudes and increasingly regulates the everyday personal life of peoples. These are focussed on the collective improvement of the quality of all facets of life of the society. This is a deviation from the movements which are about specific classes and special interest groups. These are primarily about individual choice being a human right. Hence these are also called as '**pro-choice**' movements. Homosexuality once used to be a taboo, even a criminal offence, in many of the developed societies. Today, LGBTQ rights are acknowledged even in the developing countries and many have legalised the same-sex marriage. Similarly, women have come out about the right over their own body to legalise abortion.

Today, a movement can be carried out on the streets as well as in the social media. The **digital world** has given a platform to ordinary peoples to raise their voice with extensive reach. It also provides a relatively safe space for rapid and widespread dissemination of dissent. Anyone can conveniently launch a worldwide campaign sitting at home without incurring the cost of printing leaflets and posters. These often have no clear leadership and a lone activist can trigger a chain reaction. The Arab Spring movement that kept many Arab nations in turmoil during 2011-12 started from a single video going viral of a Tunisian vegetable vendor who set himself on fire to protest against police harassment.

Today, technology is used by the new generation activists to convert a digital movement into a physical movement. The activists use compelling popular symbols to gain international attention and support. Live streaming of protests has become a very potent weapon. Show of solidarity also becomes easy through the media. Protests once started from the alternative media inevitably reach the mainstream also. Hence, movements are getting better coordinated and changing from national into transnational ones.

Of course, there is also a lot of fake news and misinformation in the media. The governments also sometimes use the same tools to stifle free speech, but once something is uploaded on the web, it is impossible to erase it.

Social movements can start due to external/non-domestic reasons as well and may have international consequences that **impact foreign relations** of a nation. Cross border illegal migration is a perfect example of the same. Influx of migrants into the North Eastern states of India from Bangladesh and Myanmar has changed the ethnic and religious demography of these states. It has led to domestic violence and has complicated India's relations with the neighbours.

There have been social movements in many European nations to check migration of Muslims from the Middle East and Africa. It has given rise to far right political parties in Europe and these have won the EU elections of June 2024. This is likely to cause tensions between European nations. While these are basically domestic social issues, they have inter-state political implications too.

# Chapter IV

# United Nations Organisation

The concept of ensuring international peace through joint action gained ground at the beginning of the First World War itself, and a League of Nations Society was formed in Britain in 1915. The Society propagated the idea that peace among the nations can be maintained only if there is a permanent organisation in which all nations participate and the members jointly discuss and resolve contentious issues that lead to conflicts through consensus. The concept was supported by US President Wilson when USA entered the war, and as a result of Wilson's efforts, the League of Nations came into being in 1920 following the Treaty of Versailles. Its primary objectives were prevention of wars through collective security and peaceful settlement of international disputes through negotiation and arbitration. The League was also given a whole gamut of humanitarian objectives like labour reforms, healthcare, and control over drug trafficking.

## THE LEAGUE OF NATIONS

The League of Nations was entrusted to ensure peace by preventing wars while it had little on the agenda to establish international harmony to prevent disputes from arising in the first place. It had no constructive economic plan to foster mutual cooperation and make nations develop a stake in peace, and hence coordinate to work towards international amity. The League thus became simply an **adjudication organisation**, and not a facilitator for peace. Its task was reduced to prevention of wars, and this could be done only in a legalistic manner - through adherence of international treaty obligations by the concerned nations.

The lofty ideal of ensuring peace by cooperative action was possible only if the nations were willing to cooperate, and the collective body was capable of implementing its decisions. Its success also depended on whether the member nations were willing to go in for arbitration at all, were amenable to accept its verdict, and the body was potent enough to take action in case of non-compliance. The concept hence also presumed that one nation could be made to act against another nation, with which it otherwise had friendly relations, just because the League as a collective body had voted to act against that nation.

Nations have multiple, diverse, and divergent concerns, and it was unrealistic to assume that a nation would forgo its own priorities of self interest at the behest of such an assorted body of dissimilar nations each having its own specific concerns. Further, collective action did not mean collective security, and certainly did not guarantee peace; it could only pave way for a minor conflict to escalate into another major war if nations again resorted to formation of power blocs to confront collective action. In short, peace depended on whether the member nations wanted peace at all or not. The League was found wanting on many of these counts, and soon turned into a league of notions that were good to talk about but hard to implement.

The **procedural structure** of the League was in itself a major handicap in ensuring any quick and collective action. The decision for taking any step had to be with the unanimous consent of all the nine primary (later fifteen) members of the Executive Council, as each had the power of veto. Certain decisions required unanimous endorsement of the entire Assembly. There was little consensus among the nations on several issues and this provision impeded any positive or rapid action. The General Assembly was held only once a year and the Executive Council had just 3 to 4 meetings a year. Thus, any immediate decision or action on critical issues was not possible. As such, the League became an ineffectual forum to express grievances, a debating society, but helpless and useless for any practical action.

There was little to doubt that it was an **assembly of the victors** of the war - primarily Britain and France - and they dominated the League. The impression that the League was neither built on trust, nor was it designed to build trust among the nations, became evident at the inception itself when both Germany and Russia were kept out of the League: Germany because it was the aggressor in the First World War, and Russia because a communist regime had taken control over the government which had betrayed the Allies by withdrawing from the war after the November 1917 Revolution.

**Germany and Russia** were kept out of the League ignoring the fact that in both these countries new governments had taken over, and these regimes had nothing to do with the war that had been fought. It was the civilian government of Germany which had ended the war and the communists of Russia had always been against the war. As a promoter for world peace, the League should have been neutral. Rather, it should have welcomed and supported the new governments of both the countries and thereby helped in allaying mutual suspicions. Keeping these nations out only aroused distrust in both the nations about the motives of the member states that dominated the League. The two nations were not allowed to make a fresh beginning, and were stigmatised from the very start even before the newly installed governments of these countries could stand on their own and decide upon their future course of action. Both never got integrated into the European community, and were to become the principal actors in the Second World War.

Keeping Germany out of the world body was impolitic also in the sense that Germany was now an aggrieved nation and it was necessary to address its concerns: treating it as a pariah did not help the cause of peace. Exclusion of Soviet Russia - only because of its communist government - was even a bigger blunder because it was the largest nation of Europe and could have played a major role in securing peace. Its exclusion signalled to the Soviet leadership that the western powers - which had supported the white armies during the civil war - still sustained a hidden agenda, and that Soviet Union would never be at peace till a communist regime ruled the nation.

The suspicion grew stronger in 1925 when Britain and France entered into the Treaty of Locarno with Germany that defined the Franco-German border. This implied that the western nations did not see the eastern frontiers of Germany - as defined by the Treaty of Versailles - as final. The suspicion was confirmed thereafter as Germany was inducted in the League in 1926 but Soviet Russia was still kept out. This left Soviet Union isolated and vulnerable and it convinced the Soviet leadership that western nations were plotting with Germany to act against Russia.

**USSR** could join the League only in 1934 - after Hitler came to power in Germany, and western nations felt the need of Soviet Union to check the rising Nazi power. Mistrust about Soviet Union however continued to overshadow the potential danger from a rearmed Germany. This seriously weakened the League because Soviet Russia was the one country that could have exercised restrain over Nazi Germany, had it been given the due support by western nations. USSR was again expelled in 1939, but by that time the Second World War had started and the League itself had become virtually defunct.

The US Senate did not ratify the Treaty of Versailles, and did not endorse membership of USA into the League of Nations, because the Senators did not want USA to get any more embroiled in European discords. They also apprehended that European nations would take advantage of US resources for their own benefit while USA had nothing to gain out of their disputes. Getting involved in such an organisation would unnecessarily commit USA into entanglements with which America had nothing to do, and nothing to gain. Further, joining the League would restrict USA from taking its own independent course of action. **Absence of USA** in the League became a serious handicap. USA - which could have exerted a sobering influence in European affairs and could have strengthened the hands of the weaker nations and of the League itself - was thus reduced to being only an 'unofficial observer' of the proceedings of the League, with no commitment to its working. On the other hand, because of the non-membership of USA, the League member nations were never sure as to what extent USA would go in supporting the decisions of the League, if at all.

USA had its own interests that differed from those of Britain and France. In fact, economic interests of USA often contradicted the security concerns of these two European powers. USA had strong trade relations with many European nations, including Italy and Germany, and it was reluctant to join hands with Britain or France to become a party in taking any action against Italy or Germany. US banks had given heavy loans to these nations, and had an interest in their economic recovery, and thus followed a policy of supporting Germany and Italy. USA suffered the devastation of Economic Depression during 1929-33 just when Nazism was raising its head in Germany, and it was more worried about its own sinking economy than about the domestic politics of European nations or their security concerns. Further, during the same period, USA was also increasingly getting involved into a conflict with Japan, and as such, USA concentrated more towards Indo-China and the Far East than on Europe.

## WEAKENING OF THE LEAGUE

This obviously meant that Britain and France were the only major powers left in the League of Nations that were in favour of peace as established by the Treaty of Versailles. Even though Britain and France had fought the war together as allies, there had been stark differences in their approach even during the war. Divergence of their outlook only widened soon after the war, and with every new issue coming up, relations between the two became more and more cold. This was so because the two nations had their own threat perceptions, and thresholds of security concerns. France had suffered the most during the war because the war had been fought mainly on French soil causing more devastation than in any other country. France was a ravaged nation and needed financial resources for reconstruction, and hence insisted on compensation by way of reparations. France also had to fear the most from Germany as it shared a long border with Germany. As such, ensuring security for future through strict implementation of the Versailles treaty was its prime concern.

On the other hand, **Britain** had not been invaded and did not suffer any territorial damage. Being an island nation, it had also much less to fear because of its naval strength. Britain needed to revive its own trade and industry to recover economically, and for that Britain desperately needed breathing space. It felt that a peaceful, stable, and prosperous Germany was the best guaranty of peace. It would also help British trade and hence was good for British economy too. Hence, while France wanted to keep Germany weak, Britain wanted it to recover. Thus, from time to time Britain also diluted and scaled down some of the restrictive provisions of the Treaty of Versailles and it increasingly started to appear as if Britain was friendlier to Germany than to France. As such, even though Britain was a signatory to the Treaty, it was seen to be itself abandoning the Treaty, as well as France, while France needed the world body to ensure compliance of the Treaty of Versailles.

While the threat of Germany remained the foremost concern for France, it was the **threat of communism** that seemed to pose a greater danger for Britain. Besides being at variance in their threat perception, Britain and France were both also too weak after the war to take any precipitate action. These factors emasculated the League making it a spineless body. The League could threaten the weaker nations, but not the stronger ones that posed the real threat. In actual functioning also, the League was able to intervene and arbitrate to resolve disputes only where smaller nations were involved. However, when Japan occupied Manchuria in 1931, the League took almost two years to decide that Japan should vacate Manchuria. This infuriated Japan. It refused to vacate Manchuria and withdrew from the League in 1933. However, the League could do nothing by way of positive action against Japan as no nation was willing to take-up the violator by the horns. Britain, in fact, looked at the rising Japan as a check on Soviet Union in the Far East, and tacitly supported it. Finding it a toothless body, Germany also walked out of the League in 1933 after Hitler came to power and repudiated the Treaty of Versailles. Several South American nations also withdrew from the League as they considered it as a worthless expenditure.

In 1935 **Italy attacked and conquered Abyssinia** but the League could only impose half-hearted economic sanctions on Italy. This failed to check Italy; instead it brought Italy into the German camp. Italy withdrew from the League and joined the Anti-Comintern Pact. This sounded the knell of the League. As it became easy to defy the decisions of the League without any fear of repercussions, it failed in its principle aim to resolve disputes where nations that mattered were involved. This provoked nations to enter into several bilateral and multilateral treaties that totally overshadowed and by-passed the basic function of collective security of the League. Unfortunately, the League continued to act only as a judge, and not as a mediator to bring about reconciliation. As nations started leaving the League one by one, the organisation became even more redundant.

The League however did commendable work on many schemes of socio-economic welfare and there was better consensus on the non-political issues. The League thus also had many long term achievements to its credit. Although the League met its demise in the flames of the Second World War, many of its subsidiary bodies survived in its rebirth as the United Nations Organisation. The present day International Court of Justice, the International Labour Organisation, UNESCO, and the World Health

Organisation are reincarnations of the ancillary bodies of the League of Nations. However, it failed to achieve the primary objective for which it was created. On the day the Second World War broke out, the member delegates of the League were deeply engrossed in feverishly debating the frivolous issue of poundage of rails on European railway systems.

## UNITED NATIONS ORGANISATION

When the Second World War broke out, the League was temporarily shut down. After the war was over, it handed over charge, along with its assets and subsidiary wings, to the newly formed United Nations Organisation in 1945. Hence, the UNO was an avatar of the League of Nations.

The Second World War proved that peace could not be ensured merely by trying to prevent wars, and a world body entrusted with the task of maintaining peace should not function simply as an arbiter of disputes. It must be a forum of resolving conflicts by removing the generic causes of discord through collective deliberation and consensual action. At the same time, it must also bring nations together through a constructive agenda, and hence, it must have objectives that go beyond the solo aim of maintaining peace.

Any such organisation must provide a platform through which nations cooperate to pursue humanitarian goals that affect the planet as a whole, and address problems which nations on their own cannot deal with. It must help nations in times of distress and develop common welfare programs for the well being of mankind. Above all, it must stand for justice for all. As such, it should represent not just the governments but the peoples at large and reflect global aspirations of the human community. It must epitomise the new world order and hence should be based on open, inclusive and democratic principles. These were to become the founding precepts of the United Nations Organisation.

The **UNO was never meant to be a world policeman** that would impose peace by the use of military force. Any international body cannot have, and ought not to have, such a character, or else it would be defeating its own reason of existence, that is, preservation of peace. As declared in Article 1 of the Charter, UNO was meant to resolve disputes by peaceful means, in accordance with international laws, and by consensus.

Any such world body can be only as successful as the member states are willing to make it succeed. Since the members of this organisation are a diverse lot, the success record of UNO has also been mixed. Like the League of Nations, the UNO has several humanitarian objectives too. As in the case of the League, while the success record of its political objective of resolving bi-lateral disputes has been uneven, at times even controversial, it has been a phenomenal success story in the fields of human welfare. It also appears as if it is meeting its primary goals through its secondary ones.

On **political issues** involving national security, consensus among nations is often difficult to achieve. Nevertheless, UNO provides a table for negotiations. Even if UNO may not directly intervene as a body, its very existence prevents a breakdown of dialogue. It also ensures that world leaders communicate in an open forum, in presence of other members, where they have to justify their position on logic. They stand to be questioned, even criticised, by neutral nations. This compulsion to explain, and to remain in constant communication, compels the member states in dispute to exercise restraint, and not to cross the red lines of international acceptance. Although nations often defy the decisions/resolutions of UNO, it is at the cost of international disapproval and reprobation, and nations want to avoid that.

UNO was dominated by USA in its formative years, and USA also succeeded in involving UNO into the Korean War to serve its own interests. (Soviet Union at that time was boycotting the UNO and could not use its veto power.) Thereafter however, as more and more nations joined UNO, US influence over UNO declined and UNO became ideologically neutral. UNO thus played a part in ending the Korean War, in resolving the Suez Crisis 1956, and in diffusing tensions in the Middle East and in many other parts of the world. Nevertheless, it is also true that USA interfered in the affairs of many nations - Vietnam, Iraq, and Afghanistan, to name a few - without bothering about the UNO and UNO could do nothing. The ongoing war in Ukraine and the conflict in Gaza also show how ineffective UNO is in preventing wars.

UNO however exercises a sobering influence on nations that keep it relevant despite its occasional failures. Perhaps it is also practically not possible to prevent all wars and UNO cannot be condemned as a dud organisation just because armed conflicts intermittently keep taking place. The onus of failure of UNO to prevent many wars lies on the member states and not on the organisation. Ultimately, its success depends on the will of the nations, and of the leaders that govern them. Nevertheless, its success lies in containing disputes, in localising conflicts, and preventing a minor spark from spreading and escalating into a serious conflagration. Its success is evident from the fact that there has been no major war since the inception of UNO. UNO has also helped develop international laws by global consensus, and the International Court of Justice plays the role of an impartial arbiter to resolve many issues.

The permanent functioning of the **UN Security Council** also helps in keeping the UNO awake. While the provision of veto power to five nations in the UNSC has often stopped right action to be taken, it has also prevented wrong actions to be taken unilaterally by a superpower. While this position of no-action has failed to stop many a conflict, it has also succeeded in limiting the conflicts, and prevented them from spreading. UN intervention without the consensus of superpowers would be a sure recipe for another world war, and a nuclear one at that. To that extent, the veto power perhaps stands justified.

Many analysts also hold - cynically though truthfully - that possession of atom bombs has done a better job at preventing escalation of wars than UNO or the veto power in UNSC.

The demand to make the Security Council more representative, by expanding the number of permanent seats, has been going on since long. There are no permanent members in the UNSC from South America, Africa, and the Global South. India, Brazil, and Japan are among the top contenders for a permanent seat. However, many nations are opposed to the idea because of their own rivalries. In the 1995, Italy, Pakistan, Mexico and Egypt formed a group called Uniting for Consensus, nicknamed as the **Coffee Club** to oppose adding permanent members in the UNSC. Instead, they supported the expansion of UNSC by having more non-permanent seats. Today there are about 50 countries in this group. They hold that increase of permanent seats would further increase the disparity between the member countries.

Today, China is the single biggest opponent of India in getting a permanent seat. Denying a permanent seat in the Security Council to India - a country with a sixth of global humanity - makes a mockery of the principle of equal rights. While there is ample justification for including India and certain other nations as permanent members, it is equally debatable if expanding the Security Council would yield any better results, other than satisfying the prestige needs of the denied nations. Too much expansion may also lead to even more dissensions and more debates rather than to any good action because ultimately everything depends on the good sense of the nations, and often the security concerns of a nation come in way of internationally expected good sense.

## UNO AND HUMAN RIGHTS

During its formative years UNO could not meet with its avowed objective of supporting rights of self-determination of the peoples of subjugated colonies and the populace under colonial role had to struggle for their own independence. This was because the founding nations of UNO - Britain and France - were themselves the main colonial powers, and had the support of USA. However, as UNO became more representative, self-determination became a firm international principle, and many more nations have achieved independence on the principle of self-determination with the support of UNO.

UNO's record in curbing **racism** has also been dismal. The South African regime rampantly continued with its abhorrent policy of apartheid well into the 1980s because of USA's unstinted support to South Africa. It was only after public pressure mounted on the American politicians that the US Senate - despite veto by President Reagan - imposed strict economic sanctions on South Africa which led to the end of apartheid and democratisation of South Africa. However, much has changed since those times. Today, discrimination on the basis of race, religion, or gender, is internationally not acceptable. Individuals may still be practising such discrimination, but it cannot be the political policy of a nation, or even of a multinational private organisation. This success has been achieved primarily by UN efforts in bringing these issues into public domain, and exposing those nations and organisations that practice discrimination.

UNO's success on **human rights** has been equally questionable. Human rights continue to be violated by China, North Korea, ultra-radical Islamist regimes, monarchies, and by several other despotic establishments. Again, these may not be called as failures. UNO's success lies in the fact that its mere existence makes nations answerable for their human rights' record before the international community, and in the fact that these issues are being raised at all on a global platform. Even if human rights are not respected at places, the concerned parties are being questioned, made accountable to the world community, and even reprimanded through the yearly reports of UNHRC. Even the most repressive regimes today cannot deny that humans have certain basic rights. They only try to defend that they are not denying their citizens of these rights. International pressure is building up, and as in the case of apartheid, it may be expected that one day these regimes may not have any option but to yield to a more civilised and internationally acceptable behaviour.

While being critical of UNO in its inability to safeguard human rights in many countries, it must also be kept in mind that even as these issues are of universal concern, they are legally and hence basically domestic matters of those countries. Interference into the internal affairs of a nation beyond a point amounts to intrusion in the national sovereignty of those countries. Nevertheless, despite such legal limitations, UNO has consistently been emphasising on these issues, and over a time, success is also evident. However, the issue of human rights has become complicated due to a mix of economic factors and racial bias. White nations are yet to get out of their colonial mindset and keep commenting adversely on Asian nations while ignoring their own long history of slavery and religious persecution. They also want to impose tariff restrictions on products of Asian nations for using child labour. Thus, extraneous factors obfuscate the basic issue of human rights.

Although **democracy** is not mentioned in the Charter of UNO, because many of the founding member states were not democratic, it remains a core value for the organisation. The opening words of the Charter, "We the Peoples", reflect the fundamental principle of democracy, that popular will is the basic source of legitimacy of sovereign states. The UNO does not advocate a specific model of government but promotes democratic governance by reinforcing the relationship between democracy and human rights. This is done through bodies like the United Nations Democracy Fund, the Office of the High Commissioner for Human Rights, the United Nations Entity for Gender Equality and the Empowerment of Women, et al.

Democratic values are also enshrined in the Universal Declaration of Human Rights. The International Covenant on Civil and Political Rights lays down the principles of democracy in international law. The UN General Assembly has also passed several resolutions endorsing respect for human rights, non-discrimination against women, fundamental freedoms, rule of law, free and fair elections by universal suffrage and secret ballot, system of political parties, independence of the judiciary, and free and pluralistic media. The UNO also provides electoral assistance like logistic support, training, and short-term observation. The UN General Assembly has proclaimed 15th September as the International Day of Democracy which provides the people an opportunity to review the state of democracy in their nations.

Even though almost half of the world's population still lives under undemocratic, semi-democratic, or pseudo-democratic rule, democracy has become such a holy cow that even the most oppressive regimes do not dare to oppose these resolutions, or the UNO for promoting democracy, because no one wants to be labelled as undemocratic. In fact, most autocracies call themselves democracies. The Chinese leadership describe their country as a democracy "with Chinese characteristics," and even have the temerity to claim that China is the world's "greatest" democracy!

## HUMANITARIAN ACTIVITIES

While UNO has been unable prevent many wars, it has played a stellar role in peace keeping activities. UNO is the only internationally legitimate institution authorised for military intervention to enforce peace and UN peacekeeping forces are ensuring that conflicts and civil wars do not resume at dozens of trouble spots in Africa, Middle East, and elsewhere. Once a resolution gets the endorsement of the world community, there is no other organisation that can perform the thankless task of keeping peace in these conflict ridden zones. The peace keeping forces protect the civilians from militant groups and have earned the reputation of being largely impartial and effective. [There are occasional aberrations also. Some aid workers of UN in Gaza actively participated in the attack on Israel on 7th October 2023.]

Even if UNO fails to prevent wars, it plays a significant role in **post-war reconstruction, and refugee resettlement**. Its role in providing shelter, food and medicines to displaced persons in war-torn areas is particularly commendable. There are estimated to be a total of about 70 million refugees / internally displaced persons spread in different parts of the world at present. Most of these permanently survive on UN aid at any given time. UN even runs schools in refugee camps. These success stories do not get media coverage, and hence the UNO gets only brickbats for its failures.

Much of this success has been due to the overt and subtle functioning of the UNO and its multiple subsidiary agencies that permeate all facets of human life. These agencies are spread across the globe and have been relentlessly carrying out economic and social development, and addressing global issues that affect mankind as a whole. While political issues keep the nations apart, UNO becomes the medium for collective efforts, and coordinates international endeavour in face of global humanitarian challenges.

UNO's true success thus lies in the field of **humanitarian work**, in its ability to provide immediate relief in case of a crisis to any part of the globe. During any catastrophe - whether man made or natural - the UNO becomes the channel for collective action which nations cannot deal individually. These can be calamities like an earthquake, a tsunami, a flood, a famine, an epidemic, or displacement of civilians due to war or civil strife. There is no other organisation that has the resources, experience, capacity, and the machinery to deal with such emergencies and deliver on the scale that UNO is able to do. It has well developed logistical strategies to deal with such humanitarian crises, and when the UNO deals with a problem, all nations tend to come forward and contribute in the endeavour in a non-partisan manner.

The World Food Programme has addressed the issue of hunger and nutrition by providing life-saving support to starving millions over the years, especially to those affected by famines and conflict related displacements. The World Health Organisation is another agency of the UNO that has played a critical role in monitoring spread of epidemics. It sends warning signals and also coordinates in development and distribution of medicines and vaccines.

UNO has taken up the cause of preservation of environment, global warming, elimination of contagious diseases and AIDS. It also addresses problems of drug-trafficking, sex-trafficking, and child labour. UNO has led campaigns to ban landmines, for improvement of labour standards, and to stop the use of child soldiers. The UNO has coordinated for nuclear disarmament and non-proliferation, and test ban agreements. UNO has worked for the preservation of heritage and protection of world cultural treasures through UNESCO.

More than the direct relief that UNO has provided, its success lies in putting these issues on the global agenda, thus evoking public reaction, and compelling nations to initiate corrective action. These problems affect the entire planet and no country on its own can tackle them. These have become the shared responsibilities of mankind and have to be dealt with collectively. United Nations as an organisation is unique in the sense that it has the internationally accepted legitimacy for such humanitarian tasks for which there is no alternative.

As nations, and their officials, work together for common non-political non-security related humanitarian goals, it brings them together. They adopt a non-partisan approach in charitable endeavours, and develop common values. As they interact and exchange views they shed suspicions. It helps in softening political differences which is also conducive for enduring political peace. Such working together helps foster common values and mutually acceptable behaviour. It carries seeds of internal reforms as well. Often this expectance of acceptable behaviour is mocked as 'aid with strings attached' but that is one non-intrusive way for achieving the non-political goals of UNO.

## UNO AND TERRORISM

Terrorism is not a new phenomenon. Extremist activities kept occurring in monarchical totalitarian regimes that did not give political space for expression of popular dissent. In a way, it was politics by other means: When other methods failed to achieve results, individuals and groups resorted to violence. Violence became a regular feature of political wrangling for power with the outbreak of the French Revolution. Later, the Nihilists, the communists, the Fascists, and the Nazis, resorted to street violence to capture power. While they were called as revolutionaries by some, they were labelled as subversives by the governments. During the colonial period, many took to violence as a way to liberation. The colonial governments called and treated them as criminals while the nationalists gave them silent support and facilitated them as freedom fighters. The debate still goes on, depending on which side of the fence one is sitting on.

Terrorism in the modern age has acquired a very different character. Today, it is neither for a revolutionary change of the government nor for capturing power. Further, while the extremists of the earlier period targeted the top functionaries of the government, the **terrorists of today pick soft targets** - the civilians. They have little or no popular support or sympathy. But they have the backing of powerful sponsors and act as proxies. Of course, some are autonomous, and although they also need sponsors, they act on their own. Some are simply like mafia gangs, indulging in extortion, drug and arms smuggling, human trafficking, and other illegal activities. As such, there is no template of terrorism.

Today, there are any numbers of terrorist groups, each having its own agenda. However, the common strategy of all is to inflict harm to their perceived enemy. Terrorism from different angles has been discussed in various other chapters in this book as well and here we will only examine the role of UNO on the issue.

Several nations have been victims of terrorism in the last few years, India being one among the most affected. Way back in 1986, India drafted a proposal for the UNO called as the Comprehensive Convention on International Terrorism. However, it has not yet been adopted because there is still no unanimity on the very **definition of 'terrorism'**. This is because many nations are either directly or through sponsoring non-state transnational actors are deeply involved in terrorism. For many others it has become a political game of international rivalry rather than a common global humanitarian issue. One nation's terrorist is another nation's freedom fighter. For example, PLO remained a terrorist organisation for long but was also recognised as a body fighting for the freedom of Palestine. Similarly, Pak sponsored terrorists in Kashmir are also described as freedom fighters, or best as 'militants', not as terrorists.

While Islamic terrorism was gaining ground in the Middle East, USA became a prominent sponsor of a rabid terrorist group called Taliban. However, when USA itself became a victim of terrorism in September 2001 (the Twin Tower attack), the United Nations Security Council immediately established the Counter Terrorism Committee. The **UNSC-CTC** is supposed to take all steps to curb terrorism. This includes taking steps to criminalise all forms of terror financing, checking safe havens of terrorists, and sharing information with other governments on terrorism. UNO has also formed many other agencies to curb terrorism. The Financial Action Task Force (**FATF**), which was formed in 1989 basically to check money laundering, has also been assigned the task of curbing terror financing. This is because terrorism cannot survive without money. Since terror financing is done through the anonymity that modern global technology provides, like use of virtual currencies, special agencies were needed to check the same.

However, UNO has utterly failed on this issue because certain of the nations have taken their selective positions on the subject. Thus China ensures that Pakistan sponsored terrorism in India is protected while USA has formally given up its so called 'war on terror' with handing over of Afghanistan back to Taliban in August 2022. Islamic nations have a very ambivalent and divided approach on the subject and none is willing to accept that Islamic terrorism is an issue. In fact, nations want to avoid the very use of word "Islamic" although terrorism is largely Islamic and Muslim nations and Muslims as individuals have been its biggest victims. FATF too has failed to act, and while it accepts that much terror funding is being routed through Pakistan, it has ensured US financial aid to Pakistan to continue because USA does not want to completely lose all its influence in Pakistan to China.

UNO also suffers from **institutional problems** on the subject. In 2006, UNO established the Human Rights Council for protection of human rights around the globe with headquarters in Geneva. None of its 47 members belong to the Islamic nations or to totalitarian regimes. Nonetheless, it has become a self appointed international referee on human rights. Most of the time it is more concerned about protecting the human rights of the terrorists rather than of the victims. Whenever governments try to take action on terrorism, the UNHRC accuses the governments of human right violations. If governments try to curb terrorist propaganda, they accuse the government of suppressing basic democratic right of freedom of speech. Hence, UNO's own two bodies are in conflict with each other on the issue. In any case, nothing much should be expected out of UNO considering that its Secretary General Antonio Guterres himself has become the chief spokesman in defence of terrorism.

## UNO AND CLIMATE CHANGE

Climate change is all too visible to be ignored. We see extremes of weather conditions unheard of earlier: scorching summers in Europe and USA and flash floods in the Arab nations (April 2024). In fact, all parts of the globe are witnessing unprecedented heatwaves, unseasonal torrential rains, forest fires due to drought, rising sea levels, receding snowlines, thinning glaciers, thawing permafrost, etc. Much of this is being attributed to human activity, primarily due to use of fossil fuels - oil and coal - for energy leading to emission of CO2 and other greenhouse gases (GHG) that cause global warming.

Degradation of natural ecological system is not a new phenomenon: It started with agriculture based settlements what we call as the beginning of civilisation of human beings. It involved large scale cutting of trees to turn forests into plains for cultivation and urbanisation. Environment took a major knock with the beginning of the Industrial Revolution, and the use of fossil fuels has kept increasing ever since. While scientists had since long started pointing out the impact of human activity on environment, and consequent impact on life on the planet because of the changing climate, it was first taken as an international issue of concern during the UN Conference on the Human Environment at Stockholm in 1972. It brought environmental issues into the ambit of international affairs by emphasising the need of global cooperation. In 1982, the UN Environment Programme (UNEP) was formulated to address the environmental threats. In 1983, the UNO appointed the World Commission on Environment and Development. Its report "Our Common Future" was released in 1987 which proposed the concept of "**sustainable development**" to balance economic development with environmental protection. In 1988, the UNO also formed the Inter-Governmental Panel on Climate Change (**IPCC**).

The UN Conference on Environment and Development at Rio de Janeiro in 1992 sought to find ways of promoting economic development of developing nations without affecting the environment. Thus came up the UN Framework Convention on Climate Change (**UNFCCC**). Its meetings were called as **COP** - Conferences of Parties. The UNFCCC was based on the principle of common but differentiated responsibilities and capabilities of the states. India stressed on the issue of historical responsibility and per capita emission as the basis for a differentiated approach. This basically meant that developed nations which had become rich in the modern age through high levels of emission in the past, and are still using more fossil fuels, should bear a proportionately higher burden of the cost of corrective action. They also have the financial resources and technologies for the same. They should also enable the developing nations to reduce emissions by funding as well as by technological cooperation. The developing countries cannot be asked to enter into binding agreements that require diversion of money that they need for economic development and poverty mitigation.

In December 1997, 84 nations became signatories to the **Kyoto Protocol** which set legally binding targets on 37 developed countries for the reduction of GHG emissions. This was on the principle of 'common but differentiated responsibilities.' However, the US Senate did not approve of the Kyoto Protocol because of this provision. Although 36 developed nations reduced emissions, total global emissions increased because developing nations like China and India, which contributed substantially to GHG emissions, were exempted. What the Kyoto Protocol truly achieved was to pave the way for future climate negotiations in which developing countries could also be included. As a result, a Green Climate Fund was set up in 2009 to make critical technologies freely available to developing nations, although contributions to it were meagre.

The Kyoto Protocol also succeeded in making climate change a global challenge. Successive IPCC reports painted a gloomy picture of the problem and stressed that global warming posed multidimensional threat to human existence on the planet. While pollution had become a health hazard in the industrialised nations, upsetting of the global eco-system affected all nations. NGOs supporting the cause became vocal all around the world and public opinion began to be built. While the level of awareness was more in the developed nations, the developing nations also realised that not only would they be the worst affected, they were also the least equipped to deal with the unforeseeable problems. Although nations continued to use fossil fuels, many of them also started working on alternate/renewable sources of energy. As such, a consensus began to emerge that this was an issue on which all have to join hands. This led to the Paris Agreement of 1915.

The **Paris Agreement of December 2015** was a legally binding international treaty accepted by 196 parties to attain the goal of limiting global average temperature below 2°C of the pre-industrial level. The Agreement provided a framework for financial, technical and capacity building support for the developing nations. Each signatory had to submit a national climate action plan (targets) called as the Nationally Determined Contributions (**NDC**s).

Today, there is little politics on the issue and all nations are working on the Paris

Agreement targets and contributing money for the same. Even oil producing Gulf States have joined the effort. Not only the governments but the large corporate houses also - including oil companies - have started taking positive action. The progress is reviewed at each COP meeting. During the **COP28** held at Dubai during Nov-Dec 2023, it was agreed to triple renewable energy capacity. However, it is a global target and not nation specific, and without timelines. Nations also agreed to create a Loss and Damage Fund to compensate nations, especially the Least Developed Countries, for climate change problems. However, there was no established mechanism to ensure that nations fulfil their financial commitments. Despite certain shortcomings, the fact that nations have agreed to work on the subject augurs well.

However, climate change is not just about GHG emissions: It is directly related to the overall ecological balance. While emissions do lead to global warming, so do all other activities of development like industrialisation and urbanisation. India needs not only energy for power, it also needs infrastructure development. India also has serious security concerns in the Himalayas and needs strategic roads for defence movement. These activities involve deforestation that alters the fragile landscape of the region which in turn affects the climate.

## INDIA AND CLIMATE CHANGE

**India** has one of the lowest rates of per capita GHG emissions but in terms of volume it is the third-largest emitter in the world after China and USA. India has also faced some of the worst climate related disasters in recent years. India cannot finance the huge investments needed to enhance its capacity to adapt to climate change unless its economy grows faster. At the same time, the losses incurred due to climate related problems seem to be exceeding the investments being made for development. Hence India has a multilayered problem on hand. While the need for development seems to be at odds with climate control measures, development itself will be in jeopardy unless climate related events are controlled. More money may be spent on rescue, relief, and restoration in environment related disasters - like floods, droughts, and landslides in sinking hills - than that on infrastructure development. Hence, India is very much on the same page with the international community on the subject, although it may differ on the specifics.

**Environmentalists** have done no less damage in complicating the whole issue. Many are professional activists hired by the opposition parties and rival corporate houses for stalling developmental projects in the name of protecting the environment. One sees the same faces on TV agitating for a wide range of causes. Whenever an activist succeeds in halting an important developmental project, he gets some unknown international award from some vague NGO. When the government wants to know the source of funding of such NGOs, the government is accused of being undemocratic, and of being callous towards environment. In some cases, this is true also.

The **federal structure** and the constitutional provisions are also a problem in India. While the central government has overarching responsibility for environment protection, the state governments too have powers on many of the subjects that are related to environment. Since different political parties are in power at the centre and in the states at different times, the two are often at loggerheads on the issue. While such tussles delay important projects, there is little coordinated policy at the national level for environment protection.

Climate change has to be tackled through adaptation and mitigation. Adaptation means accepting the facts and preparing for the same. Adaptation does give some immediate relief but has its limits. Not only funds are an issue, adaptation involves community action, and social awareness about environment is extremely poor. Politically also, expenditure on environment hardly fetches any vote. Further, unless the problem is dealt at the global level, not much can be achieved at the regional level. Since total need of energy cannot be reduced, the problem can be mitigated only by switching from conventional sources of energy to renewable sources such as wind, solar, ocean, geothermal, hydroelectric, and nuclear energy. It also needs energy conservation through efficient usage like electric vehicles, public transport, etc.

However, there are several **basic challenges** on the issue. The foremost is that switching is a very slow and costly process. Even if necessary funds and political will is on hand, there is no capacity to switch to alternative means overnight. Further, natural sources such as wind, sunlight, and descending rivers for hydroelectric power are not available in many regions. Nuclear power is very costly and is no more considered as a clean energy because of the problem of disposal of nuclear waste. Nations hence will need to continue the use of conventional sources for decades to come as there seems to be no perfect alternative immediately on hand. Thus, climate control is a race against time.

The second problem is that environmental impact of switching to alternative technologies has not yet been fully assessed. For example, renewables need batteries and Lithium is essential for batteries. However, Lithium mining and extraction is an environmental hazard. One ton of Lithium needs about 500,000 litres of water. The released water seeps into freshwater aquifers and poisons underground water as well as nearby rivers and ponds. The disposal of used batteries is even more problematic. Thus, the remedial medicine may even worsen the disease.

The third problem, which coal producing nations like India face, is that of **livelihood of millions presently engaged in coal mining** for power houses and industries. Renewables like solar energy do not need manpower. Hence, alternate means of employment needs to be considered. It has not yet turned into a problem in India despite exponential increase of solar energy because of the extensive demand for power, and hence coal mining continues as before. However, peoples of states like Jharkhand and Chhattisgarh depend on coal mining so much that closure of this activity can turn into a major socio-political crisis.

Lastly, many scientists hold that climate change is an inevitable natural cycle and human contribution may tinker a little bit but would not be able to reverse the cycle. Planet earth has gone through recurrent phases of extreme warming and glacial ages without any human involvement in the past and the same would happen in future. This view may be controversial, even cynical, but has scientific evidence. Nevertheless, it cannot be denied that human activity has contributed to climate change.

Climate change is just one aspect of environment protection. There are issues of air and water pollution, noise and light pollution in urban areas, plastic wastage and freshwater availability due to groundwater depletion, ocean acidification and loss of bio-diversity. We need an integrated and holistic approach in dealing with environment conservation. Human activity is taking away the planet from the conditions that allowed human civilisation to develop and thrive. Now is the question of survival.

## CHALLENGES BEFORE UNO

UNO has also been undergoing transformation due to increase in membership and expansion of its activities. UNO has become more representative, more open, more democratic, and less dominated by any superpower. While the Cold War and the prospect of a regional conflict flaring into a global war was the prime concern of the UNO for several decades, the developmental and humanitarian agenda seems to have overtaken the political agenda now. This is because far graver issues have come to affect the planet, like terrorism, climate change, epidemics like Ebola and Covid, and mass migration of refugees displaced from disturbed areas.

UNO also faces several **organisational problems** that often affect its efficacy. With expansion of activities, the organisation has become too bureaucratic, and wasteful. USA, the prime contributor to its funding is increasingly hesitant to contribute to a body that is often seen to be working against US interests. USA pulled out of UNESCO some time back, and now it has withdrawn from UNHRC also. (USA is likely to rejoin these bodies soon.) Such retaliatory actions are not entirely unjustified also because quite often the members in these committees keep their national biases while making reports and draw prejudiced criticisms. Despite such irritating hiccups that keep coming, these should be taken by the nations in due stride as these will keep happening in such a large organisation with such diverse membership. What is required is to take corrective steps by consensus rather than throwing the baby out with the bathwater.

While using the UNO when it suits their own interests, there also is a constant effort by powerful nations like USA, Russia, and China, to make UNO redundant by defaulting in funding, by bullying, and by taking unilateral actions through alliances like NATO, in contemptuous defiance of UNO. That is what makes UNO even more essential in this post Cold-War non-polar world, so that powerful nations are kept in check and do not start acting like wild elephants. Thus, UNO as a body acts as a legitimate counterweight to the superpowers, often forcing them to modify their stand, negotiate, and make compromises in the general interest.

Today several organisations have come up like EU, G-7, G-20, BRICKS, SCO, ASEAN, etc., where a group of nations sit separately to resolve their issues, without the need of UNO. These groups do not make the UNO irrelevant. In fact, by resolving regional or group-centric issues on specified subjects they supplement and complement the role of UNO without burdening the world community with matters that they can resolve on their own. This helps UNO in focussing on truly global issues rather than in getting bogged down by issues that are bilateral, regional, or thematic.

The United Nations is an ideal platform for the nations to find solutions through consensual efforts for shared problems, and hence is a great stabilising factor in an unstable environment. It depicts differences as well as aspirations of the international community. UNO provides a neutral ground where any nation can make itself heard, and seek attention of the world community for its problems. There is no other institution that can bring disparate nations, often at loggerheads with each other, to work together for common objectives in the collective interest. It is indispensable because there is no internationally acceptable alternative to it.

The UNO has many challenges to face, and would have many more in future. It has imperfections to correct. As an organisation the world community cannot do without, it would be for the same world community to collectively face those challenges and improve upon the imperfections. As such, the real challenge is not for the UNO as an organisation, but for the world community at large. While a large number of nations left the membership of League of Nations in disappointment, there is no country that has left the UNO. For one thing the Charter of UNO does not permit this. The other is that nations today want to be a part of the world community. It is a proof that nations are willing to face the common challenges that are before the UNO.

# Chapter V

# International Political Order

International political equations never remain the same. At the beginning of the 19th century, Russia, Britain and the Ottoman Empire were truly world superpowers. By the end of the 19th century, while Russia and Britain continued to be major powers, the Ottoman Empire had reached an advanced state of decay, and USA in the West and Japan in the Far East were emerging as great powers. With the end of the Second World War, USA and Soviet Union became the two superpowers. The end of Cold War led to a brief spell of a unipolar world with USA as the only super power. Today, Russia has resurfaced as a super power while China has also emerged as the third super power.

While the strength of the armed forces was the traditional source of power in the medieval age, the two factors that led to rise of super powers and altered the power equations in the modern era, and still do, were the developments of scientific technology and its merger with capitalism.

## RISE OF SUPER POWERS

Galileo truly started the age of science in Europe. It took a gigantic leap in England when Isaac Newton began unveiling the way the material world functioned. By the time he died in 1727, Newton had laid down the fundamental laws of motion, worked on gravitation and optics, and had invented calculus - besides exploring many other fields. Thereafter, scientists mushroomed all over Europe. Discoveries were made in every field of science, new elements were found, and systemic laws of physical existence were postulated. In fact, new fields of sciences were introduced.

Pursuit towards discovery was not limited to the academic arena: There was a desire to explore the globe as well. While Columbus landed in Bahamas - thinking he had reached India - Vasco Da Gama chartered the direct sea route to India. Since religion continued to hold sway at that time, there were many who sought refuge from religious persecution and migrated to the New World, and some went to foreign shores for propagating religion. While Portugal sailed the high seas to spread Christianity, others embarked the ships for money. They were in a society dominated by the feudal aristocracy. They did not have a religious agenda; they did not have political power and they did not own land. Their only way to prosperity was through trade. Since they were individually not in a financial position to launch an enterprise, they cooperated with each other and formed joint stock holding companies. These private trading companies, like the English East India Company and the Dutch VOC, sailed around the globe and established footholds in America, Africa, South Asia, and the Far East. These explorations laid the foundations of a **global economy through colonialism**.

While scientists and explorers were unlocking newer vistas of the intellectual and material world, Adam Smith opened the field of economics. His book '*Inquiry into the Nature and Causes of the Wealth of Nations*' - published in 1776 in England - was critical of government's regulation of trade and proposed that if people were set free, they would create prosperity for all. Smith thus sowed the first seeds of economic liberalism - capitalism. Soon, **capitalism joined hands with science** and the spirit of adventure to serve its own ends. It also helped the growth of sciences.

Science led to discoveries, inventions and innovations which in turn developed the tools of efficiency - machines. Since efficiency leads to profits, capitalism increasingly got integrated with scientific developments - the two advancing each other. Thus emerged the class of industrial-capitalists which used science and technology to modernise and mechanise the methods of production. Harnessing the power of steam was perhaps the most revolutionary of these discoveries, and was to change the way manufacturing was done. It was to reduce the costs as well. This is known as the Industrial Revolution that began with the 19th century in England, and was to alter every aspect of European society, and its relationship with rest of the world.

## BRITAIN: THE INDUSTRIAL REVOLUTION

The Industrial Revolution was a revolution of scientific inventions and the advent of railways was to lead this revolution as it completely transformed the pattern of industrial production. The 1840s was the decade of historic expansion of railway system in Britain and nearly 3000 miles of network was developed connecting most of the major terminals. With expansion of railways the volume of transportation increased hundreds of times, something that was just not possible earlier by roads. With increased throughput the size of industries also increased manifold. Previously, bigger factories could neither get raw materials nor dispatch their products at such volumes and speeds to distant places. Coal for furnaces could now be transported in bulk quantities and it led to a spurt in mining and steel industry. Rapid increase in the scales of volume led to mechanisation of all manufacturing industries.

**Mechanisation** transformed the traditional labour intensive industries and caused widespread unemployment in Britain. It thus necessitated a paradigm shift in the way industrial businesses were being conducted. On one hand rapid industrialisation was needed to cope with the problem of unemployment caused by industrialisation itself, and on the other hand, mounting industrialisation needed assured supply of even more raw materials, and at cheaper rates. Most importantly, it also needed larger and captive markets to sustain the expanding industrialisation. Since Industrial Revolution had also started in Europe, British needs could only be met by expanding in colonies, predominantly in India.

Modern and bigger industries meant larger profits. Rise of industries was inevitably to lead to growth of trade, and of the supporting financial sector. Thus, a class of industrialists, along with merchants, traders, and bankers, grew in numbers. They also gained in political influence due to money power, especially after the Reform Act 1832. The Industrial Revolution and the consequent rise of the newly rich and powerful class of industrialists impacted British internal politics as well as its policy towards India. The industrialists were now in a stronger position to steer British policies to serve their commercial needs. The interest of this class conflicted with that of the East India Company. Since profits of this class came from manufacturing - and not from trading - it looked upon the Company's role in trade with India as a problem. It wanted to export its own products to India instead of importing Indian goods, which adversely competed with its products.

British dominance had considerably expanded in India by this time, and this class wanted to have a free access to India by abolishing the role of the East India Company in trade with India. The government had been gradually increasing its control over the East India Company since the passage of the Regulating Act 1773, and had considerably reduced the Company's monopoly by the Charter Act of 1813. Since this class was now in a position to substantially influence the economic policies of the government, it was able to compel the government to completely terminate the commercial activities of East India Company by the Charter Act of 1833. Thereafter, the British government pursued a policy of unbridled **colonial expansion and exploitation** in India so as to provide captive markets as well as assured and cheap sources for raw materials. Political colonisation of India was thus followed up by industrial colonisation, all to the benefit of British trade and industry. It was a triumph of British capitalism.

While this industrial-merchant class purportedly wanted a policy of free trade at the domestic level, it pursued a policy of imposing restrictive tariff barriers as far as trade with the colonies was concerned. India thus became a supplier of cheap food and raw materials to Britain, and a net importer of British manufactured goods. Colonisation of India also led to wars and mutinies that were crushed with a heavy hand. Colonial exploitation of India along with technological advancement brought **prosperity to Britain** and made it a super power.

During the period, Portugal, Spain and France also expanded their global empires and became major powers. However, none could match Britain because of its scientific superiority, private enterprise, and sound financial management. Power now depended on technology and money, and not on sheer numbers of soldiers.

## RISE OF RUSSIA

Quite contrary to the rise of Britain, the rise of Russia as a super power was largely due to its military power, its policy of expansion through conquests, and not so much due to economic power or technological progress. In 1462 Ivan III ascended the throne of the Grand Duchy of Moscow - a small principality around Moscow - and began a policy of territorial expansion and thus laid the foundations of the Tsarist Russian Empire. In 1613 the Romanov dynasty seized power and the successive Tsars kept expanding Russia during the 17th century through wars of territorial acquisition. By the end of the 18th century Russia had expanded considerably in size. It had annexed Siberia, Ukraine, territories in Central Asia, the Balkans, and the Baltic region. Through the Russo-Persian War of 1826-28, Russia gained Armenia, Azerbaijan, and chunks in the Caucasus region. Through the Russo-Turkish War of 1828-29 Russia occupied certain territories of the Ottoman Empire. Russia also needed warm water ports and free navigation through the Ottoman straits, and thus even reached the Black Sea. Russia had thus attained its zenith of expansion and this made all the nations of Western Europe - particularly Britain - suspicious about the Russian bear.

Britain did not fear any direct attack from Russia but it also did want any European power to become too powerful. Britain was a highly war mongering nation at that time. It not only fought wars with many Continental nations, it also encouraged wars among the Continental nations so that Europe never unites against it. Rivalry with Russia became an obsession with Britain and as such it adopted a policy to stop Russian advance towards Asia Minor. Thus, Britain used the Ottoman Empire as a countervailing force against Russia. This led the **Crimean War 1853-56** in which Britain and France joined hands with the Ottoman Empire to stop the Russian expansion.

Russia was diplomatically isolated and was still a backward country with severe limitations of logistics and depended primarily on the size of its army. Its own large size created problems of mobility. On the other hand, France and Britain had modern weapons and the Ottoman Empire facilitated the issues of logistics. As a result, the Russian army started facing reverses. Facing an imminent defeat, Russia sued for peace and the Crimean War ended by the Treaty of Paris in March 1856. Through this treaty Russia had to give up some of the territories it had acquired recently while both the Tsar and the Ottoman Sultan agreed not to station any naval or military force on the Black Sea coast. This provision weakened the Russian position as regards the Ottoman Empire was concerned. The distrust between Russia and Britain continued.

It was a common enemy - Germany under Kaiser Wilhelm II - which brought Britain and Russia into the same camp at the beginning of the 20th century. The division of Europe into two armed camps resulted into the outbreak of the First World War. German power was entirely due to its technological superiority. As a result, Russia suffered massive defeat in the war and the Tsarist regime collapsed. The alliance with Britain also collapsed because of the communist coup in Russia in November 1917. The fact that the new regime had export of communism on its agenda made the western nations very apprehensive of Soviet Russia, and Britain along with some other nations actively aided the counter-revolutionary 'White Army' to fight the Bolshevik government. Though the intervention failed, the distrust between Russia and the West only increased.

**Communism** had added a new dimension to the historical hostility towards Russia, and totally disoriented the western perception. Britain thereafter tried every ruse to check and isolate Soviet Russia. It kept USSR out of the League of Nations and supported the anti-communist Nazi regime in Germany. Soviet Union was also kept out of the loop while the western powers dealt with Hitler during the Munich settlement of 1938 giving the impression to USSR that they were plotting to lead Germany into a war of mutual annihilation with Russia. Meanwhile Stalin kept strengthening Soviet Russia as a military power as he could correctly foresee the forthcoming war. Soviet Russia was modernising as an industrial power at a rapid pace. Further, and much to the disappointment and shock of British leaders, Stalin entered into the secret Ribbentrop-Molotov Pact in 1939, and Hitler got a free hand to wage a war in Europe. While Hitler overran Western Europe, there was peace in the East. Having finished his agenda in the West, Hitler surprisingly attacked USSR in June 1941. This changed the whole equation as Soviet Union in principle was now on the side of the Allies.

Churchill welcomed Soviet Union with open arms and Britain along with USA provided all the help they could in Russia's war against Germany. This was not out of any change of policy towards Soviet Russia but simply because Britain wanted Soviet Union to bear the brunt of the war and thus save Britain from German invasion: The distrust of Russia continued to linger. Even as a savage war was fought on the Eastern front, there remained an uneasy peace on the Western front, and USSR had to bear the burden of fighting Germany. Stalin kept exhorting Britain - now an ally - to open the second front in the West as a relief to Russian forces, but that was not done: Britain simply waited for Germany and Soviet Union to decimate each other. Britain engaged the Germans in North Africa only to protect Egypt - and hence the Suez Canal through which it controlled the colonies of South Asia - and not as a helping hand to Soviet Union.

From July 1943 onwards, when the Soviet army started pushing the Germans back, the western Allies attacked in Southern Europe - more to check the Soviet penetration in the Balkan region rather than as a relief to the Soviet army. When the Red Army was reaching the German borders, the Allies landed at Normandy in June 1944 and the second front was opened. Thereafter, there was a race between the Anglo-American army and the Soviet army to reach Berlin first. Thus, even while fighting a common enemy in the shape of Nazi Germany, Soviet Union and the Western Allies were also fighting a political war. The bifurcation of Germany, and the dissection of Berlin, was only one more chapter in their **age old rivalry**.

Thus, the so called 'Cold War' between Soviet Union and the West did not begin with the conclusion of the Second World War; it only resumed after the brief interval of the war. It was merely a continuation of the distrust and acrimony that had existed for long and had prevailed even during the Second World War. Communism had only added an extra colour of threat to the historical suspicion and apprehension towards Russia. However, the conventional parameters of international relationship had radically changed during the war. Soviet Union, though a badly bruised nation due to the war, was now a super power, with a cordon of satellite communist states of Eastern Europe under its thumb. It had natural resources, massive manpower, and was also developing modern technology - partly as a result of collaboration with Britain and USA during the war.

## RISE OF USA

The decades that followed the American Civil War (1861-65) was a period of reconstruction and economic resurgence of USA. Large scale migration from Europe to America during the 1840s had brought scientific knowledge, skills, and technology of the industrial revolution into USA. It was during this time that scientific education got a boost in America resulting in vital inventions in technology that placed industrial activity in an overdrive. It was also an era of spurt in innovation and individual excellence. While scientists like Graham Bell and Thomas Alva Edison created gadgets that could be put to commercial uses, entrepreneurs like Tesla, Andrew Carnegie, John Rockefeller and JP Morgan became icons of wealth creation. In fact, wealth creation became a fetish and prosperity a creed in USA. While the Europeans were squabbling on issues of constitutionalism, nationalism and socialism, Americans were only thinking about making money. It was the apogee of capitalism as animal spirits of private enterprise were set free, while the government stayed away from interfering into the economic affairs of the people.

This phase is thus also called as the **Second Industrial Revolution**, with USA now in the lead. Manufacturing of heavy industries jumped with innovations in the steel industry. There was expansion of railways, telecommunication, oil exploration and commercial use of electricity. Industrial growth was also accompanied and supported by a fresh wave of immigration from Europe bringing more labour, energy, enthusiasm and ideas. Increase in productivity led to general prosperity as well. This was also the time when steam ships ruled the high seas bringing the continents closer, and international trade increased several folds. As trade globalised, and businesses bloomed, aspirations of the American industrialists to have a larger share of the world market also increased. Prosperity also instilled a sense of power in the political leadership and a desire to enhance US influence in the world affairs.

USA modernised its navy by building steel ships and began expansion as an imperialist power. In 1867 USA bought Alaska from Russia, and annexed Midway Islands in the Pacific. In 1893 USA annexed the kingdom of **Hawaii.** In 1898 USA went to war with Spain and annexed Puerto Rico and Guam, and colonised the Philippines. At the same time USA reinforced the Monroe Doctrine and turned the whole of Latin America into a US protectorate. This was done by dollar diplomacy - by granting huge loans - as well as by use of arms. In 1903, USA sponsored a revolution in the Panama region of Colombia and helped Panama achieve independence. This gave USA control over the Panama Canal and thereby gained an overwhelming dominance in the region as well as leverage on international trade. By the dawn of the 20th century USA had become a colonial power and had started making encroachments in the Far East.

As USA became a major producer of affordable industrial goods, several European nations started buying from USA in a big way. To meet with the finances for such imports, they also took huge loans from US banks. The US industry expanded production capacity on a colossal scale to meet with this rising demand. The US government too supported this by relaxing its monetary policies. Liquidity was increased by reducing the interest rates as well as by reducing the cash to credit ratio of banks. A large number private banks and financial institutions were also opened. As a result, money supply in the banking system shot up to meet the demand of credit, and the industries got the funds to expand. This led to a spurt in the American economy and increased employment opportunities.

At this time Europe was getting divided into war camps, with each getting apprehensive of the other. Nations were seeking security through alliances as well as by enhancing military preparedness. This opened a window for the **US armament industry** which began export of arms to Europe. As tensions escalated in Europe, the belligerent nations started buying even more from USA. Britain and France were the major importers while Germany had its own well developed armaments industry. Although European nations had also spurred up their own defence related production, the major difference was that while armament industry in Europe was primarily under government departments, in USA it was predominantly in the private sector. This feature was to decide the destiny of American politics, and that of much of the planet earth, for the next century and more.

USA entered the First World War to protect its economic interests and the war ended with a major shift in the world power equations. Europe was economically devastated and lost its clout over the world affairs while **USA emerged as the sole beneficiary** of the war. While USA was a significant economic power even before the war, it became a global political power as well. It had the technology, it had the money, and it also had the manpower. American economy also got more closely integrated with Europe. International trade was facilitated by the introduction of oil fuelled ships that came about shortly before the war, and began replacing the steamships. This was to be the true beginning of economic globalisation and was soon to contribute to the Great Depression, which in turn significantly contributed to the rise of Nazism in Germany. At the same time, America's rising aspirations in the Far East brought it into a conflict with Japan that opened another chapter of the Second World War and made it truly a world war.

Much of Europe, and Japan, was reduced to rubble during the Second World War while Britain suffered economically. It was soon to lose its colonial empire as well which had made it a super power. The end of the war thus created two centres of power and to a large extent divided the world into two factions: The Soviet Union led communist bloc and the USA led western capitalist world. (China was a backward and insulated nation at that time and did not matter in world affairs.) Thereafter, there began a rivalry between the two super powers which is often termed as the 'Cold War.' However, as stated earlier, there was nothing new in this conflict between Russia and the western powers.

## STRATEGIC BIPOLARITY

By the end of the Second World War, USA had become a super power and had taken command of the western world. While USA had munificently helped USSR during the war, and wanted good relations with USSR to continue, and to bring it into the international mainstream, Britain revived the old rivalry. Winston Churchill played a key role in this and actively worked to persuade USA into joining this rivalry. * Having lost the elections of July 1945, Churchill wanted to remain in limelight and thus relevant in the domestic politics of Britain. In March 1946, he extensively toured America giving lectures about the '**iron curtain**' that had fallen between the western democracies and the communist coalition of Eastern Europe. In order to keep the frenzy of communist threat alive, he openly advocated that USA and Britain should jointly act against the communist threat. This was taken note of by the Soviet leadership, and they viewed all steps taken by USA to rebuild Europe with suspicion. Hence, it was now USA, and not Britain, that was to lead in this renewed rivalry and competition with the Soviet bloc.

*In February 1946, George F. Kennan, the US ambassador in USSR, wrote his famous "long telegram" to the US government in which he stressed that USA should forcefully resist further Soviet expansion and adopt the strategy of containment. This was not to be done by conventional warfare but through diplomacy, subversive tactics, and building economic and military alliances to isolate USSR. This later came out into the form of an article, "*The Sources of Soviet Conduct.*" As Kennan did not want to reveal his name, he signed the article as "**Mr. X**". Publication of this article had a major influence in shaping US policy and hence Mr. X also played a substantial role in initiating the Cold War.

Thus were laid the foundations what came to be known as the 'Cold War'. Since none of the two rivals wanted to enter into a suicidal open war at the battlefront, they would fight this war at the diplomatic, economic and psychological fronts, and through proxy conflicts.

When World War II ended in 1945, Europe lay devastated in ruins and its economies in tatters. Such conditions encourage communism as well as fascism. USA was wary of both such ideologies and wanted Western Europe to recover fast. At the same time, Soviet Union had come to control Eastern Europe and the West European nations looked very vulnerable. USA did not want any further expansion of the Soviet bloc. As such, USA began to directly provide monetary assistance to western countries of Europe for their economic recovery and reconstruction so as to enable them to stand on their own, so that they are in a position to check any attempt on part of the Soviet Union to expand. The US Congress passed the Economic Cooperation Act of 1948, known as the **Marshall Plan** by which a fund of over $13 billion was earmarked to provide capital for enabling West European nations to rebuild their economy.

While the Marshall Plan generated a resurgence of European industrialisation, it also stimulated the US economy as it provided markets for American goods and created reliable trading partners, besides stabilising the democratic governments of Western Europe. This also ensured US hegemony over Western Europe. The Marshall Plan was meant solely for Western Europe. It included West Germany but excluded East European nations of the Soviet Bloc. USA also ensured that Soviet Union is kept out of GATT. All these steps were viewed with suspicion by USSR and escalated the Cold War.

In March 1947, US President Harry S. Truman propounded what came to be known as the **Truman Doctrine**. It was a foreign policy principle stating that USA would provide political, military and economic assistance to all democratic nations under threat from external or internal authoritarian forces. This was a complete reversal of age old US foreign policy to stay away from conflicts that did not directly involve USA. Truman argued that USA could no longer stay aloof and permit the armed expansion of Soviet despotism into the free and independent nations because America's national security depended upon more than just the physical security of American territory. Hitherto, USA had avoided foreign commitments beyond its sphere of influence as stated in the Monroe Doctrine. The Truman Doctrine committed USA to directly intervene with arms in any part of the world in the name of preserving the political integrity of democratic nations as and when it was deemed to be in the interest of USA.

USA also took the responsibility of militarily defending Western Europe through the formation of NATO in April 1949. By that time, USSR had installed communist regimes in each of the East European nation which had been overrun by the Red Army during the course of the Second World War. [These puppet states - under the protective umbrella of Soviet Union - came to form the Warsaw Pact bloc in May 1955.] USSR thus secured its frontiers by a ring fence of stooge buffer states. By the end of 1949, USSR too had test detonated its own atom bomb. In October 1949, China also fell to communism and Mao Zedong came to power. In June 1950, communist North Korea, with the backing of Soviet Union and China, invaded South Korea. The communist coalition was now face to face with the capitalist world, with USA replacing Britain in playing the lead role in this hostility towards Soviet Union. However, the underlying motive shaping this antagonism was very different.

## IDEOLOGICAL BIPOLARITY

Prior to the Second World War, it was ideology that isolated USSR from the western nations. However, USSR fought the war not for any ideology but for sheer survival. Once the war was over, the issue was no more survival of the nation because Soviet Union no more faced an external threat. West European nations had been too devastated by the war and these petty states were in no position to enter into another war in near future against the gigantic Soviet Russia. There was also no immediate cause for a conflict with USSR. USA also had no interest or reason for entering into a war with USSR. In any case, with a cordon of satellite states as buffer, Soviet Union had little to fear about a direct aggression from the West.

For the Soviet regime, the real threat was not outside but from inside, from its own people. The issue was not survival of the nation or of the socialist ideology but that of the Communist Party, and of the clique that controlled the party, and of the individual who controlled that clique. Communism had become a baggage, a burden, and the only ideology that mattered was to somehow control the party and retain the party's rule over the nation. The Soviet leadership needed to divert this threat towards an imaginary enemy so as to justify and fortify its grip over the country. Western capitalism was the sceptre that could be accused for everything so as to rationalise the dictatorial rule of the Communist Party over the Russian peoples.

On the other hand, USA also had no direct threat of a Soviet aggression. USSR was too far away, too weakened after the war to do anything, and much too engrossed in its own problems of reconstruction. USA in any case was now much stronger, with nuclear bombs in its arsenal. Western Europe also had no such threat from Soviet Union. The cordon of satellite states of the Warsaw Pact was meant to protect Soviet Union, not to attack Western Europe, and hence served as a protection barrier for Western Europe as well. USSR also had no reason to attack the West. In any case, Western Europe had the protection of NATO.

As regards China was concerned, it was too backward to pose any threat. At the domestic front also there was no menace of communism in USA either because Americans had never had any inclination towards socialism.

The problem for America was neither Soviet Russia nor communism. The real problem was internal - the **looming decline of American industry**. With the war being over, there was a gloomy prospect of the huge armament industry closing down, causing slump and unemployment. This could be avoided only by continuing the war in some way. In fact, it was not even necessary to wage a war on ground; it would serve the purpose if threat of a war could be raised, and preparations for the same could be continued to keep the American war industry in business. That was where the chimera of communism could profitably be utilised.

The concept of Cold War was the ideal mode by which this preparedness for war could be sustained forever. To mould public opinion in this direction, and taking cue from Churchill's speeches, US Senator Joseph McCarthy began raising the bogey of communism in USA from the early 1950s. He declared that a large number of communist spies and subversives have infiltrated into the US government and in the various sections of society. *Anti-communist hysteria was thus raised to a feverish pitch in America. All this was done to keep the **phantom of communism** breathing, and to give the state unlimited powers over the citizens. During the same period, J. Edgar Hoover - the Director of FBI - accused a very large number of prominent US citizens of being communist agents. These included Albert Einstein, Charlie Chaplin and Marilyn Monroe!

*The war cry of Soviet spies infiltrating America and Britain was exaggerated but not entirely imaginary or unfounded. While USA shared the technology of making atom bomb with Britain and France, it did not share it with USSR. Nevertheless, USSR test-detonated the atom bomb in 1949. Later investigations proved that pro-communist scientists of USA and Britain had passed on the secret of nuclear technology to Soviet

Union. The Cambridge spy ring case further revealed the extent of communist sympathisers in Britain and USA who worked as spies for Soviet Union. However, communism as a political ideology never gained popularity in America.

To turn anti-communism into an official policy, US President Eisenhower propounded the theory of '**Domino effect**' in 1954 - that if one state falls to communism, the adjoining states too would fall. This also implied that USA should militarily intercede to stop communism when the first signs of its rise appear anywhere on the horizon the world over.

In order to expand US political power and its markets internationally, as also the power of the political leaders and the prosperity of the corporate armament industry, it also became imperative to make the world bipolar. Either the nations had to be in the US camp and buy US arms, or nations would be forced to go into the Soviet camp, and thereby make the threat of communism even more real, and thus justify US action of rearmament to fight a war that was nowhere. Either way, it served the purpose. Most of the western world had no choice but to align with USA in this imaginary contest.

For keeping this **ghost of communism** alive, it was also necessary to encourage and support some armed conflicts in some parts of the world going, lest the people forget that communism was a real threat. As such, wars would be fought - not to contain or eradicate communism - but to keep it alive. These wars would be fought in Korea, Vietnam, Cambodia, Angola, etc. Where a war was not erupting despite provocation, a crisis could at least be created, as was done in Cuba in 1962. The best feature of this most profitable concept was that wars could be fought far away from USA so that American soil was not soiled. The Cold War was thus a ghost war; the filmy American Superman fighting the wily communist Spiderman.

## ILLUSION OF 'COLD WAR'

This anti-communist stance of the capitalist world helped the communist regime in Soviet Union equally well. They could similarly keep their own citizens frightened of an imminent attack from USA, and thus justify their dictatorial rule. As such, a shadow-boxing competition started which was actually not a cold war anymore but only an illusion that was sustained by the successive US governments as well as by the Soviet leadership for their internal reasons and compulsions. On occasions the shadow boxing also created real warlike situations because one often gets a punch in shadow boxing. However, both the parties understood the implications of MAD (Mutually Assured Destruction) policies and avoided a direct confrontation. When the Cuban missile crisis of October 1962 escalated, USSR quietly withdrew its ships carrying missiles indicating that it was not going to wage a war for the sake of ideology.

The Soviet leadership soon became a **hostage of its own ideology**. It had no choice but to keep the flag of communism flying, and to sustain the bogey of a capitalist reaction coming in shape of an attack from the West in order hold on to their control over the party, and the country. As such, it supported quasi-communist regimes the world over, like that in Cuba, Vietnam and Afghanistan.

This in turn suited USA the most as this anti-capitalistic propaganda of USSR could sustain the US armament industry indefinitely. This war of hot words was partly for domestic consumption, and partly to create a scare among other nations about the impending doomsday. The concept of a bipolar world was an arrangement that suited both the parties. It justified manufacture and export of arms, and provided leadership roles to USA and USSR in their respective spheres of influence. The US policy of containing communism and preventing further expansion of Soviet power led to US involvement in wars all over the world - in Korea, Vietnam, Cambodia, Laos etc. USA ignored the ideals of democracy and supported racist regimes like that of South Africa, bigoted religious monarchies as those of Saudi Arabia, corrupt military dictators of Pakistan, and cutthroat brutal tyrants as Augusto Pinochet in Chile, as long as they were willing to play the second fiddle to USA.

USA was thus condemned to be perpetually at war somewhere and war became an industry in USA, perhaps the most profitable and most influential one. Besides the armament industry, a war abroad required huge supplies of packaged food, clothing, temporary residential structures, medicines, and a whole gamut of other logistical support materials. All these products were made in the private sector in USA. As this cartel of war industry bloomed, it started calling shots in the domestic politics of USA, and continuation of war abroad became a compulsion for US leaders to satisfy its never ending demands. The US national economy depended on it and no politician could afford to defy it. Thus the non-state actors had become partners - or rather a part - of the state. (It is even alleged that US President Kennedy lost his life because he wanted to stop this shady policy.) Presidents and parties kept changing but the US policy to pursue war continued.

## ARMS RACE

The Second World War concluded with the explosion of atom bombs over Japan. This shocked Soviet Union as it did not have the technology of making nuclear bombs. While USA soon shared the knowhow with Britain and France, it did not with USSR. Hence arms became the top priority for Soviet Union, even if it involved stealing technology through communist sympathisers and spies in Britain and USA. Thus, USSR tested its first atomic device on 29th August 1949. In 1950 it tested the first ballistic missile and in 1953 it tested the Hydrogen bomb. Thus, a full scale arms race started between USA and the USSR. This race was also extended to space. On 4th October 1957, USSR became the first nation to launch a satellite and in 1961 it became the first to send a human being into space. While USSR was seemingly maintaining parity or even lead in this race, it was at a great cost.

Since the Second World War had been fought primarily on Russian soil, Soviet Union was a ravaged nation at the end of the war and had to rebuild the national economy on a colossal scale. However, the socialist model of Soviet Union started to prove to be a major handicap in economic development. Reconstruction of industries and infrastructure was undoubtedly done with amazing speed, but it was very inefficient because everything depended on the state and not on competitive free enterprise.

To add to the **economic problems**, USSR had established a cordon of satellite states in Eastern Europe at the conclusion of the war for its own security. Soviet Union now had to bear the cost of not only its own reconstruction but also that of the nations of this bloc, for which it did not have the financial resources. Further, since these satellites had also been made to adopt the socialistic model of USSR, these nations also were low in productivity and failed to recover on their own, and became a huge burden on USSR. The central government of USSR was not in a position to meet with the demands of either the satellite states, or of its own republics.

The peoples of the satellite states aspired for national self-determination, individual civic freedoms and democratic rights. They resented being under Soviet dominance and despised their communist dictators who had been thrust upon them. These puppet regimes lacked popular legitimacy and frequently had to resort to state repression which only increased public unrest. When a puppet regime failed to contain popular dissent on its own, as happened in Hungary in October 1956 and in Czechoslovakia in 1968, Moscow directly intervened with military power, which further alienated the populace from their regimes as well as from Soviet Union. Gradually, it became more and more difficult to subdue the nationalistic feelings among a whole host of nations that formed the Warsaw Pact bloc.

Popular opinion in the **non-Russian Soviet Republics** was also against the central government of USSR controlled by the Russians. It must be understood here that Soviet Union was not a unitary nation: It was - as per the constitution at least - a federation of semi-autonomous republics bound by a treaty. The non-Russian republics of USSR had neither a cultural nor a traditional affinity to Russia. It was only the centralised dictatorship of the communist party that had kept the union intact. The Second World War had aroused the ethnic and nationalistic feelings in these republics, and now they faced economic problems as well. Many of the Asian Soviet republics had Muslim majority populations and they resented being under an atheistic communist regime. This was also the period of Islamic resurgence in the Middle East and these republics increasingly developed a separatist outlook.

The post Khrushchev period of USSR was the time when the old guard of the Communist Party had retired and the next rung of leadership had taken over. This was an aging and corrupt bureaucracy, mired with Marxist jargon, and totally out of sync with the realities of the new world. There was no pragmatic leader like Stalin who could steer the party and the nation on his own strength. The regime tried to continue with its socialistic policies but the inherent contradictions of the Marxian model had come out in the open. While free enterprise, competition of private capital, and incentive of personal excellence was booming the economy of USA, and that of other western nations, state control was suffocating enterprise in Soviet Russia, and the **economy was stagnating**.

The disparity in the standards of living in the Soviet bloc compared starkly with that in the West. The real threat to communist Russia was not bombs from the West but news about the West. In order to preclude such comparisons, the Soviet government resorted to curbing freedom of its citizens to travel to West, and restricted other means of exchange of information. It indulged in propaganda but that was also to be of no avail: The prosperity of West was too apparent to be camouflaged. The younger generation in the Soviet bloc saw this disparity and resented denial of opportunity to prosper. They neither had the riches nor the freedoms of the West. At this time the Orthodox Church of Russia also became assertive and the communist government was unable to curb revival of religious ceremonies any further. People increasingly would celebrate Christmas and go to Church for getting married. Communism had started to crumble.

Meanwhile, America and the entire Western world left no opportunity to **humiliate Soviet Union**. This was done by encouraging public disaffection in the Soviet bloc, by putting the communist regimes in poor light before the world community, and in the eyes of their own citizens. Pedestrian but dissident writers as Boris Pasternak and Alexander Solzhenitsyn were awarded Nobel Prize for literature, and Andrei Sakharov - a Russian nuclear physicist - for Peace. USSR was put to serious international embarrassment when Olympics were held in Moscow in 1980 and USA and certain allied Western nations decided to boycott the games, ostensibly in protest against USSR's intervention in Afghanistan. It was sheer hypocrisy that USA, a nation which had consistently been interfering in the domestic affairs of other nations, was now leading this campaign against Soviet Union's involvement in Afghanistan. However, the boycott was another way of escalating the Cold War.

The most difficult part for USSR was to sustain the Cold War in economic terms. While the arms race was a boon for US industry, this competition ruined Soviet Union as well as its satellite states of the Warsaw Pact. The assistance being given to the communist parties, and to the Marxist regimes across the globe, was also proving to be a heavy burden on the Soviet economy. While the US government could always raise money through endless public borrowing and deficit financing, the communist model provided no room for USSR for such budgetary manoeuvring. While the dollar had become the international currency for commerce, no one traded in roubles.

## COLLAPSE OF THE SOVIET UNION

When Ronald Reagan became the US President in 1981 the arms race escalated to such a level that it became impossible for Soviet Union to sustain the competition. As Soviet Union's financial health deteriorated it was unable to succour to the needs of the satellite East European states as it was doing earlier. Reagan's policies on oil led to a sharp fall in oil prices, and this further affected Soviet finances. As Moscow's financial strength declined, centrifugal forces began working and consequently Soviet Union started losing its grip on the Eastern bloc.

Soviet Union's **intervention in Afghanistan** proved to be disastrous - politically as well as financially. Soviet forces had invaded Afghanistan in 1979 to rescue the communist regime that had taken power in a coup one year back. However, the Afghans resented this and began retaliating. A large number of fighters also came from several Muslim countries and these were actively supplied with arms by USA. This rag-tag force of Mujahideen fighters inflicted severe damage to the Soviet forces and it soon became obvious that Soviet control over Afghanistan was not sustainable.

When **Mikhail Gorbachev** came to power in March 1985 as the Secretary General of the Communist Party of the Soviet Union, its economy was in a precarious state. There was shortage of all basic consumer goods and there was a general disenchantment within USSR as well as among the Warsaw Pact nations. Gorbachev realised that in order to avoid a complete collapse of the economy, and that of the nation's integrity, it was necessary to put an end to the arms race and to initiate political and economic reforms within the nation. Hence, Gorbachev initiated certain bold steps.

At the domestic front, Gorbachev introduced policies called as *glasnost* and *perestroika*. *Glasnost* meant political openness to reduce the role of the central leadership of the Communist Party in elections. It also included freedom of press and removal of restrictions on the people. *Perestroika* was a plan for economic restructuring. Soviet Union would permit market forces to play a role under government's control. All these steps were against the conventional policies adopted by the Communist Party, and Gorbachev alienated the party hardliners of the old block.

In international affairs Gorbachev abandoned the belligerence of his predecessors and began a process of reconciliation with the West known as the ***detente***. He established close relations with US President Ronald Reagan and by 1987 major agreements were made towards disarmament, thus virtually putting the Cold War in cold storage. Since the Afghan adventure was proving costly in terms of money as well as in prestige, Russian forces began to withdraw from 1988 onwards. The withdrawal was however seen as a humiliating retreat in face of defeat and showed that Soviet Russia was no more the power it once was, that it was vulnerable, and collapsing.

Peoples of the **East European states** realised that time had come to regain their freedom. As such, nationalist political agitations spread in all the states of the Soviet bloc. Gorbachev had withdrawn Soviet troops from Eastern Europe in 1987 and Soviet Union did not intervene. One by one the communist regimes began to collapse and the Soviet satellites of the Eastern bloc declared their independence from Moscow. The Berlin Wall too came down on 9th November 1989 and East Germany merged with West Germany. By 1990, all the communist regimes had been overthrown and replaced by democratically elected governments. This was natural because freedom always leads to disintegration of entities that have been kept bound by unnatural forces.

Domestically also, the reforms instead of helping towards integration only paved the way for collapse. Gorbachev's economic policies were half hearted and ill planned, and did not bring the expected results. Shortages continued, if not increased. Gorbachev had raised high hopes among the peoples and when the aspirations could not be fulfilled, the people were disillusioned. Gorbachev thus began to lose popularity among the people as well as loyalty of the party hardliners. Leaders like Boris Yeltsin became vocal critics of Gorbachev and resigned from the Communist Party. Yeltsin now became a Russian nationalist and gave up the idea of USSR as a union.

As the communist party weakened, its grip over the republics also weakened, and agitations for independence started in certain of the Soviet republics. The Baltic State of Lithuania declared its independence on 11th March 1990 and Latvia on 4th May 1990. In June the Russian republic also adopted a declaration of sovereignty. Meanwhile, Ukraine had become independent for all practical purposes. It was obvious that USSR was disintegrating.

Gorbachev made a last ditch effort to prevent fragmentation and in April 1991, he offered the republics to agree to a new union treaty that would maintain the integrity of USSR as a loose confederation. As luck would have it, just when the new treaty was about to be signed, the hardliners in the Communist Party who wanted to stop the reforms, staged a **coup on 18th August 1991**. Gorbachev was confined to a resort in Crimea where he was holidaying and soldiers came on the streets of Moscow to quell any public protest. However, Boris Yeltsin, who had been elected President of the Supreme Soviet of Russia in May 1991, confronted the coup and challenged the troops. He called for a general strike, appealed to the soldiers to join, and led demonstrations against the coup leaders. Yeltsin succeeded in mobilising popular support and the army refused to intervene. Thus, the coup failed and the hardliners were arrested.

Even though the coup had been foiled, it had also sounded the death knell for the integrity of Soviet Union. Gorbachev was released from confinement but he had lost power. Hence, he resigned as the leader of the communist party. Encouraged by the separatist movements in the satellite states, the Soviet republics also began to split out on ethnic lines. Ukraine declared independence on 24th August 1991. This was followed by other Soviet republics. As Moscow was in no position to do anything, it had no option but to recognise the independence of these republics. During night of 25th December 1991 the hammer-and-sickle flag of USSR was lowered from Kremlin and the Russian flag was raised. Thus the Soviet Union ceased to exist as a nation.

Gorbachev understood that USSR needed to change but could not have ever anticipated that by removing the shackles of Soviet state he would scuttle not only communism but also the USSR as a nation. Gorbachev certainly was a staunch communist and was keen to preserve the integrity of Soviet Union. The reforms that he initiated were to strengthen the both, and not to destroy them. Maybe opening up the economy and relaxing political restrictions at the same time was a mistake. Perhaps, he should have first implemented the economic reforms, strengthened the state finances and improved productivity, reduced the shortages and increased the per capita income of the people, and then should have initiated the political reforms. Perhaps, it was too late in the day to save the Titanic from sinking.

**Gorbachev's real achievements** were rapprochement with the West, end of the arms race, and opening of Soviet Union to the rest of the world, thereby putting an end to the Cold War. However, these were to be short lived. Today, Russia is at war with the West, and a real war at that, exactly what was feared during the fifty odd years of the Cold War during which peace was somehow maintained. As regards freedom of the people is concerned, Russia is today ruled by an oppressive regime, as intolerant as that of Stalin or Tsar Alexander III. While the West praises Gorbachev for being the instrument of dissolution of USSR, and for discrediting communism forever, many in Russia regret that Russia is no more the power it once was. They have not forgiven Gorbachev for it and Putin is trying to make Russia a world power again.

## THE NON-ALIGNED MOVEMENT

The end of the Second World War created two centres of power and to a large extent divided the world into two factions: The Soviet Union led communist bloc and the USA led western capitalist world. Thereafter, there began a rivalry between the two which is often termed as the 'Cold War.' The post World War II world was in a state of apprehensions. There were deep divisions, distrusts, and suspicions, and the two super powers wanted other nations to make their stand clear where they stood in this bi-polar world. While many countries aligned with one or the other of the two super powers, many others did not want to come under the shadow of either of the powers.

Many wanted to have good relations with both the super powers. They had nothing to do with this rivalry and did not want to get involved, and hence decided to stay neutral.

**Jawaharlal Nehru**, the Prime Minister of India (1947-64) took this policy of neutrality to a higher pitch by spearheading what came to be known as the Non-Aligned Movement, a term reminiscent of the movements during India's freedom struggle. It was initiated during the Bandung Conference of 1955, and in this so called 'movement' he was joined in by Gamal Abdel Nasser of Egypt, Sukarno of Indonesia, and Joseph Broz Tito of Yugoslavia. These three were tyrannical leaders who had come to power through violent means, and represented three insignificant nations. But this did not deter Nehru - a champion of peace and democracy - in embracing them. Nehru thought that as the leader of this 'third front' he would be at level with the leaders of the super powers. While it provided publicity to Nehru within India, and to the three despots in their own countries, it only lowered India's image and left the world leaders wondering what this self-appointed apostle of peace and non-violence was doing in this company of brutal autocrats: Prime Minister of a large country as India seeking personal glory by sharing platform with such minor players on the world stage.

The Non-Aligned Movement was joined by several recently independent African and Asian countries, predominantly non-white, underdeveloped, with a colonial past. This basically represented the '**Third World**'. Many were ruled by tin-pot dictators, and their socio-political arrangements were often at odds with the western culture, its institutions, and political ideals. Their leaders had multiple allegiances, and some had scandalous personal reputations. They used the NAM summits to air their views - largely condemnation of the western world and its value systems - often putting NAM at loggerheads with the West. Thus, NAM became a sort of front against colonialism, and the western world began viewing NAM as a subsidiary wing of the Soviet bloc.

The Indo-China war of 1962 put an end to Nehru's role in foreign affairs and the Non-Aligned Movement began losing steam. Indira Gandhi as the Indian Prime Minister tried to revive the NAM as a countervailing bloc against the West but it failed to gain traction. There were grave differences amongst the nations that constituted the NAM. In fact, other than anti-colonialism, they had nothing else in common. The Arab world was particularly divided. Further, the NAM did not have a constructive agenda to bring about cooperation, nor had the means to help any member nation. Soon after, the other nations also lost all interest in the Non-Aligned Movement. Thus, the NAM failed to make any impact on the world political order.

During 1989-90, the Soviet controlled communist bloc of Eastern Europe broke apart. Communist regimes of the Warsaw Pact fell and democracy was established. Many of these states joined the European Union and were welcomed by western countries to show superiority of capitalism over communism. In 1991, communism finally met its demise when Soviet Union also disintegrated. Communism as an ideology became outdated and went out of fashion. What once was the veneer of being an intellectual became the symptom of academic ossification and cerebral autism.

This brought a fundamental change in the world political order. For centuries, nations had been establishing their international relations basically from the strategic point of view of security. With the Cold War coming to an end, the very basis of international relations started to shift from strategic concerns to trade and business concerns and nations realigned their foreign policy from the economic point of view. This made USA the sole superpower in the world political and economic order. As the international system became unipolar, the very idea and objective of **non-alignment lost its relevance.**

With these changes, India's foreign policy also changed. While the official policy of Non-Alignment was maintained, it was put into deep freeze, and today the official policy is that of 'strategic autonomy'. Although NAM still has some 120 member nations, and after UNO, it is the largest international organisation, it has lost significance as far as its political role is concerned. Nevertheless, it continues a very large number of humanitarian activities.

## UNIPOLARITY AND AMERICAN HEGEMONY

With the disintegration of Soviet Union, USA became the sole super power on the planet, and communism as an ideology became irrelevant. Several communist governments fell, and those that still remained were communist only in name. Many of the East European states of the defunct Warsaw Pact - now free from the clutches of USSR - joined the European Union. Some even joined NATO and were welcomed by the western countries to show superiority of capitalism over communism.

While USA celebrated these developments with a hearty cheer for some time, it soon started realising the serious problem the disintegration of Soviet Union had created; the bogey of communism could no more be used as a justification for waging wars. The compulsions of armament industry however were such that USA inevitably had to find some spot, and some pretext, where a comfortable war could be waged. If no reason was available, one had to be fabricated. Thus, instead of trying to integrate the redesigned and reshaped Russia with the rest of Europe, Russia continued to be treated with mistrust and hauteur, and the bogey of Russian threat was kept alive.

Instead of winding up NATO, which also had now become irrelevant - because Warsaw Pact had dissolved - USA ensured expansion of NATO by admitting many of the erstwhile member nations of the Warsaw Pact. This was done to continue suspicions in, and about Russia, even though Russia was now a much smaller and a much weakened nation. Thus, security concerns kept festering in Eastern Europe which ultimately were to result in Russia invading Ukraine in February 1922.

USA also now needed new causes and new enemies to keep the US arms industry running. In a world where conflicts are plentiful, there was no dearth of causes to support and fight for, and the US leadership found new excuses for war, to establish peace, democracy, self-determination, and for other humanitarian reasons. USA thus fought anti-Islamic regime in Bosnia, and the Islamic regime in Libya; it fought in defence of monarchy - of Kuwait - in the first Iraq war, and fought for democracy in the second Iraq war.*

*USA attacked Iraq on the pretext of preventing Saddam Hussein from making the 'weapons of mass destruction.' This was yet another global fraud because although Iraq was soaked in blood, no such weapons were ever found. It only helped growth of dozens of Islamic terror organisations which US could fight at leisure.

Providentially for USA, there was an attack on the Twin Towers on 11th September 2001 and it provided enough justification for USA to wage a war on terror. USA fought against the Mujahedeen and the Taliban in Afghanistan - radical Islamic groups that USA itself had created to fight Russia when communist Russia had occupied Afghanistan. USA also provided funds and arms to Pakistan even though Pakistan was the sponsor of Taliban, as well as the cradle of world Islamic terrorism. USA wages war against the ISIS, and also against the Syrian government which is also fighting against the ISIS. Strange as it may sound, USA has waged the greatest number of wars the world over to establish world peace, because now establishment of peace has become a lucrative business. And US arms have killed hundreds of thousands of civilians for humanitarian purposes.

## THE NON-POLAR WORLD

For about two decades after the end of the Cold War, USA remained the lone superpower in the world. However, a unipolar state is unnatural, and hence unstable. The global scenario is transforming from a unipolar state to a multi-polar one, eventually to become non-polar. The European Union has become a serious contender as a power centre and is no more accepting the diktats of USA. However, European Union itself is showing signs of internal disquiet. This is a result of breakdown of the communist bloc due to which several East European states joined the EU. This was initially treated as a victory of the capitalist West. However, the richer nations of EU are now realising that these states are a financial liability. Migration of nationals of these states to richer West is being resented by people, and Britain has already left the EU on such issues. USA finds it difficult to adjust to this new configuration and feels funding of NATO burdensome.

There are other contenders for the top spot as well. China has emerged as a major economy that has started challenging USA in the economic arena. It is also arming itself with all types of weapons and is becoming a serious security concern as well. It has made its intention to unify Taiwan very clear. While China keeps trying to act like a bully in the South Asian region, its leaders also know that military power is a double edged sword. While brute power can keep the citizens under control for some more time, any war-like adventure can boomerang, and the totalitarian regime can collapse in no time.

Russia has also again emerged as a major power and is flexing its muscles economically as well as militarily. Under President Putin, Russia is again trying to undo the disintegration of Soviet Union and become the old Tsarist Empire. Russia has already annexed Chechnya, part of Georgia and Crimea. Now it is waging a war against Ukraine and refuses to accept it as an independent nation. USA and its allies really do not know what to do about it.

The emerging markets, and **developing economies** of nations like India, are competing with USA as well as China. There are a large number of parallel alliances like G20, BRICS, and SCO etc. that challenge the idea of a unipolar world. The World Bank and the International Monetary Fund are also power centres by their own right. These are not military alliances but based on economic issues, yet they exercise political power as well. The global wars are now being fought on the economic front: the tariff wars, currency wars, and those related to balance of payments. These wars are being fought not with battleships, but through container ships. This again is a result of the greater participation of citizens in the political process because economics directly affects the peoples.

The World Wide Web has also become an arena of warfare and cyber attacks are becoming common and menacing. There is also the Dark Web and cases of 'ransomware' are increasing. Cryptocurrencies are a challenge to the sovereignty of nations. In this type of asymmetric warfare, it is difficult to even identify who and where the enemy is. Non-state actors and professional criminal hackers sitting at home can do as much damage as an Inter-continental Ballistic Missile. Cyber security has become as important, or maybe more important, than territorial security. While the global situation remains in a flux, one thing certain is that it can no more be a unipolar or a bipolar world.

Chapter VI

# International Economic Order

The history of inter-state trade goes back to several millenniums. The Indus Valley peoples traded with the Middle East thousands of years back. The Silk Route trade that connected China with Europe also goes back to the second century B.C. International trade increased manifold after Vasco da Gama established the sea route to India in 1498. Thereafter, several European nations began trading in the East. At the same time, North and South America, much of Asia, and most of Africa, were colonised and trade further increased. By the end of the 19th century, the planet had turned into a global village and international trade along with colonialism became the key drivers of a nation's economic prosperity. These also became vital to a nation's security. Hence trade became an essential part of international politics.

To ensure their trading advantages, nations adopted various policies and also entered into bi-lateral / multi-lateral agreements with trading partners. The policies that nations adopted varied from one extreme of high protectionism to the other of free trade, depending on what was more advantageous to them. This also led to rivalry and bitter disputes, even armed conflicts. While there were international navigational laws, there was no international body to regulate or arbiter on economic matters, that is to say, there were no rules of the game. By the beginning of the First World War, protectionism and high tariff barriers had become more common than free trade.

The disruptions caused by the First World War brought out the need of a world economic order based on consensus for mutual benefit. Hence the League of Nations formed the **Economic and Financial Organisation** in the early 1920s. Its purpose was to consider methods of removing inter-state trade barriers and promote free movement of goods. A Financial Committee was formed which focused on monetary and fiscal issues with a greater participation of state and private bankers. The EFO also developed tentative ideas about European integration. American delegates participated in these bodies even though USA was not a member of the League.

Initially the EFO was largely successful in cementing international policy consensus on the problems of financial stability and fiscal management. However, it was less successful in making much headway on the issues of trade and tariff matters. Further, since USA was not a member of the League, there was insufficient supervision on banking practices. When the Great Economic Depression began from USA in 1929, the EFO had no means to check the spread of recession and the entire Europe was devastated. The Economic Depression also led to extreme protectionism the world over. Nationalism, isolationism, exchange manipulation, import barriers, and high tariff rates aggravated the world-wide recession. This soon made the EFO redundant. The outbreak of the Second World put an end to the League as well as to its organisations.

## BRETTON WOODS AGREEMENT

By the mid 1944, as the Second World War seemed to be coming to a healthy conclusion, there emerged a consensus among the Allies to address the common economic issues and arrange for post-war reconstruction. The war had convinced the Allies that international economic cooperation was also necessary for world peace. Hence the United Nations Monetary and Financial Conference was held in July 1944 at Bretton Woods (New Hampshire, USA) where delegates from 44 nations joined hands to establish a new international economic order known as the Bretton Woods system. Learning the lessons of the Great Depression, and realising the problems of restrictive trade policies that had worsened the recession, the new system was intended to remove the rigidity of the earlier international monetary systems and to ensure cooperation among the nations. Since nations differed on several issues, the decisions were taken in piecemeal after successive rounds of talks.

The Bretton Woods arrangement conceived of an **international monetary system** that would ensure exchange rate stability, prevent competitive devaluations, and thus promote economic growth. It sought creation of an institution with the resources and authority to intervene in times of crises when imbalances occur. The plan envisioned of a global central bank called the Clearing Union. This bank would issue a new international currency which would be used to settle international imbalances. Each country would receive a limited credit that would prevent it from running a balance of payments deficit so as to ensure exchange rate stability.

In December 1945, the **International Monetary Fund** was created to monitor exchange rates and lend reserve currency to nations with balance-of-payments deficits.

The International Bank for Reconstruction and Development, now known as the World Bank, was made responsible for providing financial assistance for reconstruction after the World War II and for the economic development of the less developed countries. The countries agreed to keep their currencies fixed but adjustable to the dollar, and the dollar was fixed to gold at $35 an ounce. The Gold Standard, which had been abandoned after World War I, was thus restored and nations assumed the responsibility of upholding the exchange rate. As the currencies became convertible, nations settled international payments in dollars, and the US dollar became the world currency. USA had the responsibility of keeping the price of gold fixed and had to adjust the supply of dollars to maintain confidence in future gold convertibility.

Backing currency by the Gold Standard started to become a serious problem for USA by the late 1960s. Constant balance of payments deficits on part of USA led to foreign held dollars exceeding the value of US gold reserve. There were apprehensions that USA may not fulfil its obligation to redeem dollars for gold at the stipulated price. By 1971, the situation was so bad that US President Richard Nixon gave notification that the ability to convert the dollar to gold was being suspended "temporarily." The move was inevitably the final straw for the system and the agreements that created it. Although the fixed currency exchange rate system eventually failed, it however did provide much-needed stability at the time of its creation.

Despite the eventual collapse of the Bretton Woods agreements, they have much to their lasting credit. Institutions like the IMF and the World Bank survived and remain vital to the global economy to this day. Further, the agreements united 44 nations and brought them together to strengthen the world economy and facilitate international trade. This was done through GATT.

## GATT

While the Bretton Woods conferences had created the International Monetary Fund and the World Bank to address the currency related issues, it was felt necessary to also institutionalise the trade side of international economic cooperation, which had not yet been done. Hence, 15 countries had begun talks since December 1945 itself to reduce and rationalise customs tariffs. This went concurrently with the Bretton Woods conferences. These nations wanted to boost their economy by liberalisation of trade and to correct the protectionist measures which had increased since the Economic Depression.

Thus the **International Trade Organization** came into being as a specialised agency of the United Nations. The draft ITO Charter included rules on commodity agreements, business practices, international investment, and services. The primary tasks of the ITO were to boost international trade through lowering of tariffs and abolition of restrictive business practices, monitor commercial policies, assist in economic development and reconstruction, and regulate capital flows. The group had expanded to 23 by the time the deal was signed on 30th October 1947 in the form of the **General Agreement on Tariffs and Trade.**

On the other hand, even though USA had been one of the driving forces in the formation of ITO, the US Congress refused to ratify the ITO Charter in 1950. Thus, the ITO came to a dead end. This resulted in separating the GATT from the United Nations legal framework, making it a stand-alone multilateral legal entity. As such, the GATT became the only multilateral instrument governing international trade. Even though it always appeared to be a provisional arrangement, the GATT provided the rules for much of world trade from 1948 to 1994 and presided over periods that saw some of the highest growth rates in international commerce.

The guiding principles of the GATT included most of the commercial policies of the ITO Charter. GATT was based on four major tenets:

(i) **Non-discrimination** in trade on the basis of origin or destination of the goods, i.e., equal treatment of foreign and national goods and services in the domestic market: the Most-Favoured-Nation or MFN principle.

(ii) **Reciprocity**: Concession granted to one member of GATT must be extended to others.

(iii) **Transparency**: Nations must provide accurate information about their economy to others.

(iv) **Reduction of tariffs**: Trade to be based on prices and not be affected by use of non-tariff barriers like subsidies, quotas, etc. Where protection of domestic industries is necessary, it should be given exclusively.

The basic objective of GATT was to increase international trade by reducing tariffs through mutual cooperation and consensus. This was expected to bring prosperity as well as peace. The efforts to reduce tariffs were done through a series of multilateral negotiations. In the mid 1960s, agreements on anti-dumping duties were made. By the 1970s over a hundred countries were participating in the GATT meetings. The increase of membership demonstrated that GATT was being recognised as the chief instrument of economic reform and the sole vehicle for promotion of trade. GATT's efforts progressively resulted in reduction of tariffs and customs by almost one-third. Continuous reduction in tariffs helped spur very high rates of increase of world trade during the 1950s and 1960s - around 8% a year on average. On certain issues, like agricultural products, no agreement could be reached. In cases where only a small number of - mainly industrialised - GATT members agreed, the arrangements were called as "codes".

However, **reduction of tariffs** to very low levels created problems for the developing countries which faced increased foreign competition in many sectors. It led to closure of factories, unemployment, and consequent recession. As such, certain governments in Western Europe and North America began to seek bilateral arrangements with the competitors. They also increased subsidies to maintain their control over trade, mainly in the agricultural sector. These moves undermined the very purpose of GATT and its effectiveness began eroding.

While GATT was acclaimed for promoting growth, it was also subjected to constant **criticism**. Not all agreed that an open global economy was universally beneficial because open markets divide nations between the beneficiaries and the losers. Global trade was as much a domestic political issue as an international economic one. GATT's challenge was to establish a balance between the national and international economic priorities. Since no two nations are equal, it was difficult to achieve the same.

The communist bloc led by Soviet Union denounced the GATT as a tool of American capitalistic imperialism meant to enrich USA and impoverish the developing countries. [While some communist countries like Soviet Union and China remained as 'observers' in the GATT, some others became full member.] Many non-communist developing nations - also called as the 'Third World' - too held this view and described it as a '**rich man's club**' that supported an inequitable global trading system. They described globalisation as 'universalisation' of western capitalism. They complained that they hardly benefitted from the system, but their complaints were ignored as coming from countries that were not developing fast enough to join the elite club. Farmers were extremely critical of GATT's attempts to liberalise trade in agriculture and held protest marches in many nations.

Undoubtedly, American leadership was necessary to run GATT but its interests were not consistent with those of other nations. Hence its leadership was fluid and opportunistic. Despite their marginalisation in the GATT, the developing countries continued to remain in the organisation and also critical and cautious about it. As its membership increased, general consensus became cumbersome and GATT members resorted to regional or group specific agreements. It only showed the limits and possibilities of what an international organisation can and cannot do.

**India** was a participant of the Bretton Woods conference since 1944. Since India was a British colony at that time, it was represented by the British-run government of India. Because of the tenuous nature of their rule over the subcontinent, British officials recognised the political need to involve Indians in the negotiations. Hence India became a founding participant of the GATT too and remained the major spokesperson of the interests of the developing countries. India called for reduction of tariffs on the MFN basis to create market access in the developed country markets.

At the same time, India supported trade measures that were used by governments for their own domestic economic development, including import restrictions. India also stood for introduction of **special and differential treatment for developing countries**. This was to give flexibility to the developing countries in meeting their balance of payment obligations. India also became prominent in targeting non-tariff barriers like the arbitrary quotas imposed by the rich nations on import of goods like textiles that generated employment in developing countries. India led the **G-77*** countries in resisting the unrestricted opening of their domestic markets to investments by major corporations based in developed countries.

*The Group of 77 was an association of 77 developing countries that came into being in June 1964 to protect the interests of developing countries in international organisations. This also led to the formation of United Nations Conference on Trade and Development. The **UNCTAD** was an organisation of the UNO meant to address the issues of developing nations which the GATT was unable to address. UNCTAD worked in parallel with GATT. Today it works along with the WTO.

While the world economy was getting more and more complex by the early 1980s, the GATT was not reinventing itself and was becoming irrelevant to the realities of the modern world. The reason was that reduction of tariffs was not the panacea for all problems. GATT was created to promote the growth of global trade by opening markets and thus make the world more prosperous and therefore more peaceful. However, this strategy was not a substitute for technological advancement, without which prosperity through development was not possible. It brought more bitterness than peace. The problem was neither in the structure of GATT or its principles. The problem was its limited scope of jurisdiction and tunnel vision that failed to see the economy in a holistic sense and anticipate the future.

Further, **GATT was only about commodities**, not about trade in services which was increasingly becoming important. International investment in services had expanded and was closely tied to world trade. Trade in agricultural products was an area where consensus and application of agreements could never be achieved. GATT's institutional structure and its dispute settlement system also provided no solution. These factors convinced the GATT members that a new institution should be created to resolve the contentious issues in a more integrated and inclusive manner.

The Uruguay Round of talks (1986-94) was the last and most extensive of all discussions. It put an end to GATT and the Marrakesh Declaration made way for the creation of the World Trade Organisation on 1st January 1995.

## NEW INTERNATIONAL ECONOMIC ORDER

By the beginning of the 1970s, the Third World nations began asking for reformation of the Bretton Woods system which seemed to favour only the richer nations like USA. They clamoured that despite political independence from colonial domination, these nations still suffered from discrimination and various forms of neo-colonialism, and that the benefits of technological progress were not being evenly shared by all. In 1973, the Chairman of the Non-Aligned Movement requested the UNO to intervene. In September 1973, the UN General Assembly adopted the 'Programme of Action for the Establishment of a New International Economic Order'.

The New International Economic Order (NIEO) was a set of proposals put up by the developing countries to safeguard and promote their interests. The NIEO was based on the principles of equity, sovereign equality, non-interference in the internal affairs of other states, and cooperation among all nations irrespective of their economic systems. It aimed to provide non-discriminatory and liberal terms of trade, reduce inequality between the developed and developing nations, restructure the debts of the developing countries, and provide financial assistance to developing, and especially to the least developed nations through IMF and the World Bank. It also included scientific assistance from the advanced nations through transfer of technology. At the same time, the NIEO recognised the right of every nation to adopt the economic system that it deemed most appropriate for its own development.

While all nations of the Global South agreed with the objectives of NIEO, there was **no consensus** about the roadmap to reach to the goals. In fact, there was no clear roadmap at all. The NIEO was more of a political statement against the West rather than a blueprint for advancement. It had also ignored the evolving world economic order of high global interdependence and competition. While some of the nations were willing to step out of their conservative ways of managing national economy, much of the Global South remained stuck to their old ways.

This was partly because the NAM nations had predominantly been erstwhile colonies of the western nations and had an anti-West bias. Further, socialism seemed to be gaining ground the world over and the peoples of the developing nations looked forward to the state to deliver goods rather than to stand on their own feet. It must also be remembered that it was the peaking period of Cold War and the developing nations were also politically much divided. As a result, while the developed nations kept blaming the developing nations for economic mismanagement, the developing countries kept blaming the developed nations of the West for discrimination.

Except for a few nations that began to enter the increasingly globalised economy, not much progress was seen in the Global South. **India's role during the whole period was extremely negative**. As the most populous democratic developing nation and founder of the NAM, India should have shown the way. However, at that time India had adopted extremely regressive domestic economic policies of redistributive justice. Income tax had risen to a maximum of 97.5%, there was Wealth tax as well as Inheritance tax, and wealth creators were migrating to tax havens. Crony capitalism flourished under the garb of socialism and industrialisation stood stand still. Black money increased and so did bureaucratic corruption. As a result, absolute poverty increased manifold as compared to the times of British rule.

Today, no one talks about the NIEO seriously, not even the NAM nations who once rallied against the advanced nations. Developing nations today are reconciling to the situation because globalisation has become a reality which no one can ignore any longer.

## WASHINGTON CONSENSUS AND NAFTA

Meanwhile, some of the nations in Latin America faced major economic problems and communism seemed to be creeping into the region. USA wanted to check this and hence came up with what came to be known as the Washington Consensus.

The "**Washington Consensus**" was a set of 10 economic policy measures formulated by the IMF, the World Bank, and the US government in 1989 to improve and stabilise the crisis-stricken economies of the Latin American nations. The 10 principles were:

(i) Fiscal discipline and budgetary restraint to control inflation and national debt.

(ii) Diversion of public spending from subsidies to expenditure on pro-poor services and investment in pro-growth infrastructure.

(iii) Tax reforms to broaden the tax base.

(iv) Interest rates to be market driven.

(v) Exchange rates to be competitive.

(vi) Trade liberalisation by reducing imports barriers and lowering of tariffs.

(vii) Liberalisation of foreign direct investment.

(viii) Privatisation of inefficient state owned monopoly state enterprises.

(ix) Abolition of regulations that restrict competition.

(x) Legal security for property rights.

Adoption of these principles was also a condition for assistance from USA, the IMF and the World Bank. The principles of the Washington Consensus later became applicable to all the Third World nations. Since these principles needed structural changes in the domestic policies of the nations, many of the developing countries criticised them as 'aid with strings attached', and that it violated the tenets of sovereignty and non-interference as stated in the NIEO. However, institutions like the IMF did not want to impose restrictions. They only said that if you want us to help you, then you also must help us in helping you. If you do not help yourself by putting your own house in order, our help wouldn't help and we wouldn't be able to help. Ultimately it didn't help and USA came up with NAFTA to solve its own problems with its immediate neighbours.

The **North American Free Trade Agreement (NAFTA)** was a free-trade zone agreement between USA, Canada, and Mexico which came into effect on 1st January, 1994. NAFTA lifted tariffs on majority of the goods produced by the signatory nations. It also aimed for gradual elimination of remaining tariffs and non-tariff barriers over a period of 15 years. There was to be free exchange of goods and services among the three countries. The nations also agreed to set standards on health, safety, and industry. NAFTA was later expanded to include protection of workers from job losses and protection of intellectual property rights. However, NAFTA had mixed results. While USA was able to expand its markets, thousands of American workers lost their jobs after US companies relocated their manufacturing facilities to Mexico to take advantage of the lower wages and lax workers' health and safety regulations. In July 2020, USA terminated the NAFTA and replaced it by US-Mexico-Canada Agreement (USMCA).

## WORLD TRADE ORGANISATION

The creation of WTO in 1995 marked a major revamp of international trade arrangements. It replaced bilateralism with multilateralism in international trade and provided a rule based world economic order. Whereas the GATT mainly dealt with trade in goods, the WTO treaty and its agreements covered about 60 areas, including trade in goods, services, intellectual property rights (TRIPS), trade related investment measures (TRIMS), and development. The WTO is thus the major global international organisation dealing with the rules of trade between nations. [The TRIMS agreement forbids discrimination against foreign investments while Trade-Related Intellectual Property Rights (TRIPS) covers patents and copyrights and thus protects the innovators/inventors of their creation.] WTO's multilateral dispute settlement mechanism is way out of bilateral trade disputes with major trading countries, something the GATT was unable to do. While it aims for an overall reduction of tariffs on manufactured products and phasing out of the quantitative restrictions, WTO also supports the developing countries to protect their economic interests.

The **WTO has 164 members today** representing 98 % of the world trade. Some 20 more countries are seeking to join the WTO. This popularity has shown the strength of the organisation in promoting overall development. The growth of world trade has helped reduce absolute poverty. Increase of exports has been an important factor in raising the living standards, especially in South East Asia, which has benefitted from the remarkable growth of world trade. WTO also deserves credit for helping to avoid /

resolve trade disputes. The institutional structure of WTO provides for transparency, monitoring and review mechanisms for trade policies, peer-reviewing, and potentially subjecting governments' actions to international scrutiny. In fact, there is practically no field related to economy that is not covered by the WTO. However, its overarching command on world economy has also brought it to much **criticism**.

Firstly, it must be understood that WTO is not a homogenous organisation. There are many countries like Russia and China (PRC) which have joined WTO under **Article XII**. This clause provides that a country "*may accede to this Agreement, on terms to be agreed between it and the WTO*". The terms of accession are decided on a case-by-case basis and are different for each applicant. Article XII sets no limits to the terms that may be agreed to and the terms of accession are different for each new member. Article XII also allows the contracting party to restrict the quantity of imports in order to safeguard its external financial position and its balance of payments. Hence, the ambit of fields covered by the WTO varies. Thus, while the WTO is a multilateral organisation, it has bilateral element as well. As such, all members are not equal in the organisation, and some have benefitted more having acceded under Article XII which provides room for certain exemptions and concessions, and leeway for bi-lateral arrangements.

It is also logical that free trade would benefit the developed countries more than the developing countries. The developing countries - the **Third World** - demand protection to be able to develop new industries and diversify their economy. They rightly point out that the developed nations of today used protection to enrich themselves at one time to become developed nations. The concept of MFN, a core tenet of the WTO, that each country should trade without discrimination means that a domestic company, or even the government, is not allowed to favour a local company. This gives an unfair advantage to the foreign multinational corporates over the local ones, and hence, denies the right of developing nations to promote their own emerging industries.

Free trade is also not equally implemented across different industries. The WTO also selectively brings in **non-economic factors** like environment, CO2 emission, use of child labour, etc., into consideration which puts the developing nations into defensive. USA and EU impose high tariffs on agricultural products which hurt export of agricultural products from developing nations and affect their farmers. At the same time, USA and EU heavily subsidise domestic agriculture while demanding removal of subsidy and stockholding by the governments of developing countries like India. Developing countries have primary products - agricultural and mining - and need to diversify. For this, they need short term protection. This has led to several disputes that still continue.

Since the decisions of WTO affect the **domestic laws of nations**, these have forced nations to change their laws accordingly. This affects domestic politics, especially in democracies where pressure groups do not like amendments that adversely impact their interests. In the earlier decades, the richer countries dominated the WTO and got what they wanted. However, the developing countries have become more vocal, and more important in certain sectors, and can no more be ignored. This has resulted in a large number of disputes. The negotiations are slow in WTO and it is often difficult to reach to an agreement. Nevertheless, the WTO has made efforts to ease the problems of developing economies in recent years and the developed countries are being asked to reduce restrictions on imports from the least-developing countries. The integration of special and differential treatment provisions in favour of developing countries provide them scope for a phased approach to trade liberalisation.

This has irked many developed countries like USA and they want to remove the **special and differential treatment for developing countries**. In fact USA, the prime founder of WTO, is so cheesed off that it is on the way to sabotage the WTO. USA has recently blocked consensus on appointments to the dispute's body of WTO. This has paralysed the dispute settlement mechanism of the WTO and has the potential of destroying its integrity and effectiveness. This would be a return to the disorder of the 1930s.

Donald Trump's war cry of 'America First' is a call in the direction of protectionism. Rogue nations like China and Russia also care little for WTO now. China has blocked many global giants from entering its market on various pretexts. India's slogan of 'Atmanirbhar Bharat' is also paving the way towards protectionism. Thus **unilateralism** seems to be becoming the order of the day and many nations are again entering into bi-lateral or limited multi-lateral free trade agreements. There are dozens of such agreements today. The European Free Trade Association (EFTA) is one such example with which India has recently concluded an agreement. The Regional Comprehensive Economic Partnership (RCEP - which India refused to join) is another such example. These undermine the very idea of WTO which aims at a comprehensive and uniform world economic order.

The fact is that a uniform and universal world economic order is not possible because each nation has its own strengths and weaknesses. As stated in an earlier sub-chapter, nations prospered due to their scientific and technological excellence. This made Europe and USA economic giants and controlled the world economy. Russia was a distant third while China was a non-runner. However, in the last two decades major changes have taken place. China is now technologically highly advanced while many smaller nations, called as emerging economies, have also joined the race. This has made the world economy interdependent.

At the same time, **primary products** - agriculture, dairy, animal husbandry, fishery, mining, etc. - have become equally important. However, primary products do not generate as much wealth as the technology based products. Hence the nations that still depend on primary products lag behind. Hence, the 'Third World' is demanding a new world order. The problem is that they do not know what that should be. Worse still, they are shy of taking the challenge by the horns and want protection. Without competition they may never gain strength. At the same time, there is also the genuine fear that competition with a giant may end up in fatal consequences for the infant. Hence, they do need protection. It is a sort of Catch 22 situation for which there is no easy solution. While such problems will continue, WTO is not likely to disintegrate in near future. This is because of globalisation and inter-dependence and because there is no perfect alternative to healthy cooperation. There are only a few countries which are still not members of WTO, the only significant being Iran. Even Iran wants to join but USA has obstructed its entry for political reasons.

## INDIA AND THE WTO

India has had a love hate relationship with the WTO. India has benefited in many ways due to WTO. Increase of India's exports of commercial services has contributed substantially to India's GDP. Indian global exports of labour-intensive sector products like textiles and clothing have also risen. The financial sector reforms initiated in 1991 have resulted in a regulated banking sector. As a result, India's financial and telecom services sector has also benefited and India is emerging of as a knowledge-based digital economy on the global stage. WTO provisions helped Indian software professionals to use computers and peripherals imported at zero tariffs to significantly augment the export of Indian software to the world market at the turn of the century generating employment to millions. Today, India is the world's second-largest telecommunications market and a major exporter of mobile phones (though largely only assembled in India). These are people-centric developments that use digital technology for trade, development, and empowerment.

However, there are problem areas also. This is because of the peculiar **structure of Indian economy**. While Indian economy is now primarily based on industrial and services sectors, almost half of its population is still surviving on agriculture which contributes to just about 15% of the GDP and a fraction of the exports. India can neither ignore the rural masses nor the industrial and services sectors which help India meet the international financial obligations.

Further, India's industrial sector still depends on high end foreign technology. Much of what India manufactures is basically assembling of components from abroad. If export / import duties are high, then input costs rise and the product becomes uncompetitive in the world market. If duties are lowered, then foreign products inundate the Indian market, killing even the assembly based domestic industry. Thus, India wants a very selective tariff structure on industrial products.

**Agriculture** is another problem area. There was a time when India needed food from abroad. Today India is surplus in foodgrains and deficient in pulses and oilseeds. Because of political compulsions, the government is unable to effect diversification to correct the imbalance. Food production is also heavily dependent on seasonal rains and the government cannot take any risk at the food front. Because of small landholdings and input costs, agriculture has also become unremunerative for small farmers. However, due to lack of enough jobs in the industrial sector, masses still remain glued to agriculture, with low per capita income, which in turn leads to poor purchasing power, low demand of consumer goods, and hence a damper to the industrial sector.

While the industrial sector has not grown due to the socialist policies of the government since independence, populist policies have forced governments to heavily subsidise agriculture by way of free electricity, subsidised fertilisers, waiver of loans, government purchasing foodgrains above the market price (MSP) over and above the needs, and direct cash transfer of money (Kisan Samman Nidhi). The government then distributes the unnecessarily purchased foodgrains free of cost to nearly half the Indian population. All this expenditure is a drain on government resources. Money which could well be spent for employment generation, health, education, etc. is being spent to win votes. Thus, socialism and populism have become the bane of Indian economy and lack of a clear policy has consistently put India in an ambiguous position at the WTO.

USA has challenged India's **export subsidy schemes** and high tariffs on many products. Many nations accuse India for levying excess duties to give impetus to its local manufacturing. India contends that such products were not covered under the Information Technology Agreement as these did not exist in 1996. Hence these are outside the jurisdiction of WTO. India also asserts that the subsidies it provides are in the form of production subsidies, which are permitted under the WTO. The export subsidies too are given for production and marketing purposes, which are also permissible under the WTO rules. Indian exports are also not significant enough to cause a surplus in the global market, as is being alleged by other WTO members. India holds that it is not obliged to implement the recommendations of WTO's dispute panel about its export promotion schemes and has appealed at the WTO's appellate body.

Regarding the subsidies on food, India has invoked the **Peace Clause** which protects a developing country's food procurement programmes against action from WTO members in case subsidy ceilings are breached. India contends that adequate buffer stock of foodgrains helps to deal with fluctuations in production and helps meet with the vagaries of nature. There are other issues also like the Agreement on Countervailing Duties, Anti-dumping Duties, etc., which affect India. India has also sought a clear dispute settlement mechanism in the global agreement to end subsidies for illegal and unreported fishing being done by many other nations.

There are also problems regarding lack of provisions in Indian **laws for protecting patents** on trade related intellectual property rights in several sectors because Indian economy is not based on knowledge and innovation. India is the pharmacy of the world, but it basically makes generic drugs. There also, India depends on China for almost 80% of the Active Pharmaceutical Ingredients (API) - the raw material for drugs. Indian bureaucratic control over every activity, despite some liberal economic reforms, on the pretext of balance of payments issues is also a cause of complaint by India's major trading partners like USA and EU. However, WTO's ruling against India has resulted in major legislative amendments to Indian laws to bring India's trade measures in conformity with its WTO obligations.

After India recently banned a large number of Chinese mobile Apps, China claimed that India has violated WTO rules. India holds that there is no bilateral agreement between India and China related to smartphone Apps. As per the rules of the WTO, a country can take action against companies if it is a threat to national security and the sovereignty of the nation. WTO has set up a dispute panel against India to clarify whether India's duties on imports of certain information and communications technology products infringe WTO norms or not.

**India has its own disputes** with the WTO. India accuses that some of the measures practiced by certain nations flout the provisions of WTO and adversely impact exports of certain products by India. India is seeking support from countries facing similar situations, and along with these nations, aims to collectively bring about changes in the WTO rules.

While the aim of 'Atmanirbhar Bharat' has merits, and India needs to stand on its own feet on all strategic products - weapons as well as chips - care needs to be taken that the policies do not make India insular. India must remain in the world community as a worthy partner. It also needs to compete with the best. The success story of human evolution - from a fearful ape to an adventurous hunter to a cosmic explorer - is the story of inspiration, competition, adventure, endurance, endeavour, and enterprise - a story of the desire to excel, to out-perform and to achieve more. India cannot afford the safety of coffin that protectionism provides. In fact, as a champion of the causes of the 'Global South' it must show the way.

## SOCIALIST ECONOMIES AND THE CMEA

International relations depend on economic factors as deeply as on the political ones because economics and politics are intrinsically interwoven. This is especially true regarding the relations of Soviet Union and the communist bloc with the western world after the Second World War.

Soviet Union wanted money for reconstruction after the war and generally revive its economy. Hence USSR took an active role in the Bretton Woods conferences and supported the Western proposal of creating the ITO. American and British aspirations to create a truly international organisation led to a Soviet-friendly drafting of the ITO Charter which was extremely tolerant of economic centralism of the Soviet led communist bloc. It also provided room for compatibility between the goals of free trade and the Soviet policy of state monopoly over foreign trade. **USSR was in favour of the ITO** and expected to fully participate in the post-war economic institutions.

However, after Churchill began ranting about the bogey of Cold War through his 'iron curtain' speeches in USA since March 1946, Soviet-West relations started deteriorating and rapidly turned into a Soviet perception of Western hostility. In 1947, the "Truman Doctrine" came up to check Soviet Union's growing influence. A key component of this doctrine was the European Recovery Program - known as the Marshall Plan - aimed to help in the reconstruction of West European countries but not for the communist bloc. Soviet Union's request to participate in the GATT was also rejected by USA as the Soviet system was considered as incompatible with the free-market principles of the GATT. USSR also seemed to have little to offer by way of reciprocal trade concessions and Soviet intentions were suspect for political reasons.

As such, **Soviet Union was not invited to the GATT** Conference in mid-1947 and could not join the IMF and the World Bank. Its demand for loan for post war recovery was also rejected. USSR was given 'observer' status but observers don't participate in the real negotiations unless they have some concrete concessions to offer. GATT participation as observer could not have protected Soviet trade from sanctions imposed by the West. Thus, Soviet Union was excluded from all international economic organisations. Having been turned into a pariah, Stalin created the **Council for Mutual Economic Assistance** (CMEA) in January 1949. Also known as COMECON, it initially included the communist nations of Bulgaria, Czechoslovakia, Hungary, Poland, and Romania, with USSR heading the table. Later, Cuba, the German Democratic Republic, Mongolia, and Vietnam also joined the organisation.

USSR also had its own reasons to remain alienated from the Western institutions. USSR knew that USA would dominate the post-war world - economically as well as politically - and saw the Bretton Woods institutions as an opportunity for USA to use the principles of free trade to further its goal of global hegemony at the cost of the less developed countries. The concepts of non-discrimination and multilateralism would not allow USSR to develop a system of bilateral economic agreements with the communist East European bloc under Soviet control. This would undermine Soviet economic control over the Eastern bloc. USSR also did not want American dominance to spread into its sphere of influence.

USSR's reasons for remaining insulated from international institutions were also based on certain ideological assumptions. **Stalin believed that capitalism would eventually collapse.** Participation in a globalised market system would subject the Soviet economy to world economic problems, as had happened during the Great Economic Depression 1929-31, which had not affected the USSR as its economy was insulated from the Western economy. The Soviets also felt that requirements of multilateralism, non-discrimination, reciprocity, transparency, and the use of tariffs were not compatible with their own state trading system. Multilateralism and non-discrimination contradicted the country specific planning policy of USSR and were impediments in its policy of using trade relations as a political negotiating tool.

The **communist leaders believed that protectionism was necessary** for their own industrialisation, and that a multilateral trading system was not in their interest. An open Soviet economy may give rise to unemployment and inflation. The concept of transparency also was not acceptable to Stalin because of his obsession for secrecy. He feared that the West could use sensitive information to brow beat the Soviet Union. The Soviet model was based on centrally planned pricing structure. This made it difficult for other countries to negotiate on a level playing field. This could create uncertainty in the stability of a market-based trading system. Because of these issues, the Stalinist regime promoted autarky and took little advantage of gains from free trade.

Stalin died in March of 1953 and East-West relations relaxed for some time. USSR had firmly established its dominance over the Eastern bloc and had improved relations with the developing countries. USSR also wanted technologically intensive industries. This led to an increase in East-West trade activity. The communist regimes of Eastern Europe, including members of CMEA, were more open to multilateralism. Some became observer or associate members of the GATT. (In the 1970s, some became full members.) This suited the Western Europe as well because many of these nations wanted to get out of American dominance. It was also an antidote to communism.

In 1985 **Gorbachev** came to power and started political and economic reforms in the Soviet Union. He also wanted full membership in the GATT but his request was rejected by USA. Nevertheless, Soviet trade with other nations, especially with the West European nations increased. In June 1988 the CMEA and EEC established formal relations. Gorbachev wanted to bring USSR into the international economic mainstream and as such CMEA lost relevance. In any case, it was a small group with little to offer to the members. In fact, it had become a liability for the USSR. As USSR itself started disintegrating, the CMEA became redundant and was formally dissolved on 28th June 1991.

Even after the collapse of Soviet Union, the western nations kept obstructing Russia's entry into the WTO. It was only in August 2012 that the Russian Federation could become a member of the WTO.

## CHINA

China is a superpower today, militarily as well as economically, and hence needs a special mention here. At the turn of the 20th century, China was a feudal and fragmented nation, militarily weak and economically colonised. For the next five decades China remained engrossed in civil wars and in wars with Japan. The Chinese (KMT government) did participate in the Bretton Woods negotiations since 1944 and also became a member of the GATT in 1948. However, in October 1949, the communists took over power and the revolution put an end to any further Chinese involvement in international organisations.

Having come to power, Mao Zedong introduced his own brand of dictatorial but nationalistic communism. While China became unified and militarily strong, and literacy levels too improved, Mao's various schemes also brought famines and economic ruin. Agricultural as well industrial productivity remained poor because of state control, and the state did not have money to invest for modernisation. Private players had neither the right nor the incentive to invest. China also remained internationally isolated and backward. It did not even join CMEA as its relations with Soviet Union were also not good. US President Nixon wanted to bring China into the US camp and also visited China in 1972. While certain agreements were made between USA and China, these were mainly on strategic issues, not on economic matters. China continued to be insular, isolated, poor and backward.

Mao Zedong died on 9th September 1976. There was a brief period of power struggle after which **Deng Xiaoping** came to power in 1977. Unlike Gorbachev who tried to open the economy as well as politics in USSR at the same time, Deng was fully committed to the absolutist power of the state through the instrument of the Communist Party. At the same time, he understood that economy needed to open up through moderation, modernisation and globalisation. Deng was not dogmatic about Maoism, or even about communism. He was a pragmatic nationalist who wanted to strengthen China irrespective of the ideology. While maintaining the façade of supremacy of Maoism, Deng admitted that Mao was '70% right and 30% wrong'. This was an acceptance that things needed to change, and it was to transform China.

China had certain basic advantages. It was the fourth largest nation by way of landmass, rich in mineral resources, and its strategic position gave it access to the sea, and hence to global trade routes. It was also the most populous nation, although peoples were largely engaged in low productivity agriculture, and some in inefficient state owned industries. There was severe unemployment as well. Deng's basic plan was to use China's geography as well as demography as assets by improving productivity. To that end, Deng formulated the policy of 'four modernisations' - agriculture, industry, technology, and military.

**Private ownership and enterprise were encouraged**, although under state control and supervision through centralised planning. In the agriculture sector, the farmers were permitted cultivate land like private property and sell a part of their crops in the free market on the condition that they allocate a set portion of the produce to the state. Agricultural reforms raised incomes, and savings of millions began generating demand for consumer goods. However, it was essential to move millions from agriculture to the more productive and income generating industrial sector. Savings had also provided the government with the necessary money to invest in the industrial sector. Thus began industrial and market reforms.

In the industrial sector, the state-owned units had to produce a certain fixed amount for the government and the surplus could be used as profit. This did not mean privatisation, but it gave the managers of the state enterprises freedom to use profit as they wanted. However, modernisation needed technical knowhow and big money for investment. Since China had neither, it had to come from abroad. Thus Deng formulated what is known as the "**Open Door**" policy and invited foreign companies. It was a complete reversal of Mao's policies.

In order to bring foreign investment, autonomous Special Economic Zones were created exclusively for exports. They were also given privileges and tax cuts. The existence of a large underemployed workforce meant that foreign companies could employ low-cost labour which could produce goods which could easily compete in foreign markets due to cheap prices. Dictatorial control of the state also meant that there were no labour or trade union issues to confront. USA particularly backed China's opening up and market-oriented reforms.

Thus a large number of **US and European companies entered China** and made huge investments. China began producing technologically low end products in large quantities for export to the western world and in the third world markets. Production and profitability increased generating employment, income, and savings for further investment. In enriched the state with money in dollars and gave employment to the Chinese masses, and thus increased purchasing power of the people. Restrictions on religious activities were relaxed and tourism was promoted to bring in foreign exchange. China also joined the World Bank, the International Monetary Fund, and the Asian Development Bank.

As many Western companies opened/shifted their operations to China, they brought not only money but also technology and Chinese products became even more competitive in the global markets. While its cheap goods flooded the world, decline in poverty led to growth of an enormous domestic middle class of prosperous consumers. A flourishing middle and upper class meant that companies could open firms in China for the domestic market also. With the expansion of manufacturing and services sectors, a largely agrarian economy began to shift into an advanced industrial economy. At the same time great emphasis was given to technical education. Generous scholarships were offered to Chinese students to seek higher education in the West.

The State-Owned Enterprises (SOEs) nevertheless remained the key players in the national economy and got full support of the Chinese government. These were handed over to the provincial and local governments and were allowed to compete on free market principles which made them more efficient. Private businesses were also encouraged. The state adopted a wide range of supportive policies for employment generating industries like the provision of inputs at affordable prices, favourable export credit terms, simplified paperwork, tax incentives, and subsidised land prices along the coastal areas and in the underdeveloped hinterland. Investment in infrastructure and improvement of social and financial institutions was also done.

Deng Xiaoping lost power in 1989 and was succeeded by **Jiang Zemin** who further carried out the policies of economic reforms and integration with the global economy. The Chinese government made innovation a top priority in its economic planning. By the turn of the 21st century, China had become the largest supplier of a number of consumer goods. In 2000, China initiated the "go global" strategy which meant foreign investment by Chinese firms - primarily the SOEs - to develop globally competitive Chinese firms, and acquire modern technology. In 2001, China joined the World Trade Organization. As a result China fully entered the international commerce and became the leading producer and distributor of goods around the world.

As China entered the global economy, Chinese businesses were in a position to further attract investment and expand their markets. China also started manufacturing high-tech products. Greater interconnectivity meant that Chinese manufacturers became integrated into various global value chains. In 2007, the Chinese government launched the **China Investment Corporation** (CIC) in an effort to diversify away from its US dollar holdings. By 2010, China had become the world's second largest economy and the world's largest manufacturer.

## CHINA AND THE CHALLENGES

While China is an economic superpower today, it has many challenges ahead, at the domestic front as well as in the international arena. On one hand, its economy is slowing down, and on the other hand, China has made more enemies than what is good for it. The two are interconnected and of China's own making.

China is no more a poor country where companies can hire workers at low wages and manufacture low cost goods which could be exported for sale around the world markets at cheap prices. As per capita income and standard of living has gone up, so have the salaries, as well as the cost of products. China's 'one child only' policy to control population has also created a demographic challenge. An **ageing population** and restriction on immigration means that it will increasingly have more of the elderly to take care of and less for productive work. As a result of these factors, labour cost has risen now and foreign companies are seeing falling profits.

Overreliance on exports for economic growth is also a problem now because nations are putting restrictions on Chinese goods. China also heavily subsidises many of its products, and in a way, dumps them in foreign markets. While this is being resisted by many nations, it is not a profitable way of conducting trade in the long run. Government control over the exchange rate of Chinese currency, the Renminbi (RMB), against the dollar in order to boost exports is also a matter of dispute.

On one hand the Chinese economy is showing signs of distress, and growth is slowing down, and on the other, China has landed into a severe **debt problem**. Its realty sector is in deep crisis due to unrealistic expansion of housing. The Chinese government uses the banking system to boost credit in order to help meet its GDP growth objectives. Hence GDP figures of China are also suspect.

**Economic diplomacy** was always central to Chinese foreign policy and China uses its money power to spread its influence all over the world. Hence, China is investing heavily in several poorer countries of Africa and South America to gain access to their natural resources as well as to spread its political footprint. Many of these projects are unremunerative and are only putting smaller nations into Chinese debt trap. China thus seems to be pulling off its geopolitical objectives without military confrontation. China's **Belt and Road Initiative** (BRI), also called as "One Belt, One Road" (OBOR) project, launched in 2013, is seen as another move to expand Chinese influence. While the ultimate outcome of BRI is suspect, it is apprehended that it would saddle many countries with large debts. Nations like Italy have already started to opt out of it.

China is also investing heavily in all of **India's neighbours** - Pakistan, Nepal, Bangladesh, Myanmar, Bhutan, Sri Lanka and Maldives. India perceives this as China's attempt to cordon India and finds itself trapped in the quagmire of Chinese economic diplomacy. India needs good relations with the neighbours for security reasons. However India cannot match the Chinese financial resources in helping these nations. India has also often failed to keep its promises: The development projects that India undertakes in these nations get bogged down in bureaucratic delays and sometimes never take shape. On the other hand, these nations need money for infrastructure development. They also use the leverage of China's help to extract more concessions from India. Even where India has helped, political parties in these nations use the bogey of 'big brother' approach of India for electoral purposes. Many of these political leaders adopt a positively hostile posture for domestic popularity.

While all these investments may put the borrowing nations into a debt trap, their inability to repay the loans would ultimately add to China's own debt crisis. A huge loan is more a lender's problem than a borrower's headache. Whether China gains anything politically or not through such means, it surely is likely to stand to lose much economically. Perhaps, China would lose money as well as influence.

At the same time, China has become extremely obsessive about **state control**, especially after Xi Jinping came to power in 2012. Xi is so paranoid about his own power that he does not want any private enterprise, including a Chinese one, or any billionaire, to become too powerful. Thus restrictions are again being put on private enterprise. Totalitarianism has led to opacity and government corruption. President's Xi Jinping's recent anticorruption drive is more about consolidating his own political power than about reforming the system. Even Chinese businessmen are being harassed. Local officials hesitate to pursue projects because they feel it will lead to scrutiny from the central government. On the other hand, income disparity has widened within China exposing the socio-political fault lines. China continues to be a closed society where there is no personal freedom. The utter chaos during Covid 19 and the concealment of truth has exposed the weaknesses of the foundations of the Chinese system.

Lack of an independent **judicial system** means absence of rule of law. Many western companies now find it difficult to do business in China because regulations are not transparent, contracts are difficult to enforce, and intellectual property rights are not protected. The state owned enterprises are being protected while established foreign firms have to face restrictions. Many have thus started to relocate.

China is using its economic and military power to spread its political influence in the neighbourhood. It has openly declared its aim to annexe Taiwan and has laid claim over the entire South China Sea - its transit as well as its maritime resources. This has brought China into direct confrontation with much of the international community. China's growing alliance with Russia, a powerful country now also at odds with the West, has further emboldened Xi Jinping to embark on brinkmanship. While Putin portrays himself as a modern Tsar, Jinping thinks of himself as a Manchu king.

All these steps are being seen as a security issue and a concern for the international political order by many nations - India, USA, Australia, Japan and many EU members. They want to reduce their dependency on China and decouple their economy from that of China. **USA is particularly irked** with China as it poses economic as well as a security threat. China is the largest merchandise trading partner of USA and biggest source of trade surplus. China is also the largest foreign holder of US dollars. However, China is being accused of using unfair trade practices, such as an undervalued currency and subsidies given to domestic producers, to flood US markets with low-cost products. This threatens American jobs, wages, and the overall economy.

Hawks like Donald Trump want to raise tariffs on all products from China. USA also accuses China of large scale infringement - and theft - of US intellectual property rights. Storage of data by Chinese companies has also become an issue and USA is about to ban TikTok. USA has also formed the QUAD to counter China in the Indo-Pacific region. While China has become a global producer and a major user of clean and renewable energy technology, it is also the world's leading polluter and is facing flak at the international platforms on environmental issues.

While an escalating **trade conflict** between USA and China would have negative consequences for the Chinese, as well as the world economy, the potential of a military confrontation is an even more a horrifying prospect. This is becoming more and more threatening as the Ukraine war continues and no side willing to resolve the issue. China continues to fish in troubled waters and Xi Jinping has become excessively powerful. The leaders of the Chinese Communist Party have followed these policies of domestic despotism and regional hegemony even after the death of Mao because that is only the way they can retain power. However, this policy goes quite contrary to the very basics of economic prosperity through technological excellence. How long this would continue, and to what end, remains to be seen. It should also be remembered that Xi Jinping is an aging leader and how long will he remain in power is a question.

## GLOBALISATION AND THE GLOBAL SOUTH

Globalisation basically means interconnectedness of nations in all fields of activity. It is a process that involves integration of economic, political, social, and cultural systems across the borders, resulting in increased flow of goods, services, capital, people, and ideas. However, globalisation largely refers to economic affairs - trade and investment.

Globalisation is not a new phenomenon and inter-nation trade existed in the prehistoric age. However, it increased substantially from the 16th century onwards with the beginning of colonialism. It got a further boost after the **Industrial Revolution** in the 19th century. The Industrial Revolution promoted capitalism, improved productivity and made Europe and USA rich. At the same time, while colonialism led to increased exploitation of primary commodities - minerals, ores, and agricultural produce - Europeans also brought modern technology, investment and institutions for development to the colonies. As a result, nations like India came out of the medieval age and entered the modern era. While colonialism ended by the middle of the 20th century, the newly independent nations kept lagging behind and the legacy of colonialism led to the North-South divide that still continues.

Today, globalisation is viewed as a panacea for all economic problems as well as a cause of many problems for the Third World nations. This is because while some give importance to poverty reduction through development, the others are more concerned about **increasing economic disparity** among nations due to globalisation. The paradox is that while globalisation has reduced absolute poverty, it has also increased disparity. Further, it has brought income disparity not only among the nations but also among the peoples within the nations. Those who took the road of scientific innovation and entrepreneurship - individuals like Bill Gates and nations like USA - became richer. Those who did not, or could not, have been left behind and the gap is increasing.

Globalisation is not only about flow of goods and services. **Globalisation has eased flow of money** as well. Today governments and financial institutions can move money for investment and safe keeping freely from one nation to the other. Foreign Portfolio Investors keep moving money from one capital market to another depending how the stock market is performing. US FPIs hold almost 20% of the investment in Indian capital markets and their flows affect the Indian stock market and hence the wealth of millions of Indian investors. US Federal monetary policy similarly affects the monetary policies of other nations. This affects the value of currencies of nations and hence affects trade as well. Free movement of money also allows MNCs evade national taxes by locating in tax havens. Nobody, nation or any organisation, has any control over this free flow of money while it has a crucial role in the overall economy of nations and the financial position of individuals.

Globalisation is a difficult issue for the Third World: It can neither be ignored nor fully compatible with the national interests as it undermines the power of the state. **Globalisation empowers the MNCs** of the technologically advanced countries over the state in developing nations. While critics of globalisation have their own justified objections, there are two realities that have to be accepted by all. The first is that globalisation is inevitable and no nation can remain isolated. Every nation needs something which it cannot produce and has to buy from somewhere else. Many also have something to sell and hence need to trade with others. The other is the harsher reality that all - individuals as well as nations - are not equal. Everyone was equal in the Stone Age but we cannot return - and would not like to return - to the Stone Age. Hence, globalisation is not really the issue: The issue is how nations respond to the global forces. The only option is to strike a right balance between prosperity and equality, with prosperity having a higher priority.

Globalisation of economy today basically means all nations being in competition in an open and free market. Thus, it means opening of opportunities. It is for the nations to make best of the opportunity or avoid competition for fear of losing out. At the same time, interdependence between the industrialised and the developing countries has deepened. A growing number of developing countries have been integrated into the international economic system. If the developing countries want to remain in competition, they have to undergo considerable modification in their domestic policies to make best of the opportunities. They cry about inequality of opportunity due to lack of technical deficiencies. But then, it is for them to upscale the same.

Globalisation does not mean only free trade. It also includes **exchange of ideas and technology**. There can be no doubt that globalisation has improved productivity through spread of modern technology which has led to poverty reduction and improvement of living conditions in much of the world, including the Third World. China is today an economic superpower only because it opened itself to foreign investment and technology - the inevitable fruits of globalisation. India is today a world soft power because of the IT sector, a product of globalisation. Globalisation has also created Global Capability Centres* and India is a major beneficiary of this development. Globalisation also brought the Green Revolution to nations like India in the 1960s that solved the problem of starvation deaths. Globalisation has universalised distribution of vaccines and medicines that have saved millions of lives in the Asian and African countries. Control of epidemics has been a result of global efforts.

**Global Capability Centres** are offshore units established by multinational corporations to perform various business functions for the parent company. They help companies to concentrate on their core competencies while using skill of the local centres. There are primarily aimed at innovation initiatives for conducting research and development of new products and services. GCCs are involved in managing IT infrastructure, software development, cyber- security, Artificial Intelligence, Cloud Computing, Data Analytics to support decision-making, handling back-office processes such as finance, human resources, and customer support. GCCs serve as innovation hubs as they bring together specialised talent and provide space for experimentation and global knowledge/skill exchange, sharing, assimilation, and collaboration. These are cost efficient as these are established at centres which provide savings in salaries, infrastructure, and operational expenses. Spreading of their businesses across different places helps companies to deal with regional fluctuations and acts like a safety net. India has become a frontrunner in this field and a large number of GCCs have come up in various cities providing high income jobs as well as revenue for the government.

At the same time, it is also true that poverty has increased in a few regions of the third world. However, this is more due to poor governance, domestic political strife, ethnic and religious conflicts and climate change related problems rather than due to globalisation. In fact, many get aid from richer nations and from the very financial international organisations which are blamed for all the ills of globalisation.

Globalisation increases trade opportunities that allow businesses to expand their customer base and access new markets, which helps to boost sales and increase profits and thereby create wealth. Global competition among businesses facilitates sharing of innovative and efficient technologies that increase productivity. Competition also provides higher quality products at lowers prices for the **consumers**. This has led to higher levels of economic growth, employment, rise in income and general poverty mitigation. These developments have contributed to greater economic growth, improved productivity, and job creation in numerous areas worldwide. At the same time, those nations and individuals which are not able to compete face job losses and decline in income. Hence, globalisation is by itself not the problem, but the way it is managed.

Globalisation has certainly made **nations vulnerable to international economic downturns** over which they have little control. There is no one-size-fits-all formula for such problems. Each state is unique in terms of strengthens and weaknesses. Each has to have its own strategies for adaptation and realignment. Hence nations have to be flexible, diversify, and adjust to turn a crisis into an opportunity. The fundamental step that all have to take is investing in education and skill development. Without a proper environment for scientific research, there is no way a nation can compete in this global race. The other is infrastructure development to facilitate all types of economic activity that provide employment. Governments should also have laws that promote economy and regulate it when necessary. Laws should also make economic growth inclusive. As a last resort, the governments must have a backup plan and financial reserve to directly help the peoples in times of crisis, as was done in USA during the Economic Depression of 1929-33.

## ECONOMIC REGIONALISM

Regionalism stresses upon geographical identity as the primary basis of cooperation between states of a territorial zone. Peoples of a region also have closer cultural and traditional trade links. Hence, it is also recognition of the commonality of issues of an area, and of the idea that it is easier and desirable for the nations in the vicinity to join hands for mutual common good. This has led to formation of countless regional blocs around the world. Success of regionalism depends on the relative economic and political nature of the states that comprise a regional bloc and their mutual bilateral relations. Hence, some blocs are more conducive for regional cooperation than the others. Since there are always political rivalries with the neighbours, regional cooperation has come to largely mean economic cooperation.

Liberal trade between nations of a regional bloc forms the foundation of economic regionalism. Economic regionalism can be consistent, conflicting, as well as complementary with globalisation. Regionalism does help smaller nations with developing economies to face the **challenges of globalisation**. A regional bloc can ring fence the region and protect it against the forces of global competition. Joining hands can also strengthen each of the member nations to better negotiate and compete by taking a common and united stand in trade agreements with richer and powerful nations. They can jointly resist global pressures better than what they can do on their own. Being a member of a powerful bloc adds power to each of the member and their integration makes the bloc more powerful than the sum of power of each individual state.

However, while membership of a free trade area provides access to a larger market and enables free flow of capital and labour, the concept of regional free trade agreements is **inconsistent with the idea of a truly global economy**. Regionalism generates intra-regional trade amongst its members rather than globalised trade with non-members. Regional blocs have also created trade barricades against outside states. Access to a large and profitable market is difficult for those outside the organisation and is a barrier for the less developed countries that need export-led growth. A powerful regional bloc like EU can even dictate terms to the poorer economies of the Global South. The practice of protectionist measures imposed against non-members also contradicts the aims of the World Trade Organisation.

Regionalism also comes in way of national sovereignty as states cede their rights to regional bodies and lose their ability to make their own policies. While reduction of trade barriers leads to economic growth and development, and the consumers benefit from a wider choice in terms of prices and quality, some nations benefit more than the others. This creates acrimony within the group and it is a major reason why none of the regional organisations other than the EU has been successful.

The limitations of regionalism have also been discussed in a later chapter in the context of SAARC and ASEAN. We need to discuss why EU has been more successful and has become the most politically influential and economically powerful regional group.

## THE EUROPEAN UNION

The idea of a united Europe was first mooted by Napoleon. He considered Europe as too small a region to be divided into nation-states. His vision of Europe was as an integrated body with a single currency and without customs barriers. However, racial differences, rising nationalism, and personal lust of power of the rulers, led to wars and fragmentation of Europe. The end of the Second World War divided Europe into two groups: the democratic capitalist West and the dictatorial communist East. The West European nations had two fundamental issues. The first was to prevent any further war and the other was of reconstruction and economic recovery from the ravages of the war. The twin objectives could best be achieved by having functional institutions that encourage cooperation as the nations were too weak to stand on their own.

The process of cooperation progressed in steps. In the early 1950s, the European Coal and Steel Community came to be formed. In 1957, six nations signed The Rome Treaty to establish the European Economic Community **(EEC)**. The aim of EEC was to revive the economy through regional cooperation. Removal of trade barriers led to high levels of economic development and the economic benefits of this step attracted other nations also to join the EEC. With the end of the Cold War and the disintegration of USSR, nations of the Soviet bloc as well as the newly independent nations of the fragmented USSR also began joining the group. As the membership increased, its scope of activities also increased. Finally, the Maastricht Treaty 1992 led to the creation of European Union which provided for free movement of goods, services, and capital. The EU kept expanding its agenda and the Schengen Agreement 1995 enabled unrestricted visa-free travel of citizens within the EU. In 1999, the concept of **Eurozone** was accepted which introduced Euro as the single currency of EU and the region was declared as a zone of peace.

The EU also developed a nominal security apparatus on the principle of collective self-defence through the Common Security and Defence Policy. It can deploy troops to preserve peace. Its success lies in the fact that there has been no armed conflict among its members. This is no mean achievement considering that these petty states fought some of the most brutal and blood soaked wars with each other for centuries till the conclusion of the Second World War. However, the EU is not a military alliance and it is dependent on NATO for security with which it closely coordinates. Neither USA nor any member nation wants the EU to become an alternative to NATO.

Today, EU has 27 members. Attempts have been made to have a **common foreign policy** for EU but success in this field has been marginal because of the large number of members who have different needs and different perceptions. However, the EU as a group uses its soft power - diplomacy and economic clout - and thus exerts considerable influence in the global affairs. In the economic arena, the EU as an entity is a significant actor on the world stage. It is represented in the G20 and the WTO, and holds observer status in the IMF, the UN General Assembly, and the G7 summits. The EU has its own free trade agreements with a large number of countries and other regional groups. The Euro is only the second to US Dollar in terms of world trade and reserve currency.

The EU has a **quasi federal structure** and is a hybrid of supranational and inter-governmental institutions. While the supranational institutions can take decisions applicable to all in certain matters, the inter-governmental institutions accept the state's sovereignty for the protection of national interests on other matters and decisions are taken on the basis of unanimous consensus. EU has common laws on varied subjects like respect for human rights, democracy, agriculture, environment protection, etc. Thus liberal policies are for economic as well as political matters.

While the relative success of the EU provides a useful blueprint for other regions of the world, it must be understood that the circumstances which led to its formation and enlargement were contextual. EU nations are also culturally much more homogeneous than those of any other region. However, like any other organisation, EU has its own challenges because of the basic fact that all nations are different. Unrestricted movement of goods and services has benefitted the technologically advanced nations like Germany more than, and often at the cost of, other nations. To deal with this problem and to maintain the integrity of the union, EU has the provision of regional funding. EU's budget allocates a substantial amount to improve the living standards in the poorer nations of Eastern Europe. This is resented by the peoples of the richer nations that certain nations have become a drag on their purses. The poorer nations on the other hand resent that EU is imposing terms on their domestic policies.

**Migration** - legal as well as illegal - due to porous borders is a major problem within EU. As many nations of the erstwhile Soviet bloc and the newly independent nations of the disintegrated USSR joined the EU, the initial homogeneity of the EU was diluted. Most of these nations had been communist dictatorships with poor economy. Constant enlargement of EU has provided opportunities and also created problems. Cheap labour from Central and Eastern Europe has been one of the main causes of dispute. Concern over uncontrolled immigration has also been a decisive factor in Britain leaving the EU in 2020, a step that has been a major setback for the EU. The victory of the far right parties in the EU elections of June 2024 is an indication that EU nations are very concerned about migration.

The **Russian invasion of Ukraine** is the single biggest challenge for the EU today. While most of the EU nations consider it as a threat to Europe, nations like Bulgaria, Hungary, and Slovakia are taking a pro-Russia posture. Although the EU nations want to help Ukraine in stopping the Russian advance, they can help Ukraine only financially and by armament supply. However, all nations do not have the financial or military resources to help, and the burden has to be taken by a few. The EU has imposed several sanctions against Russia but at the same time many nations cannot do without Russian oil and gas. Hence, they also pay Russia for its war expenditure.

The invasion has led to exodus of Ukrainian families to immediate neighbours like Poland which have to accommodate the refugee migrants. Ukraine is a major exporter of foodgrains. Since it is unable to send its produce through the Black Sea, it is trying to send the same through Western Europe. This has impacted the prices of foodgrains produced in Western Europe. The EU nations are much divided about to what extent they can bear the burden of this war. So far, the burden is being borne largely by USA but the future is uncertain.

## INDIA AND THE EU

While EU has certain common international political principles and strategies, the EU nations largely conduct independent foreign policies. Although India and the European nations differ on many international issues like the Ukraine war and the Middle East, it really does not matter because the European nations themselves are divided and ambivalent on many of these issues. Many have double standards where their own interests are involved. Indian Foreign Minister S. Jaishankar aptly said that "*Europe has to grow out of the mindset that Europe's problems are the world's problem, but the world's problems are not Europe's problems.*" Hence, India's relations with European nations on political issues are more on bilateral basis than with EU as a bloc.

Since EU is more of an economic bloc, India has to conduct its trade relations with Europe largely through EU. While the EU is India's second largest trading partner, India is the ninth largest trading partner for the EU. Negotiations for a free trade agreement are going on since 2007 and are always on the verge of being finalised but never reaching a conclusion because of clash of interests from both the sides.

The agreement proposes to facilitate and liberalise trade in goods and services. The EU is critical of India's high tariff rates on certain products and has sought larger access to Indian markets for its own products. The EU is concerned about India's intellectual property rights regime, especially about patent protection. It demands domestic laws that go beyond the obligations of the Trade-Related Aspects of Intellectual Property Rights (TRIPS) Agreement. The EU also wants an investor-state dispute settlement mechanism which will allow EU investors to challenge the Indian government in front of an international tribunal. This compromises Indian sovereignty and is also incompatible with current Indian laws.

Like other white western nations, EU as a bloc indulges in hypocritically taking the high moral road where it suits. **EU imposes** a large number of non-tariff barriers. While some are desirable, like the condition to have conformity with standards, many are designed to act as a hindrance to others while helping the EU. The EU and India have different perspectives on issues related to climate change. EU also comments on India's sovereign internal decisions. It has raised concerns about human rights in India, including about religious freedom and the treatment of minorities. EU has even expressed its unease about the Citizenship Amendment Act 2019. These are irritants that come in way of having a deal.

India has its own concerns in dealing with EU. India wants to include free flow of white-collar experts as a part of the deal. However, the EU does not have a uniform working visa system due to which **migration of Indian professionals** is restricted. Further, India does not have a clear, comprehensive, and consistent domestic economic policy and hence trade negotiations keep hanging because it is always difficult to take care of the interests of Indian manufacturers and the consumers at the same time. There are also pressure groups that condemn the ruling government irrespective of the merits of the decision. Hence, the ruling regime has little elbow room to negotiate and has to tread very carefully keeping the elections in mind all the time. Lastly, India has still not given up its socialist protectionist policies and is still not ready to compete. Hence, delaying a deal and denouncing the West for neo-colonialism is still a very populist electoral stand.

While a free trade deal with the EU remains in suspended animation, India has signed a free trade agreement with the **European Free Trade Association** in March 2024. The EFTA is a four-member non-EU European bloc comprising of Switzerland, Norway, Iceland, and Liechtenstein.

## INDIA AND LATIN AMERICA

South America is one of the richest regions of the planet in terms of natural resources - minerals, ores, oil, and agricultural products. Persons of Indian origin - predominantly Hindus - are present in almost all nations of South America and they comprise about 40% of the population of nations like Suriname and Guyana. Yet for decades India ignored the continent. This was partly because India had adopted a pro-Soviet policy under the garb of non-alignment. Cuba - a prominent communist nation and a close ally of USSR - had become a vocal member of NAM and India had developed close relations with Cuba. This was a major hurdle because Cuba was trying to instigate communist revolutions in South America while the South American governments, supported by USA, were fighting against communism.

Secondly, many of the Latin American states were military dictatorships while India under Nehru had become a world champion of democracy. It was a very strange stand because Cuba was also a dictatorship! Hence, India had no political leverage or interest in Latin America. Further, India's protectionist socialist policies were also not conducive for trade relations. Thus, for decades due to lack of political will and vision, **India failed to explore the benefits** of the opportunities that existed of the Latin American resources, and of the presence of Indian diaspora.

With the end of the Cold War, democracy began to gain ground in South America and India's foreign and economic policies also became more realistic and liberal. While the government still did not give much attention to Latin America, private Indian companies realised the untapped potential that existed in Latin America and began entering various sectors in the region. Since then, India's export-import with the Latin American nations is steadily increasing. The major items of Indian export are petroleum products, vehicles, chemicals, machinery, and pharmaceuticals. India imports crude oil, gold, vegetable oil, copper, etc., from Latin America.

It must be remembered that Latin America is part of the Global South, and if

India intends to play a leadership role in the Global South, it must be proactive in its approach with Latin America. Today, there is hardly any political issue between India and the Latin American nations. Relations with these nations can be advantageous to both only by way of improving trade relations. However, the overall **trade level is very low** because the government and the private sector are working in silos.

There are certain challenges also that India needs to address. The first and foremost is that the Foreign and Commerce ministries must join hands and give a coordinated strategic direction to the private sector to enhance business relations with Latin America. For this, it is essential to facilitate trade by simplifying procedures and reducing trade barriers. India also has to promote digital platforms for trade.

Latin America has a growing and aspirational middle class. India thus also needs to diversify the trade by moving from natural resources to sectors like infrastructure, information technology, and manufacturing. It should also encourage bilateral investments. Some success has also been achieved in these areas. Tata, Reliance, and Birla groups have made their presence felt in Latin America. TCS has offices in 16 cities of 9 countries in Latin America employing some 25000 personnel. Both India and Latin America are giving importance to renewable energy and many countries are members of the International Solar Alliance. Suzlon has undertaken wind energy projects in Brazil and Uruguay. Bolivia has the world's largest reserves of Lithium - a major component of electric batteries - and is gaining importance as India seeks to shift to electric vehicles. India is a major exporter of pharmaceuticals to Latin America. The low priced Indian generic medicines have helped Latin American consumers and governments to reduce the cost of healthcare.

For long, language remained a barrier as Spanish and Portuguese are the main languages of Latin America. India should take a lesson from China which has hundreds of Spanish and Portuguese language institutes and study centres. India should do the same.

Much also depends on the political climate of Latin America. Many of the nations are in domestic political turmoil while a few have high levels of crime due to drug trafficking. Nevertheless, India has to adopt a selective strategy to deal with nations that can provide mutually beneficial relations.

## INDIA AND AFRICA

India and Africa have historical people-to-people ties and trade links. Due to British colonisation of certain parts of Africa, there is also a considerable presence - about 3 million - of peoples of Indian origin in Africa. While some were transported as indentured labour, many others went for trade and ancillary services. Since entire

Africa had been colonised by the European nations in the 19th century, India and Africa shared the same past of colonialism. India and the African nations became independent almost at the same time after the Second World War and hence had much in common to share. Both were opposed to colonialism and racial discrimination and most of the African states joined the Non Aligned Movement. Hence, India's political engagement with Africa was much closer than that with Latin America after Independence.

Although Africa and Latin America are culturally two different worlds, they also have much in common in terms of resources, potential opportunities, and problems. The two also have the largest numbers of members in the Group of 77 - the Global South. While relations with Latin America are basically transactional and based on economic imperatives, relations with Africa are multi-dimensional and cover cooperation in a wide spectrum of sectors as education, health, trade, technology, infrastructure development, energy, security, and agriculture. This is because of the geo-strategic position of Africa as well as because of the large numbers of sovereign African nations being members of various international organisations like the UNO. Their combined strength gives them political power as a bloc and it is important for India to have their support.

Nevertheless, India's footprint in Africa remained stagnant for decades. This was because during the Cold War period, many African nations became communist and Africa was deeply divided on political and religious lines. The Indian government also gave little attention to Africa because it was considered as a poor region with little to offer India. There was also lack of awareness about Africa. This is despite a large Indian diaspora in Africa. It was so because the Indians settled in Africa had been living there for a few generations and had lost connections with their mother country.

India-Africa relationship has taken a more **positive turn after Narendra Modi** became the Prime Minister and gave impetus to the policy of 'South-South cooperation'. Due to his efforts, the African Union was admitted as a full member of the G-20 at the New Delhi Summit in September 2023. His views on India's position on the nature of relationship were best expressed during his address to Uganda's Parliament in July 2018, *"Our development partnership will be guided by your [African] priorities. We will build as much local capacity and create as many local opportunities as possible. It will be on terms that are comfortable to you, that will liberate your potential and not constrain your future."*

This basically means a policy of "*developing together as equals*" for the sustainable development of Africa without interfering in its domestic policies. While India helps the African nations in all fields, the relationship is not one of donor-recipient but that of partners without conditions attached. African nations also understand India's economic and political clout. India's diplomatic assertion on behalf of the Global

South for a more equitable world order resonates well with the African nations who are disenchanted with the North dominated western order. Hence India is perceived as a trustworthy partner in Africa.

On the economic front, Indo-African relations have been sustained by the government as well as the private sector. India is the second largest lender in Africa. This is being done through public-private partnerships. The government aid is routed through the African Development Bank which India joined in 1983. India's EXIM Bank* devotes a considerable portion of its international financing for technical assistance and trade promotion schemes in Africa. Many African nations are worried about taking loans from China, which have proved to be debt traps for many nations, and prefer to associate with India through direct investment. They also appreciate India's stand to restructure global financial institutions to prioritise the Global South.

*The Export-Import Bank (EXIM Bank) was established in 1982 by the Government of India as a financial institution for providing credit for export oriented sectors. It provides loans to Indian exporters to help them expand in overseas ventures.

Africa is rich in natural resources like minerals and ores, including gold and rare earths, and is a major producer of pulses and lentils. India imports all of these items from Africa. On the other hand, India exports cereals to Africa. Hence the two complement each other's food security. Africa has a growing aspirational middle class. As such, Africa is a buyer of Indian goods as well as a supplier of commodities. Hence India-Africa trade is also growing. Today, India is Africa's third largest trading partner after the European Union and China. India has observer status in the Common Market for Eastern and Southern Africa (COMESA), Southern African Development Community (SADC), and the Economic Community of West African States (ECOWAS).

India not only supplies affordable generic medicines to Africa but also assists in developing its public healthcare services capacity. India provides scholarships to African students for studies in India through the **ITEC.** [The Indian Technical and Economic Cooperation Programme is an international capacity building platform instituted by the Government of India in 1964. It provides scholarships to officials of developing nations from the civilian and the defence sectors for training in institutes in India.] India and the African nations share similar views on climate change and India is helping African nations to switch to renewable energy through the International Solar Alliance.

As regards **defence and security** cooperation is concerned, India stands for assistance for self sufficiency of African nations. The Indian army has long been a part of UN peacekeeping missions in Africa. Indian military academies train army officers of a number of African states. This is not limited to conventional methods but also covers modern areas of technologies like artificial intelligence, cyber security, and drones. India also supplies hardware like tanks, patrol boats, combat helicopters, interceptor boats, and armoured vehicles. This helps African nations in dealing with terrorism which is a serious threat to regional security.

In **maritime security**, Indian navy is prominent in the Arabian Sea as well as in the Indian Ocean. Indian and African navies regularly hold joint exercises. India also trains Africa in maritime surveillance and undersea scanning technologies. Indian engineers help in shipbuilding and port development, and strengthen African capacity for repair and maintenance of equipments. Being the littoral states in the Indian Ocean, India and many African countries join hands to ensure freedom of navigation in the Indian Ocean and India has been active in checking piracy around Somalia.

India has limited **expectations from Africa** in return. In the political field, India expects diplomatic support of African nations in the international arena, like support in India's bid for a permanent membership in the UN Security Council. The two also need each other's support in restructuring the world economic order for mutual benefit.

There are **challenges** for India as well as for the African nations in developing this relationship to a higher level. The foremost is the division among African nations on various issues. Africa is also afflicted by ethnic and religious conflicts, especially in the Sahara region. There are also law and order and governance issues in some countries. These factors make Indian investors cautious about venturing in the region.

**China's growing presence in Africa** through soft loans to mineral rich African states is also a challenge because one of the aims of China is to dislodge India from Africa.

However, India's biggest challenge is not outside but within India. China's reach in Africa is primarily state led. On the other hand, Indian activity in Africa is largely led by the private sector. But India still has no coordinated Africa policy where the government institutions and private businesses can join hands for leverage. The Indian government has to understand that high level visits and summit meetings, declarations and honour decorations, are useful but have limitations. Ultimately, intentions have to materialise on ground and start delivering. Further, India may never become an alternative to China as far as money power is concerned.

However, India has its own strengths. Africa is still a largely untapped market, especially for goods like textiles, pharmaceuticals, automobiles and light machinery. Indian investments in Africa also need to diversify beyond the traditional sectors. India is a world soft power due to its IT sector. India can help Africa bridge the digital divide by leveraging its strengths in institutional connectivity, IT infrastructure, banking, and telecommunications. Indian private sector is playing its part in this sector and Bharti Airtel is a major telecom operator in Africa. Indian government should prioritise local skills and thus help improve productivity in a transparent manner.

India also needs to improve people-to-people contacts. Many of the African nations are as cricket crazy as Indians and the game can become another tool of soft power. The success of Indian Premier League in Africa in 2023 is a pointer in this direction.

❖❖❖❖

# Chapter VII

# Evolution of India's Foreign Policy

India became independent at the break of 15th August 1947. It was the shining hour for Jawaharlal Nehru - his own tryst with destiny. He read a brilliant speech in English, and those of the Indians who could understand it listened in awe and admiration. Nehru's supremacy at this time was unchallenged. As the Prime Minister, he was now determined to carry on the baton with elegance and charm - qualities that had placed him on the high pedestal.

## THE NEHRUVIAN PERIOD

Unlike many of the khadi clad boorish leaders of the Congress, Nehru was urbane and debonair. He had been educated in England, spoke good English, had visited foreign countries, and was convinced that he alone among all understood the foreigners and could interact with them at level. Thus he took the charge of foreign policy in his own hands. Even during the freedom struggle, Nehru had been formulating the foreign policy of the Congress party. At that time struggles for national liberation were going on against colonialism in Africa and Asia. Congress had condemned imperialism, and had passed resolutions supporting the cause of nationalism and independence. Nehru had also declared that India stood for world peace and non-violence, and these moral ideals became the corner stone of his foreign policy. These were also to become millstones around India's neck.

With the lofty ideals of world peace, liberation of subjugated peoples, anti-colonialism, anti-imperialism, and faith in the United Nations, Nehru set about with the unenvious task of putting the chaotic post-war world to order. Nehru wanted to show that India might be a poor underdeveloped country, unable to feed or clothe its own millions, but it was a spiritual master, and as the leader of a great civilisation, it was his moral duty to teach the world leaders how to conduct world affairs. He also wanted to show Indians how *he* was putting the world affairs into order. This unnecessary exhibition of moral superiority was to prove costly for India.

Nehru envisaged his role on the world stage and his approach towards India's immediate neighbours was of benign neglect. They were too insignificant to deserve his personal attention. But it was a neighbour that created the first problem. When **Pakistan attacked Kashmir**, almost immediately after Independence, Kashmir had not yet acceded to the Union of India. After dilly-dallying for quite some time till it became inevitable, the maharaja of Kashmir fled from Srinagar and consented to accession. Thereafter, the Indian army moved in, but just when the army was about to drive out the Pakistani invaders from Kashmir, Nehru sought the intervention of UNO.

This over-confidence on UNO was misplaced because India did not have a single friendly nation by its side. India was made to agree not only for a cease-fire but even for a plebiscite although there was no provision of plebiscite in the instrument of transfer of power regarding the Princely States as stipulated in the Indian Independence Act 1947. Pakistan did not agree to withdraw its forces for the conduct of plebiscite, and Nehru took no action. Thus Pakistan not only succeeded in retaining control over a sizable chunk of Kashmir forever but also got a perpetual cause to create trouble.

Despite the bloodshed of partition, Nehru had failed to understand the true nature of the newly created immediate neighbour. He refused to acknowledge it even after the war of 1948. While the Kashmir issue remained unresolved, Nehru accepted the arbitration of UK and the World Bank, and magnanimously signed the **Indus Waters Treaty in 1960** with Pakistan - imagining that it would improve relations. This gave Pakistan a very generous share - over and above international norms - of the waters of Indus. It was a decision that could never be reversed and India regrets it to this day.

These issues - that concerned India - were however trivial matters for Nehru: he had graver issues of international concern to attend to. His craving to pose as a world statesman - shaking hands with the world leaders - while at the same time, passing homilies of peace to one and all proved to be a great obstacle to Indian interests.

## NON-ALIGNMENT

The post World War II world was in a state of apprehensions and the world was divided into two camps. On one side was the Communist bloc led by Soviet Russia and on the other side was the Western bloc led by USA. There were deep divisions, distrust, and suspicion. The **Cold War** had started and nations wanted others to make their stand clear where they stood in this bi-polar world. Nehru didn't want India to be in either of the camps - perhaps he was not sure where India stood.

In 1945, when USA had dropped atom bombs on Japan to end the World War, Nehru had condemned the US action. This had irked the US administration even though USA had supported India's cause for independence. Nehru was enamoured by socialism, and by the Soviet brand of planned economy. Various resolutions passed by the Congress Party prior to Independence against capitalism had only antagonised USA and the West European leaders. However, this didn't bring India any closer to the Soviet Union either. At that time Soviet leadership was contemplating of overthrowing the government of India through a communist revolution, and since Congress Party was against communism, relations with Soviet Union remained distrustful. Nehru's visit to USA in 1949 stirred even more suspicions among the Soviet leaders. Hence India did not earn the goodwill of any group. Nehru did not even want India to join any faction. He wanted to play the role of a neutral peacemaker.

In 1950 civil war started in **Korea**. India had no geo-political stake in the region or any moral ground for taking sides. Yet India supported the cause of the communists - who were in fact the invaders - and condemned US military intervention in the UN General Assembly. Perhaps this was done to earn the goodwill of China. India earned no goodwill of China but conclusively lost the support of USA for good. Cold War distrust and American dislike of Nehruvian socialism further cooled relations with USA as it suspected Nehru of being a supporter of Soviet Union and an advocate of communism.

USA was in search of allies and military bases in Asia to check the expansion of communism. After India refused to side with it, USA found a compliant minion in Pakistan. While Nehru kept sermonising USA on moral principles, Pakistan joined the US camp. Pakistan made a strategic agreement with USA in 1954 and joined SEATO (South East Asia Treaty Organisation) as a member in 1955. For decades Pakistan got substantial financial and military aid from USA - which armed and encouraged it to wage a war against India in 1965 - a war in which no country supported India.

Nehru opposed the Anglo-French action during the **Suez crisis** of October 1956 - which further alienated the western world. The same month Soviet army invaded Hungary to crush a domestic uprising. Nehru criticised Soviet action as well. India had no stake in either of the two events, yet Nehru voiced his concerns. In fact, India expressed an opinion on every international issue, whether it concerned India or not, and whether India could contribute to a resolution on the issue or not.

India's liberation of Goa in December 1961 by armed intervention had made Nehru talking about peace look hollow to the western world. Not that India's unsolicited opinions mattered, but it made many nations to view India with distrust. That too, coming from a country that was itself deeply poverty stricken, barely able to feed its millions, and unable to resolve its own problems.

Being neutral was understandable, but to be critical of all was unwarranted. India had become an international preacher of morals, with neither of the super powers on its side. Instead of correcting this precarious situation, Nehru made a virtue of it and glorified it by calling this state of friendlessness a policy of non-alignment. Thus began the so called **Non-Aligned Movement**. Soon, NAM became a sort of front against colonialism, and the western world began viewing NAM as a subsidiary wing of the Soviet bloc, and India as a supporter of Soviet Union. While the annual jamboree of NAM conferences did India no good, such discordant notes at a forum of which India was seen as the cheerleader only raised distrust about Indian motives. While NAM countries were of no help to India, it did considerable damage to India's relations with the powers that mattered. When China attacked India in 1962 none of the NAM nations supported India.

While the NAM was basically against colonialism, Nehru's desire not to miss any opportunity where he could be seen in international limelight drove him into joining the **Commonwealth of Nations** - a residue of the once British colonial empire - an organisation to create an illusion that even though the Crown may have lost its colonies, it still retained their loyalty. The member nations were dominion status nations like Canada, Australia, New Zealand, etc., which still retained the British Crown as their head of state. India as a sovereign Republic had no logic to be a part of it. It was strange that while Nehru held strong views on colonialism yet he had no hesitation in joining it. The Commonwealth had nothing in common and no wealth to contribute. India gained nothing out of it - except winning some medals at the Commonwealth Games. Yet the foreign affairs ministry spent money, time, and energy for the futile activities of this dud organisation.

India was among the first countries to recognise the newly created state of **Israel**. At the same time Nehru decided not to have diplomatic relations with it. For decades India kept voting against Israel at every international forum whereas Israel never opposed India. This was done to win the friendship of Arab states but these consistently supported Pakistan on every issue. The ruling Congress Party also intended to win the votes of Indian Muslims by opposing Israel. This communalisation of foreign policy had a very dangerous message - that Indian Muslims were not patriots. It also hyphenated India's foreign policy to domestic issues and for long proved to be an impediment in pursuing a policy of bi-lateral relations with each state of the Middle East on the basis of mutual common interests.

## INDO-CHINA WAR

Nehru's foreign policy was to finally meet its own tryst with destiny when China attacked India in 1962. Historically, China had pursued a policy of hegemony and expansion towards south, especially over Tibet. By 1900, Tibet was left with nominal autonomy in internal affairs, while Beijing had curtailed Tibet's right to conduct international relations. Beijing also claimed all territories under Tibetan control as a part of China. At that time, the British were expanding in the Himalayan region and came to control certain territories that Tibet had for long claimed as its own. The Tibetan claim was on the basis that these areas were predominantly Buddhist, and the Dalai Lama - as the spiritual head of the Buddhist sects of the region - had sovereignty over peoples that owed allegiance to him. The Tibetan claim was thus more religious - or cultural - in nature, rather than political or territorial. It was factually also incorrect because majority of the peoples in the region were not Buddhists.

It was the era when frontiers were often not clearly demarcated on ground or on paper. British expansion in the region in the late 19th century had become a cause of tension between the Government of India and the Tibetan government. In order to de-escalate the situation, hectic negotiations took place between the Tibetan and British officials in the presence of Chinese officials. At that time China was in internal turmoil and the Chinese officials often could not attend the meetings. In March 1914, the Tibetan authorities agreed to a line of demarcation called as the **McMahon line**. Since Chinese officials were not present in this meeting, and the officials of the Autonomous State of Tibet did not have the mandate to decide international matters, the Tibetan officials made a condition that this demarcation would be considered valid only after the approval of the Chinese government.

The McMahon line was not accepted by the Beijing government. Hence the Tibetan government also declared it as void. Thereafter, China got more and more embroiled in its own internal problems and the issue of border remained undiscussed and undecided. Nehru visited China during August-September 1939 and established personal relations with the Chinese dictator Chiang Kai-shek. Chiang also visited India in February 1942. However, despite Nehru's public posturing of bonhomie, Chiang summarily rejected the validity of McMahon line. India thus inherited an unsettled border and an unresolved dispute at the time of Independence.

In 1949, communist forces led by Mao Zedong took control over Beijing and established the People's Republic of China. Chiang Kai-shek fled to Taiwan and established the Republic of China. Mao did not recognise Chiang's government and declared Taiwan as an integral part of China. This was called as the **'One China'** doctrine which meant that no part of China could remain separate from China. There was no place for an independent Tibet or Taiwan in this doctrine. Hence the territories that Tibet considered as its domain also had to be incorporated into China. In October 1950, Chinese troops entered Tibet and annexed it. Mao also rejected the McMahon line and laid claim over the disputed regions. Thus, the unresolved issue of boundary became a sore point between India and China and tension started brewing at the borders.

India was among the first nations to recognise the communist regime of China, and supported it at every international forum - at a time when China was isolated and had USSR as its only ally. Nehru even signed a treaty of friendship with China in 1951 without resolving the border issue. He was under the illusion that by keeping an underdeveloped but populous nation as China by his side, his own stature would be strengthened on the world stage. The communist leadership of China on the other hand distrusted Nehru because of his past close relationship with Chiang Kai-shek. Mao also resented his efforts to act like a mentor. The distrust increased even more because of Nehru's vacillation regarding Tibet and his ambivalent relationship with the Dalai Lama.

The **14th Dalai Lama** - then only 15 - formally took over charge as the spiritual and temporal head of Tibet in October 1950 - just after the communists had occupied Tibet. He played no small role in fomenting suspicions. On one hand he wanted to get rid of the communists and restoration of his political power, and of Tibet's sovereignty. He even wanted India to help him in this endeavour. On the other hand, he rejected India's right over the disputed territories that India inherited after Independence. Nehru did not want to displease the Chinese leaders - with whom he developed personal friendships - by helping Dalai Lama. At the same time, Nehru showed close bonds with the Dalai Lama. Thus, the Chinese leadership became suspicious of Dalai Lama as well as of Nehru.

While India's ambiguous relationship with Dalai Lama continued to cause distrust, instead to trying to resolve the issue diplomatically, Nehru tried to gloss over it. As he was wont to do, Nehru conducted relations with China on the basis of vague idealism, with a view to display himself as a world statesman, desperately working to defuse global tensions. He was also beguiled by the principles of *Panchsheel*, which China raked up to bluff Nehru. Just as he had failed to understand and address the issue of communalism during the freedom struggle, Nehru thought that his oratory skills and slogans would subsume ground realities.

The success of foreign policy of a country depends on its **internal strengths**, of its military, economy, and technology. In fact, foreign policy is meant to further these aspects, and should be so adapted that external strategies serve the domestic interests. Without first putting India on the path of economic development and ignoring its defences in the name of peace and non-violence, Nehru went about the international arena hectoring all and sundry on morals with a supercilious disdain when India had nothing to offer and much to obtain. This condescending approach was resented by the underdeveloped nations and was viewed with unconcealed contempt by the developed ones. The long term damage was that Indians as a nation began to be viewed as arrogant babblers, and a permanent prejudice and hostility evolved towards Indians in the international forum. Indians were seen as inveterate speakers in search of spotlight, never to be taken seriously.

During this period while Nehru was hopping all around the globe trying to catch media attention, China remained isolated, cloistered, building its own internal strength. When it finally emerged out of its self-inflicted seclusion, it was a powerful nation. As China started flexing its muscles, Nehru became fearful and acquiesced to Chinese sovereignty over Tibet in 1957. This emboldened the Chinese and they reasserted their claim over the disputed regions.

In 1959 an **uprising took place in Tibet** against the communist rule. The rebellion was brutally suppressed and a large number of Tibetan refugees came to India - along with Dalai Lama. India granted asylum to Dalai Lama and he was personally welcomed by Nehru. He was even allowed to form a government-in-exile. This was strange because once Nehru had accepted Chinese sovereignty over Tibet, there was no room left for Dalai Lama to form a government-in-exile. All these actions were viewed with even greater misgivings by China. Although the Chinese kept the chorus of *Hindi-Chini-bhai-bhai* alive, they started physically encroaching upon Indian territories, and no action was taken by the army as the government had no policy on the issue. By this time Nehru had become positively terrified of Chinese power and wanted to avoid a direct confrontation at all cost.

By 1961, border clashes started between the Chinese and Indian forces. Even as a war with China started to look more and more likely, Nehru could not address the issue diplomatically as his foreign policy had ensured that no significant world power was with India to act as a mediator and restrain China. The trivial countries that were most vociferous in the NAM were too insignificant to be of any help, and the super-powers simply watched. Nehru had ignored the harsh reality that only a strong country could remain non-aligned. In October 1962, the Cuban missile crisis brought USSR and USA close to a nuclear war. Finding India weak and isolated and the two superpowers engaged in their own confrontation, the Chinese army crossed the borders and the war began.

It is futile to go into the details of the war. By the standards of a major war, the Chinese intrusion was very trivial. Nevertheless, Nehru capitulated and conceded to an abject cease fire in November '62 when the Chinese decided to end the war. Though they suffered heavy casualties, the Indian army did not lose morale. The army had also not lost the war. It was Nehru who lost the nerve and India had to bear the ignominy of defeat for ever - a defeat that never was. Nehru never recovered from the shock and died in July 1964.

## PERIOD OF REALIGNMENT

The war with China was a salutary lesson in many ways as it exposed the fallacies of Nehru's foreign policy. It put an end to his dream of playing the role of a world statesman and also put a final end to his hope that Indo-China friendship could form an Asian Axis to counteract the increasing influence of the two superpowers. No other Indian Prime Minister was ever to try either of the two again - make alliance with China as a pillar of policy or try to become an alternative to the superpowers - the third pole in a bi-polar world. Indian Prime Ministers thereafter - realising where India actually stood - also never tried to play the role of prima donna on the world stage.

Further was the realisation that foreign policy cannot be guided by rigid ideological dogmas but only by the needs of realistic self interest. In fact, there could be no such thing as a permanent policy in international matters: there had only to be flexible strategies to serve national concerns - depending on the evolving situations. India's foreign policy henceforth was to be shaped by pragmatism and by the developments in the international arena. The objective was no more to establish world peace but a more modest aim to secure its own well being.

While the war put an end to Nehru's role in the foreign affairs, it also put an end to the way Nehru conducted foreign affairs. It had become tragically evident that it is nations - and not individuals at the helm - that have to establish common strategic interests, and that personal friendships can further the strategic interests but cannot be a substitute for the overall policy in international relations. Thus the end of Nehru period also marked an end to the personalised style of conducting diplomacy.

**Lal Bahadur Shastri** as the Prime Minister (1964-66) had to face many problems during his brief term. There were famines and food shortages. He also had to face aggression of Pakistani intruders that culminated in a full scale war in 1965. Shastri took bold decisions in confronting the enemy head-on. Even though Pakistan had US made Sabre Jets and Patton tanks - thanks to Nehru's policy of annoying USA - the Indian forces made mincemeat of both. While the Indian army overwhelmed Pakistani forces and made substantial territorial gains as well, the war was terminated by a ceasefire under international pressure. India was still weak and the remnants of Nehruvian principles still lingered within the government. The Tashkent Agreement frittered away all the territorial gains, with India getting nothing in return - not even the Pakistan occupied territories of Kashmir - nor a pledge from Pakistan to maintain peace. Shastri died at Tashkent soon after signing the agreement - under disputed circumstances. Nevertheless, his tenure marked a singular shift in India's outlook.

The two wars had taken toll of two Indian Prime Ministers, one being her own father, and this weighed heavily upon **Indira Gandhi** when she became the Prime Minister in 1966. On one hand, Pakistan continued to be hostile and had the support of USA while India was internationally isolated. On the other hand, China had test detonated the atom bomb in July 1964. Taking a lesson from the wars of 1962 and 1965, Indira Gandhi was determined to make India stronger, militarily as well as by alliances.

In September **1967, China again attacked** the Indian posts at Nathu La and Cho la. However, this time Indian army retaliated with a heavy hand and inflicted severe casualties on the Chinese. The Chinese army retreated in humiliation and thereafter the Chinese did not ever dare to enter into any direct armed conflict with India. Soon after, Indira Gandhi gave the green signal for developing the atom bomb. She also began changing the direction of Indian foreign policy from rigid neutrality to a tilt towards the USSR.

There were other developments in the international arena as well. China had started drifting away from Soviet Union and Mao Zedong had begun to claim the leadership of world communism. It split the Communist Party of India and the pro-China faction became the CPI (M). The pro-Soviet CPI abandoned the agenda of revolution in India and started supporting the Congress Party government. Indira Gandhi had adopted a distinct anti-capitalist program and hence it was ideologically also compatible for the CPI to support the government. This made it comfortable for Soviet Union to support the Government of India.

**USSR** had its own concerns too. It was anxious about US military presence in Pakistan. As tensions of the Cold War escalated and Soviet Union became increasingly isolated, it started to see the importance of India as a strategic partner in Asia. Meanwhile, from March 1971 onwards, Pakistani army started genocide in East Pakistan resulting in millions of Bengali refugees pouring into India. As tensions across the borders started to escalate, no diplomatic resolution of the problem could be achieved. The world community also remained indifferent to the plight of the refugees, and to the problems India was facing. With war as the only option left, Indira Gandhi shelved the policy of 'splendid isolation' of non-alignment and made a formal pact with Soviet Union. The **Indo-Soviet Treaty** of Friendship and Cooperation of August 1971 was not a military alliance. It was an innocuous pledge of friendship and mutual cooperation based on internationally accepted norms of peace and as per the UN charter. Nevertheless, the message to the world community was loud and clear - that Soviet Union was now on India's side.

During October-November 1971 Indira Gandhi made a whirlwind tour of Europe and USA. World leaders were apprised of the appalling situation in East Pakistan, and through brilliantly handled press conferences, peoples around the world were informed of the grim conditions. The efforts bore positive results, and when war broke out on 3rd December 1971, the world community was either sympathetic to India, or neutral. USA made certain gestures to come to the aid of Pakistan - the US 7th Fleet moved towards India - but then decided to stay put. Beyond issuing certain statements in favour of Pakistan, China and the Islamic nations also kept away. The upshot was that Pakistan faced a resounding defeat. It lost its eastern wing with the creation of Bangladesh and some 92,000 Pak soldiers became prisoners of war.

Despite gaining such decisive leverage, Indira Gandhi failed to turn it into a long term resolution of the problems with Pakistan. All the military achievements of the war were thus lost during the **Shimla Agreement of 1972**. It only showed that Indian leadership was yet to fully learn the basics of realpolitik - that international relations are conducted on the basis of national self-interest by every nation and not on the basis of moral values. The only positive feature of the Shimla Agreement was that the two nations agreed to resolve all issues through bi-lateral interaction. This meant that no third nation or institution like the UNO had any further role in the Indo-Pak disputes.

The war of 1971 raised India's stature and in a further display of its military strength, India tested the atom bomb in May 1974. The 1970s remained a period of strong Indo-Soviet friendship. Indira Gandhi however continued with the rituals of NAM although it was not the mainstay of her foreign policy. NAM was predominantly used only to chide and castigate the western world, which only worsened India's relations with the West.

## WINDS OF CHANGE

The Congress party was defeated in the elections of 1977. Although this had nothing to do with economic or foreign policies of the Congress, the message for the international community was clear - that India as a nation was breaking the shackles of its past. The perception that India was a socialist hanger-on of Soviet Union was changed further by **Atal Bihari Vajpayee** who became the Minister of External Affairs in the Janata Party government. Relations with USA - which had been under considerable strain after the war of 1971 - were eased and in 1978 US President Jimmy Carter visited India. Vajpayee also went to China in 1979 and diplomatic relations - which had broken after the war of 1962 - were restored. The two nations also decided to initiate a regular process of bilateral dialogue to address the border issue and to improve trade relations.

The Janata Party government was an unstable coalition and full of contradictions. In December 1979, USSR invaded Afghanistan. Indian position on the issue was ambivalent. On one hand India opposed the Soviet invasion of Afghanistan. On the other hand, USA wanted India to collaborate in repelling the Soviet forces but India refused to cooperate with USA. Hence USA turned to its close ally Pakistan. All this confusion did little good to India. The Janata government was short lived, and though nothing significant could be achieved, nevertheless, in terms of the vibes sent globally through the few steps taken, it was apparent that India was coming out of the ideological closet.

Indira Gandhi's second tenure (1980-84) was rather uneventful as regards the foreign affairs are concerned. She remained occupied with domestic issues that ended in her tragic assassination in October 1984. Her son, Rajiv Gandhi, who became the next Prime Minister, was a pilot by profession. As the PM (1984-89), he captained a plane without a flight plan. He naively got drawn into Sri Lanka's civil war with Tamils by sending the IPKF in 1987. This soured India's relations with Sri Lanka for good. After he lost the elections of 1989, a coalition government was formed and India's foreign policy remained in a state of flux. The three Prime Ministers during the period 1989-91 represented different political dispensations and remained more preoccupied with party politics. Partly this was also because of the developments taking place in different parts of the world that changed the global power balance. India was a mere spectator to the unfolding events and its foreign policy saw only organic growth during the period.

During the 1980s, China had started to shed off socialism as the model of national economy and started establishing trade relations with the capitalist world. Vietnam and some of the other communist regimes also took the same path. On the other hand, the Soviet controlled communist bloc of Eastern Europe broke apart during 1989-90. The Communist regimes of the Warsaw Pact fell and democracy was established. Many of these states joined the European Union and were welcomed by western countries to show the superiority of capitalism over communism. In 1991, communism finally met its demise when Soviet Union also disintegrated. Communism as an ideology became irrelevant, outdated, and went out of fashion.

This brought a fundamental change in the world order. For centuries, nations had been establishing their international relations basically from the strategic point of view of security. With the Cold War coming to an end, the very basis of international relations started to change from strategic concerns to trade and business concerns and nations realigned their foreign policy from the economic point of view.

## COMMENCEMENT OF REALPOLITIK

While socialism had destroyed USSR, socialist policies being followed in India for decades had also brought the Indian economy to the brink of disaster. In June 1991, when **P.V. Narasimha Rao** became the Prime Minister of India, the domestic as well as the international situation left no option for the government but to change course - in internal as well as external policies. Thus, while economy was opened to private sector, India's foreign policy also became more open to the dynamics of the changing international power equations because foreign policy is a part of the overall system of a nation. India thus also started joining the global mainstream. As soon as economic policies of the government became liberal for foreign investment, India's relations with the western world started improving.

Since economics had become the basis of foreign policy of all countries, hence no nation was now hesitant to join hands with India. India was a big consumer market and there was profit potential for everyone. With policies of economic liberalisation, the western world saw ample business opportunities in India. In any case, with Soviet Union itself finished, India's pro-Soviet image had lost its meaning. With these changes, India's foreign policy also changed under the leadership of Narasimha Rao. India also joined the WTO in January 1995.

On one hand India's foreign policy shifted significantly towards the West, and on the other hand India also began a '**Look East**' policy by forging closer relations with the Southeast Asian nations so as to integrate India's economy with the growing economies of the emerging nations. Ties with Japan, South Korea and Australia were also strengthened. While Rao kept the Non-Aligned Movement alive, it was put on a ventilator. Rao's most significant step however was that he took the courage to establish full diplomatic ties with Israel. Israel has not only proved to be a true partner from the strategic point of view but has also been beneficial for India from the economic point of view. This step is a reflection of the foresight of Narasimha Rao.

During 1996-98 an unstable coalition government remained in power and two Prime Ministers headed the government with short and directionless tenures. **In 1998, BJP led NDA** came to power and Atal Bihari Vajpayee stayed as the Prime Minister till 2004. Even though it was also a coalition, it was much more stable and for the first time assertive nationalism became the hallmark of Indian foreign policy. One of the first things that Vajpayee did was to go ahead with the nuclear program and India test detonated a series of nuclear bombs. He also tried to improve relations with Pakistan but the Pak army sabotaged the effort by starting the Kargil war in 1999. No nation tried to intervene and Indian army succeeded in driving out the Pak intruders. India's relations with all nations remained stable although the nuclear tests led to many problems on the sidelines as well.

In 2004, a **Congress led UPA coalition** formed the government. Besides the fact that it was a hotchpotch alliance of disagreeing parties, there also came up two centres of power: One was official, of the Prime Minister, and the other of the Congress president Sonia Gandhi, who controlled the strings of the puppet PM Man Mohan Singh. Sonia Gandhi also formally created an extra-constitutional supra-government body called as the National Advisory Council (NAC), of which she was the chairperson, to guide the PM. This practically made the PM dysfunctional. It must be understood that while the Ministry of External Affairs is the leading ministry for foreign policy, the Prime Minister and the PMO play the key role in foreign affairs. This is not only because of the importance of foreign affairs in national security but also because foreign affairs have become very complex involving a large number of ministries and only the PMO can do the coordinating job. As a result, the PMO and the NAC pursued separate directions and the foreign governments did not know with whom to interact.

The Congress party was more concerned about domestic politics and many of its decisions were guided by vote bank factors. Thus the government remained soft on Pak sponsored terrorism and played down on radicalisation. In 2008, the Congress party made a pact with the Communist Party of China. This must be an act without precedent in history, that the ruling political party of a nation made a pact with the ruling party of an enemy state. While the details of this pact are shrouded in mystery, this alliance opened the gates to Chinese companies to have a free run in India. As a result, while India had a trade surplus of $1.75 billion with China in 2004, by 2014 the deficit with China had risen to $38 billion. The Chinese came to so dominate Indian economy that India has never been able come out of its grip, which is a serious challenge to Indian sovereignty and security. The UPA government remained in power during 2004-2014 and the overall lacklustre performance in foreign affairs did little good but much harm to India.

## MODI POLICY

In 2014, **Narendra Modi led BJP** formed the government for the first time with absolute majority. Since then, national interest has been the centre of Indian foreign policy with the Prime Minister leading from the front. Modi has revitalised and reconstituted the **Cabinet Committee on Security** and the NAC of UPA regime has been dissolved. The CCS is headed by the PM and the other three members are the Defence Minister, the Home Minister and Minister of External Affairs. The National Security Advisor also joins the meetings of CCS when needed. The CCS reviews all issues related to defence, foreign affairs, internal security, intelligence, nuclear issues, and space policy. The CCS also approves all significant defence acquisitions.

Some of salient features of the Modi government's foreign policy have been:

* Strategic autonomy - India will pursue its own independent course of action guided by flexible pragmatism of national self interest, strategic concerns, and economic development.
* India would actively participate in international organisations but would not compromise sovereignty to multilateralism.
* While maintaining good relations with all nations, India will not be brow beaten by any power nor would it tolerate interference in the internal affairs by any power.
* India would stand for the Global South.
* Neighbourhood First Policy - to give priority to relations with the nations in South Asia and the Indian Ocean region.
* Act East Policy - to strengthen economic and strategic relations with nations in the Indo-Pacific region.

- Special relations with the Gulf nations while maintaining good relations with Israel.
- Hard stand regarding enemy nations like Pakistan and China.

India's foreign policy since 2014 has followed this path. Today, India's growing economy has become its strategic power. India is still non-aligned in foreign policy, but it is not a fetish any more. India is not opposed to any nation. India is also not on any side: It is on its own side. This has become most evident in the ongoing conflicts in Ukraine and the Middle East. While Russia and Western countries are fighting, India has remained neutral and both sides are seeking India's support. The nations that are far away from the war also want India to take initiative to establish peace. This is a reflection of the changing nature and status of India.

Although the BJP could not get an absolute majority in the elections of 2024, Modi led NDA has formed the government again. Although it is a coalition government, the change is unlikely to impact the foreign policy. The composition of the CCS remains the same indicating continuity of the policies. Heads of governments of Bangladesh, Bhutan, Maldives, Sri Lanka, Nepal, Mauritius, and Seychelles attended the swearing in on 9th June '24 indicating India's stature in the region and reemphasising the 'neighbourhood first' policy of Modi. Pakistan and China were not even invited for the ceremony indicating the continuation of stiff stand against the adversaries.

## INDIA AND THE ATOM BOMB

Work on development of nuclear technology started around 1944 at the Tata Institute of Fundamental Research. Use of nuclear power for energy was given importance after Independence and in 1948 the Atomic Energy Commission was set up. In 1954, the Bhabha Atomic Research Centre and Department of Atomic Energy were established with the objective of peaceful use of atomic energy and to achieve self reliance in the field of nuclear technology. Nations like USA and Canada helped India in this endeavour. In 1958, the Defence Research and Development Organisation - DRDO - was formed to develop defence technologies and became a party to India's nuclear progress.

By that time, USA, Britain, USSR and France had developed nuclear weapons and a section of Indian nuclear scientists wanted India also to develop the atom bomb. However, Nehru declared that India's nuclear program is only for peaceful purposes and no attention was given to develop the atom bomb. The wars of 1962 and 1965, and China's testing of atom bomb in 1964, changed Indian perspective. In 1968, Indira Gandhi finally gave the go ahead to develop the atom bomb.

Meanwhile, the issue of nuclear disarmament had begun to be raised in the UNO. China's development of the atom bomb alarmed many nations. While no agreement could be reached among the nuclear weapons states on disarmament, they agreed to stop further spread of nuclear arms. Thus, in 1968 the **Nuclear Proliferation Treaty** came into being. This was not to the stop the nuclear arms race but to keep it restricted to the elite group of five nations which had already developed nuclear bombs. India was among the few nations that did not agree to this treaty as it was discriminatory, selectively applicable, and only **legitimised the monopoly of the nuclear powers**. It also meant China's inclusion and India's exclusion. India's position was that unless all nations give up nuclear weapons, such arrangements had no meaning.

On May 18, 1974, India carried out an underground nuclear explosion in Pokhran. However, India's official position was that the test was not for making an atom bomb but to use it only for peaceful purposes, like mining. While the detonation did not cause any international problem, the fact that the explosion was done by using Plutonium diverted from a civilian programme was a matter of concern to certain nations. This led to the formation of the **Nuclear Suppliers Group**, an exclusive club of nations that could control the supply critical inputs like Uranium. India was kept out of the NSG. After 1974, India's nuclear weapons progress remained in limbo for a decade for reasons not clearly understood. In 1991, P.V. Narsimha Rao became the PM and the initiative was again taken up. However, USA intervened and testing of the bomb was halted.

In 1994, the UNO came up with the **Comprehensive Nuclear-Test-Ban Treaty** (CTBT) banning all nuclear test explosions anywhere in the world. During the course of the negotiations on CTBT, India proposed that the CTBT should be truly comprehensive in the sense that it should be aimed at eliminating all nuclear weapons. However, Indian proposal was ignored and India was asked to sign the treaty before it became operational. India was thus forced to declare its opposition to the CTBT. The Treaty was opened for signature in 1996. While most of the nations signed the treaty, India did not because it held that its structure was discriminatory. In 1998 when NDA formed the government with Atal Bihari Vajpayee as the PM, a series of thermonuclear tests were done in May 1998.

At the same time, Prime Minister Vajpayee declared a '**voluntary moratorium**' on nuclear weapons testing. He also formulated the policy of a 'credible minimum nuclear deterrence' and 'no first use of atomic weapons' as the standing principles of India's nuclear programme. Soon after, Pakistan also detonated nuclear bombs proving that hostile nations like China had been helping it for developing atom bombs since long. China also blocked India's bid to join the NSG on the ground of it being a non-signatory to the NPT. With two hostile nations in the neighbourhood having atom bombs, there was no question of India giving up its own nuclear programme by signing the NPT or the CTBT.

In a way, India is already following the spirit of the CTBT by declaring its unilateral moratorium on nuclear testing. India has been a consistent supporter of global nuclear disarmament and was compelled to become a nuclear weapons state only because of the two nuclear neighbours. Nevertheless, India still remains committed to a universal and non-discriminatory treaty banning all nuclear weapons. However, with rogue states like Pakistan and North Korea becoming nuclear powers and Iran also on the verge of developing an atom bomb, the CTBT has become redundant and nuclear disarmament a mirage.

The proliferation of nuclear weapons has also changed the concept of **nuclear deterrence**. Since the major powers know that actual use of nuclear arms would bring retaliatory nuclear attack, they refrain from crossing the red line. However, it has not stopped conventional warfare as seen by the Russian invasion of Ukraine. It has clearly displayed the limitation of nuclear weapons. Since no power can use them, or would rather not dare to use them, these are no more than 'paper tigers' as Mao Zedong said. Hence nations are increasing their conventional weapons and the arms race continues. When a conventional war takes a nuclear turn can never be predicted. It can even happen by mistake, not only by an inadvertent human error but even a mistake of the computer systems that control and command the nuclear shield.

## INDIA-RUSSIA RELATIONS

India-Russia relations have remained steady and unaffected by the political changes in either nation since Independence. Till the 1990s, the relations were that of partners who shared ideology as well as mutual concerns. Both were anti-western and shared the common ideology of socialism. During the Cold War period, while USSR saw India as a stable nation which was becoming a leader among the non-aligned and anti-colonial nations that could counterbalance the growing influence of USA in Asia, India found USSR as diplomatic bedrock in the international arena, as a crucial ally that could act as security insurance against Pakistan and China, a reliable source of weapons, and a contributor of technology for economic development. India and USSR also backed each other in the UNO on several issues.

The decade that followed the disintegration of USSR in 1991 was a **decade of decadence for Russia**. While the communist structure had been dismantled, there was no alternate system in place. [The Soviet national anthem was abandoned but no new anthem could be composed. As a result, in the Olympic Games of 1992, only the music was played for the Russian contingent.] The economic situation became worse, law and order went to dogs, corruption skyrocketed and certain powerful individuals who had connections in the erstwhile state machinery took control of state companies and became very rich. They were called the oligarchs but were more like mafia bosses.

President Boris Yeltsin, a chronic alcoholic, failed to control the situation and his health also deteriorated due to excessive drunkenness. The domestic chaos affected Russia's stature in the international arena as well. Russia had lost its satellite states as well as its republics and hence lost its clout in the world power equation. Russia was a pale shadow of its former incarnation as Soviet Union. As Russia lost much of its value as a strategic partner, Russia-India relations went through a period of neglect. In 1993, the Indo-Soviet Treaty of 1971 was renewed but Russia clarified that it was no longer willing to make any security commitment regarding military threat to India. The security clause constituted the very essence of the Indo-Soviet Treaty 1971, and thus the renewed treaty had no meaning.

On the other hand, India had started to become a more liberal and open economy with policies more favourable to the West. India also wanted to reduce its dependence on Russian weapons and was keen to acquire cutting edge modern western technology. However, **the West never understood India's security concerns** and USA could never replace Russia either as a reliable ally in international diplomacy or as a strategic partner in security matters. USA was also closely collaborating with Pakistan on issues related to the Taliban regime in Afghanistan. When India tested the nuclear bombs in 1998, the US government imposed a series of sanctions against India. These included termination of sale of defence related equipments and services to India, and denial of financial assistance, including loans, to India. The Kargil war of 1999 further showed the double dealing of USA. This compelled Atal Bihari Vajpayee to renew India's engagement with Russia.

Meanwhile, the Russian peoples yearned for the lost glory and power of the erstwhile Russian empire and wanted a strong leader to set things right. Boris Yeltsin also wanted to hand over power to some capable leader and retire. On 31st December 1999, he handed over charge to **Vladimir Putin** as the acting President. Putin was regarded as a strong man and won the election of March 2000 to become the next President of Russia. Putin had seen how Russia had been reduced from a world superpower to a minor player and was determined to restore the pre-eminence of Russia. He also understood that his own political power depended on making Russia powerful again. [Putin restored the Soviet era national anthem.]

While Putin took strong steps at the domestic front to restore order, he also went about revitalising Russia's traditional relations with India. Putin had a healthy respect for Atal Bihari Vajpayee. Putin came to New Delhi on the evening of 2nd October 2000 and immediately after landing went on an unscheduled visit to PM's residence and had a private dinner with Vajpayee. This led to the signing of **Indo-Russian Strategic Partnership Treaty in October 2000**. This treaty provided for bilateral cooperation in the fields of defence, energy, space, nuclear, science and technology, etc. Thus Russia again became a staunch ally of India.

## US-RUSSIA RELATIONS

While Russia's support for India continues without conditions, the relations have become very complex. This is almost entirely due to the renewal of Cold War rivalry between Russia and the West. It may be recalled that during 1989-91, the satellite states of USSR overthrew the communist regimes and thus the Warsaw Pact bloc was shattered. However, USA and the western nations did not dissolve the NATO. Instead, in 1990, three erstwhile members of the Warsaw Pact - Poland, Hungary, and the Czech Republic - were made members of NATO. The message was clear that the West was not willing to ease relations with USSR. After the fragmentation of USSR in 1991 also, the West made no effort to help Russia or to establish a rapprochement so as to admit it as a respectable member of the European family. Boris Yeltsin visited USA and Britain to improve relations but the West did not reciprocate. This was resented by the Russians.

After Putin came to power, he also made efforts to improve relations with USA and met George Bush in June 2001. In September 2001, when Islamic terrorists attacked the Twin Towers in New York causing hundreds of casualties, Putin expressed his solidarity with the Americans. At that time Russia was fighting its own war with the Islamic rebels in Chechnya. On 23rd October 2002, Chechen terrorists seized an auditorium in Moscow and some 150 Russians were killed. Hence, Putin felt that Russia and USA had a common cause which could be the basis of a lasting friendship. However, **in March 2003, USA invaded Iraq** on the pretext of preventing Iraq from developing Weapons of Mass Destruction. Iraq was occupied by US forces but no such WMDs were found because these had never been developed. The invasion was done because USA needed a war for its armament industry. However, US invasion of Iraq was seen as a serious breach of trust by Putin because Iraq was a traditional ally of Russia. This marked the turning point from where Putin's grudges against USA and the West began to escalate.

While Putin had no choice but to ignore the domestic developments in the erstwhile Warsaw Pact East European satellite nations, he considered the breakaway erstwhile Soviet republics, though independent nations now, as very much under the Russian zone of influence, as these were a part of the once Tsarist Russian Empire. In 2004, the three **Baltic States joined NATO**. This was considered as a serious provocation by Putin. In 2004, elections were held in Ukraine in which while one of the candidates was pro-Russia, the other was supported by the West. This was seen by Putin as US interference in Ukraine which Putin considered as under Russian sphere of influence. During the 2008 NATO summit, the issue of admitting Ukraine and Georgia also into NATO was discussed. While the two could not be made members of NATO because of the differences among the NATO members, the proposal was considered by Putin as a part of western strategy to encircle Russia.

By this time, Putin had strengthened the Russian armed forces and in order to show its muscle power, the Russian army invaded **Georgia** in August 2008 and occupied a fifth of its territory. This was the first war in Europe after the end of WW II and the western powers could do nothing. On the other hand, US President Barrack Obama described Russia as a 'regional power' which was taken as a direct insult by Putin. During the elections of 2012 in Russia, there were certain protests against Putin for which Putin blamed the West. Putin was re-elected as the President and he wanted to show that Russia was again a superpower.

In 2014, **Russia formally annexed Crimea**. Crimea was officially a part of Ukraine but had a sizeable Russian population. With the support from the local Russians, there was no need for war to occupy Crimea. At the same time, in the border areas of Ukraine, which also had Russian majority population, rebels began a low intensity conflict of secession. In both the cases, the western powers could do nothing beyond criticising Putin and expressing solidarity with Ukraine. However, USA imposed severe economic sanctions against Russia and Russia was expelled from the G8 group. This further embittered Russia-West relations.

Ukraine wanted to join NATO for security but could not be admitted as certain NATO members opposed the move for ideological reasons as well as out of fear that such a move may precipitate a full scale war. The NATO charter also prevents a nation with ongoing border disputes from being admitted as a new member. Ukraine also wanted to join the EU but was not admitted for similar reasons. Hence Ukraine was left defenceless as well as a hostage of western alliance. At the same time NATO kept supporting Ukraine which made it a target of Russian aggression.

It needs to be pointed out here that at the time when Ukraine had seceded from USSR, it had a sizeable stockpile of nuclear weapons, because it was a part of USSR. However, in 1994, at the instance of USA through the Budapest Memorandum, **Ukraine joined the NPT and decommissioned its nuclear arsenal**. However, in return, Ukraine was given only 'security assurance' by USA but not 'security guarantee' as Ukraine had been promised. This did not commit USA or the NATO to come to Ukraine's help militarily in case of a conflict.

Putin demanded that the western powers should not interfere in the internal affairs of Russia nor should incite the Russian neighbours to act against Russia. Putin was particularly against any further expansion of NATO. As the NATO allies could not resolve the issue diplomatically, Russia attacked Ukraine on 24th February, 2022.

During the whole period, USA also remained in confrontation with China on a whole host of issues. This brought Russia closer to China. Putin has also signed a security pact with North Korea on 19th June 2024. Today, a new axis has come into being with Russia, China, North Korea and Iran, along with Iran sponsored terrorist organisations on one side, and the US led western nations on the defensive. This axis is not the Germany-Japan axis of WW II which USA could deal with simultaneously on its own strength. Russia and China are superpowers while North Korea is a nuclear power. Iran is a regional power and with terror organisations by his side can cause serious problems. USA, despite its immense economic power, is not in a position to militarily confront this new axis. American ignominious withdrawal from Afghanistan in August 2021 has already shown that it is losing the heft it once had. With war erupting in Gaza since October 2023, the situation has become even more difficult for USA. Further, the NATO allies and the EU nations are not united on many of the issues and are not on the same page with USA. Hence, **USA is increasingly getting isolated**.

While USA or the NATO have directly not entered the war on Ukraine's behalf, they are supplying arms and providing intelligence, training, and funds to Ukraine. *During the G7 summit of June 2024, a large amount of money has been pledged to Ukraine to continue fighting the war. Hence, Ukraine has become a victim of Russian invasion as well as a casualty of western friendship because only Ukraine is suffering severely in terms of loss of lives - soldiers as well as civilians - and wanton destruction of its cities.

*It would be interesting to point out the role of US armament industry in this war. The share value of the companies that manufacture arms has skyrocketed since the war began.

The West is also not taking any step to enter into a dialogue with Putin to reach to a compromise, at least to a ceasefire. USA is only putting up resolutions against Russia in the UNO which is not helping the cause of peace. India's position is that condemnation of Russia is not the solution and hence abstains from voting in the UNO. During the G7 summit of June 2024, a peace plan was also put up by the western nations. However, India did not support the initiative because Russia had not even been invited to discuss the peace plan, and hence had no meaning.

USA and the western media portray Putin as a dictator and call the Russian elections, which Putin has been consistently winning, as rigged frauds. While it is true that Putin is dictatorial in nature, and the truth about Russian elections can never be known, it is also true that he commands a sizeable popularity among the Russians. People like strong leaders and Putin is admired for restoring the lost glory of Russia, for punching the West on the nose, as well as for reviving the Russian economy. Today, Russia is much more prosperous than it ever was. Western criticism of Putin seems to be not only an expression of cynical frustration but also not helping the situation in any way.

From the way the war in Ukraine is progressing, it does not seem likely that Putin wants to occupy Ukraine for good. Such a step would be too provocative, and may draw Russia into a larger war that may not be in Russia's interest. Occupying Ukraine would also entrap Putin in administering a region that is intrinsically hostile to him and may domestically involve him in a situation that would be basically untenable. That is the reason that Russia has not embarked on a whole scale operation against Ukraine.

Perhaps, all that Putin wants is recognition of Russia as a super power, acceptance of his position as the legitimate head of Russia, assurance of security, and non-interference by the West in the region that Russia considers as its sphere of influence. That leaves room for a compromise solution for peace. How that compromise is reached at is difficult to predict and remains to be seen. It should also be remembered that Putin is an aging leader and how long will he remain in power is a question. The US presidential election of November 2024 may provide some way out.

## INDIA-US RELATIONS

The present situation has put India in a very delicate position. USA and the West expect India to be on their side, and support democracy. However, India cannot take sides at this juncture. For one thing, the Ukraine conflict does not directly affect India. There are also no ideological or moral issues involved because both the sides are to be blamed. India taking sides would also have no impact on the ground realities. Lastly, India has to take care of its own interests. While India is not supporting the Russian invasion, it has to maintain its relationship with Russia for its own concerns.

India's concerns are on the security front as well as on the economic front. On the security front, India's threats are from China and Pakistan. While Russia has stood as an unwavering friend of India, USA and the West have been unreliable partners. India has been procuring **Russian weapons** for decades because Russian weaponry was easy to get and was also less expensive than that of the West. While India has tried to diversify its weapons procurement, buying the French Rafale fighters for instance, the process has not been smooth because of USA's reluctance to transfer cutting edge technology to India. Further, USA keeps arming Pakistan which is a major irritant for India-US strategic partnership.

In any case, India constantly needs spare parts for the large Russian arsenal it has imported over the years, and hence India will continue to need Russian equipments for years to come. Russia and India have also collaborated on military technology and the joint development of Brahmos missile in 2019 is a perfect example of such joint ventures. The two nations have also joined hands to manufacture AK 203 assault rifles in India to replace the obsolete INSAS rifles. India is also importing Russian S-400 surface-to-air missiles. Russia is also collaborating for the development of nuclear submarines. Indian defence personnel are familiar with Russian weapons having used them for a life time. Russia is also expanding the Kudankulam Nuclear Power plant. In fact, Russia is the only nation which is supporting India's nuclear needs. Hence, India-Russia collaboration on defence and technology would continue for long.

At the diplomatic front, Russia and India continue to support each other and never comment either on the domestic issues of either nations or on their positions on international matters. Even when PM Modi told Putin point blank in an open forum in September 2022 that this is '*not an era of war*' in the context of Russian invasion of Ukraine, Putin and the Russian government took the remark in due stride and did not react. Other than this, India has never commented upon the Russian invasion of Ukraine. In fact, Modi's comment was as much for Russia as to the West, to find diplomatic solution to the problem rather than escalating the war.

To avoid any misgivings and to further India-Russia relations, Modi visited Moscow on 8th July 2024 and had a private dinner at Putin's residence. Modi was warmly hugged by Putin and was also given the highest civilian award, much to the chagrin of USA and its western allies. US incoherence about the event is evident by the fact that while the US State department commented that India should contribute to the peace effort, the US ambassador to India retaliated by saying that India should not take US-India strategic partnership for granted.

In fact, **USA also keeps commenting on the domestic issues of India** as if it is India's political party in opposition. USA has questioned the Modi government on democratic values and calls the ruling BJP as a Hindu party that is intolerant towards Muslims. USA has criticised the Modi government for revoking Article 370 and for violating human rights and curbing freedom of expression. USA has also commented upon the Citizenship Amendment Act passed by the Indian Parliament. Similar has been US reaction on Modi's inauguration of the Ram temple in Ayodhya in January 2024. The US government funded NGO called as the Freedom House has commented that Modi's government engages in the "harassment of journalists, NGOs, and government critics" and that "the BJP has increasingly used government institutions to target political opponents." USA also criticised the arrest of Arvind Kejriwal on corruption charges. The Indian government has officially told the US government that it considers such unwarranted commentary as unhelpful interference in India's domestic matters but USA maintains a supercilious attitude belying the fact that USA is no more the power it once was.

The US Embassy in New Delhi regularly invites Kashmiri separatist leaders. USA also supports the Khalistani separatists based in USA and Canada and has accused the Indian government for the assassination of Sikh separatist leader Hardeep Singh Nijjar in 2023 in Canada. India holds that Canada has given no evidence about the charge and that the Canadian government has provided a safe haven to separatists who are also indulging in all sorts of criminal activities. However, USA has refused to take cognisance of the Indian point of view. Proclaimed terrorists roam about freely in USA and Canada but USA remains blind to what is going on and deaf to Indian protestations. This shows American hypocrisy and double standards that allows USA to use drone strikes to kill suspected terrorists with impunity wherever it wants.

**USA has major issues with China** regarding trade as well as security, particularly in the Indo-Pacific region. India is the only power that can help USA in containing China in the region and USA has also taken steps to take India on board through bodies like the QUAD to face China. However, frequent criticisms of India's domestic affairs are a serious roadblock in turning India-US relationship into one of true strategic partners. India can never be sure of USA when it comes to India's problems with Pakistan and China. Thus, India has to use its ties with Russia in restraining China as the two nations have come close. India has no option also.

On the **economic front**, India's trade with USA and the western nations would continue as before because unlike the state driven relations with Russia, much of India-US trade is market driven and outside the control of governments. On the other hand, USA wants India to fall in line with US sanctions on Russia. However, India has refused to abide by Western wishes. For one thing, West European nations themselves have adopted a very selective stand on the issue. While imposing embargo on many items, they continue to purchase Russian gas (at much higher prices) as they have no alternative. Hence, they are paying Russia for fighting its war with Ukraine and also paying Ukraine for fighting with Russia.

India has taken its own position on the economic front and has been **purchasing**

**crude oil from Russia** in large quantities at discounted prices. India's exports to Russia have also increased of items that Russia earlier imported from the West. USA has not taken any retaliatory steps against India on these deals because it has already created more enemies that it can deal with. Further, USA also understands that if India does not import oil from Russia, and buys only from the Gulf States, oil prices around the world would shoot up and the western nations would be equally affected. Hence the West has accepted India's position of neutrality. In any case, India's current stand does not really affect Europe. Insisting on India condemning Russia is meaningless because such a condemnation would have no impact on the outcome of the war. In fact, India is perhaps the only nation which can help bring about a peaceful diplomatic resolution, provided the West wants a solution at all.

Lastly, India is most useful for Europe and USA in the Indo-Pacific, where their interests truly converge. India can act, though not as a countervailing force, but certainly as a sobering and moderating force. However, USA and the West seem to be at a loss on the strategy to be adopted about the China question and are unable to decide their next step. What would be the impact of US Presidential elections to be held in November 2024 remains to be seen.

## INDIA'S INTERNAL CHALLENGES

While India finds itself at the crossroads of a difficult international situation, its real and far graver challenges are at the domestic front.

When Covid spread in China during 2019-20, it came as a startling revelation that hundreds of Indian students have got stranded in China due to lockdown. They had to be airlifted back home. When war broke out in Ukraine, the news that some 20,000 Indian students have been trapped in the war zone came as a total shock to most of the Indians. India's diplomacy did give results, and despite a very difficult situation, all but one was evacuated safely. Why were thousands of Indian students studying in such places where the language and the culture are totally alien? Why are thousands going to USA, UK, and other places to study?

It may be an eye opener to some to know that about 150,000 Indians are giving up their citizenship every year for good and permanently settling abroad. Of these, some 5000 are millionaires! Why everyone with talent, intelligence, skill, and entrepreneurship abandoning the soil of their birth? What is wrong here that the brilliant among the young and the enterprising wealth creators are giving up on their own nation? Those who can develop India and make it strong are literally flying away to migrate.

The reasons are many. For one thing, the Indian political system has given up on merit and is **promoting mediocrity**. Poor educational level is causing underemployment and unemployability. While the high tech sector is facing problems of hiring and retention due to shortage of skilled professionals, the unemployables are getting low wage jobs or resorting to poor income generating self-employment. This is leading to low demand and hence is a damper for the manufacturing sector which alone can solve the problem of unemployment.

Some of the other challenges are as under:

* Lack of political will to formulate a clear roadmap for economic development.
* Lack of socio-political consensus regarding development and growth.
* Regional political parties becoming powerful but have no cohesive national agenda or policy.
* Federalism - laws differing from state to state.
* An overweight ruling bureaucracy of generalists.
* Corruption in every sphere.
* Poor governance at the micro level.
* Difficulty of starting and doing business due to excessive and complex regulations.
* Cost of money – high interest rates.
* Complicated and wavering taxation system.
* Difficulty to acquire land.
* Labour laws.
* Frequent change of policies.
* A lifeless judicial system making dispute settlement and contract enforcement difficult.
* Lack of infrastructure and poor quality of work as seen by collapsing newly constructed bridges, tunnels, roads, and airport roofs.

If India wants to retain its territorial integrity and diplomatic sovereignty, it has to become an economic power in order to become a military power. For this more action is needed at the domestic front than in the international arena. While India has become the fifth largest economy, its per capita income is among the lowest in the world. Although certain economic reforms were introduced in 1991, large scale reforms and restructuring of the government machinery and its agencies are required.

There are some 53 ministries in the Government of India. Why do we need a Cabinet Minister to make T-shirts (Ministry of Textiles) or a minister for making tomato sauce (Ministry of Food Processing)? Modi's promise of 'minimum government and maximum governance' remains just a slogan.

While a major revamp of the government apparatus is urgent, even more important is to change the popular mindset. Unfortunately, during the entire course of the elections of 2024, none of the above issues were brought forward by any of the political parties. No one sold the idea of economic growth, wealth creation, and overall prosperity by expanding the opportunities. In fact, the main opposition party launched a vicious campaign against the industrial business class and propagated the theme of redistributive economic and social justice. The entire election was about caste and religion. This is not the solution to problems and certainly not how nations become strong.

Although coalition politics is very unpredictable in India, the Modi (NDA) government of 2024 is likely to complete a full term. While no change in foreign policy is expected, it would be equally futile to expect any major reform on the aforesaid issues. In fact, there is fear that in order to overcome the electoral setback, the Modi government may step up unproductive but expensive populist measures. Since the political discourse shows no sign of changing direction, India's future is a cause for worry.

❖❖❖❖

# Chapter VIII

# South Asia and Southeast Asia

Before the Second World War broke out, most of the South Asia and the Southeast Asia was under the colonial rule of Britain, France, Spain and the Dutch. During the war, Japan occupied much of Southeast Asia and the colonial rule was broken. In 1945, Japan surrendered and USA became a major player in Asia-Pacific. While the Cold War began soon after the end of the war, the communists came to power in China in 1949. In 1950 the Korean War started. In the meantime, the entire region became independent. At the same time communist insurgency spread in many of the newly independent nations of Southeast Asia. In Vietnam it took the shape of a civil war. To counter communism, USA formed a military alliance called the South East Asia Treaty Organisation (SEATO) in 1954, with France, Britain, Australia, New Zealand, Pakistan, the Philippines and Thailand. As USA got more involved in the Far East, Indo-China, and Southeast Asia, the eco-political architecture of the region changed.

The newly independent nations had many issues to address. The whole region was underdeveloped and there was no cohesion among the states. While all the states were small, there were severe differences on the grounds of ethnicity and ideology. The nations had long lost their traditions of self governance due to colonial rule and the governments took time to stabilise. India was an exception in the sense that besides being the largest nation of the region, it was also the most stable. India had very close cultural and trade links with the states of the region in ancient times, but the links had been broken during the mediaeval age and by the colonial rule of different European nations.

India had the highest stake in developing cooperation in the region and had the right and obligation to play the lead role. However, the region was ignored during

Nehru's period. Not only India had its own myriad problems, Nehru visualised his role on the world map, and not in regional groupings. Since he did not want to join any camp, India kept out of SEATO. Instead, Nehru sponsored the Non-Alignment Movement. While certain of the nations of Southeast looked upon USA for security, some others joined the NAM. This created further divisions in the region.

## ASEAN

Meanwhile, certain nations of Southeast Asia realised the urgency of joining hands for containing the spread of communism in the region. They also began to see solution to their common economic problems in the global context through regional collaboration. Southeast Asia was one of the poorest regions of the world and regional cooperation could offer substantial benefits to all. They also needed to adjust with the advance of western capitalism and adapt to the new order of globalisation. But the nations did not have the necessary financial means and institutions to develop on their own. And thus came up the idea of formation of ASEAN.

The Association of South East Asian Nations was established in 1967 with the aim of developing cooperation for economic integration, regional stability, and peace. Indonesia, Malaysia, The Philippines, Singapore, and Thailand were the founding five members. [Brunei, Cambodia, Laos, Myanmar (one time Burma), and Vietnam joined later in stages]. Although the nations belonged to the same region and shared borders, they had nothing in common other than geographical contiguity. Their cultural, economic and political orders were very different and each was riven by ethnic conflicts and communist insurgency.

Indonesia and Malaysia were largely Islamic with an authoritarian democracy and a moderately developing economy. The Philippines was largely Christian with an authoritarian democracy, and a struggling economy. Brunei was a despotic Islamic sultanate and rich in crude oil and natural gas. Thailand, Myanmar, Cambodia, Laos and Vietnam were predominantly Buddhist. While Thailand was a constitutional monarchy with an authoritarian democracy, Burma soon became a military dictatorship. Vietnam, Laos, and Cambodia were engaged in civil wars. Singapore was a small city state and the outlier in the group. It had recently seceded from Malaysia. While it was a potpourri of races, it was extremely progressive under an authoritarian but democratically elected government, and resembled more a developed western state than an Asian nation.

Due to the Cold War politics, and differences among the nations, not much was achieved by ASEAN for a decade. The Vietnam conflict came to an end in 1975 and in 1977 the SEATO was dissolved. These developments prompted fresh thinking in the region.

**India** is not a part of Southeast although it shares an idealistic notion of Asian brotherhood based on the common experience of colonialism and ancient cultural ties. However, times had changed and relations depended more on political and economic factors rather than on history and culture. India really did not fit in this group. It had adopted strong protectionist economic policies after Independence. This was not conducive for trade cooperation with nations like Malaysia, Thailand, the Philippines, Singapore, and Indonesia which pursued relatively free trade policies. Politically, India was looked upon as a pro-Soviet socialist nation, and not truly non-aligned, and hence on the opposite side of the Cold War divide. On the other hand, Indian leadership viewed ASEAN as an American "imperialist surrogate". As a result, India's engagement with ASEAN was negligible for the initial two decades.

**1991** proved to be a turning point for India as well as for world politics. In June '91 P. V. Narasimha Rao became the Prime Minister of India. Realising the bankrupt position of Indian economy due to the insular and socialist policies adopted since Independence, Rao quietly began the process of liberalisation. He also opened the doors to foreign investment and India thus entered the world market. In December the same year, Soviet Union disintegrated and thus the long Cold War came to a quiet end. The end of Cold War bipolarity also reduced the relevance of India's non-aligned position. The two events changed the eco-political matrix of Asia.

## LOOK EAST POLICY

The 'Look East' policy (LEP) was formulated by the government of Prime Minister Narasimha Rao in 1991. The objective was strategic security as well as economic development of India in general and of the North Eastern region of India in particular. This was to be done by strengthening bi-lateral relations with the Southeast Asian nations as well as by associating closely with the multilateral organisations of the region like ASEAN. It was also to be a counterweight to China's growing tentacles in the region. The Look East policy was thus a significant step in India's entry into the region.

While rapprochement with the capitalist western economies was the prime motive of Rao's policies, East Asia's dynamic **'tiger' and 'tiger cub'*** economies were also vital to this externally oriented economic diplomacy. By the early 1990s, some of the countries of Southeast Asia had begun to be called as "Asian Tigers". These nations were attracting foreign investment and promoting export-led growth. ASEAN gave them a forum for regional cooperation. Narasimha Rao understood that cooperation with this region would help India in multiple ways. India needed to integrate into the global economy and the dynamism of India's eastern neighbours made Southeast Asia an attractive place to start with. Since cooperation with the immediate neighbours (SAARC) had limited prospects at the time, treating Southeast Asia as part of India's extended neighbourhood made much more pragmatic sense. Further, nations were entering into regional preferential trade agreements and Rao did not want India to be left out or discriminated against through tariff and non-tariff barriers. Associating with ASEAN would make it easy for India to deal with the region as a group.

* Singapore, Taiwan, and South Korea were called as 'Tiger' economies while Indonesia, Malaysia, The Philippines, Thailand, and Vietnam were called as 'Tiger Cub' economies.

On the other hand, Rao's liberal policies had changed the erstwhile perception of India as a socialist country and as a threat to regional stability. It began to be viewed as a benign and stabilising force with ample economic opportunities for the region. ASEAN chose to engage India 'gradually and on an experimental basis' in order to assess India's commitment to economic liberalisation. India was hence admitted in the ASEAN as a Sectoral Dialogue Partner in 1992. In 1996, it became a Full Dialogue Partner and also a member of the ASEAN Regional Forum (ARF). India started attending ASEAN summits from 2002 and became a Strategic Partner of ASEAN in 2012. Thus, within a brief span of time, India's relations with ASEAN had graduated to cover economic as well as strategic dimensions.

**Singapore** played a prominent role in facilitating India's renewed engagement with Southeast Asia and Rao described Singapore as India's 'gateway' to ASEAN. Expansion of ASEAN during the late 1990s with the inclusion of Cambodia, Myanmar, Laos, and Vietnam deepened India's interaction with the entire Southeast Asian region. The admission of Myanmar in 1997 gave India a contiguous land border with the regional body and literally brought ASEAN to India's doors.

However, LEP has never been a purely ASEAN-centric initiative. Bilateral and multilateral engagements outside the ASEAN framework have always been an important component of the policy. At the inter-regional level, India was also an architect of the Indian Ocean Rim Association (IORA) established in 1997. Even the geographic scope of LEP expanded over time from Southeast Asia to East Asia and into the Indo-Pacific.

This led to the formation of **BIMSTEC** [Bay of Bengal Initiative for Multi-Sectoral Technical and Economic Cooperation] in 1997. This is a sub-regional group of Bangladesh, India, Sri Lanka, Myanmar and Thailand. [Bhutan and Nepal became its full members in 2004.] It was to create an alternative and more specialised platform for interaction. Development of a transport network linking member states was a key area of focus for BIMSTEC so as to provide seamless movement of goods and passengers along the Bay of Bengal. BIMSTEC was also critically important for the development of the volatile north eastern states of India.

Humanitarian aid and disaster relief operations have been a key component for

India to expand its maritime presence in Southeast Asia. During the Indian Ocean tsunami of 2004, Indian Navy provided assistance to Indonesia and Thailand.

The **North Eastern states of India** have a vital stake in India's foreign policy regarding East Asia as they share land borders with China, Bangladesh, Myanmar, and Bhutan. Partition of 1947 had increased the distance between NE states and the rest of the country. Linking them by a long and circuitous route through a difficult terrain was an arduous task. The states were underdeveloped and were also neglected by the central governments for long. The region has hydro-energy potential due to Brahmaputra and its tributaries, possibly oil and gas reserves, coal, and limestone.

When the Look East Policy was launched in 1991, the significance of geographical proximity between the North East region and Southeast Asia was not taken into consideration. This was one of the major factors that limited the possibilities of developing regional economic relationships. However, in 1997, Myanmar was admitted into ASEAN as an active member and the North East became a part of the Look East policy. Though LEP facilitated India's economic and strategic relations with Southeast Asia, the North East region gained nothing.

In the last few years however, there has been growing realisation that development of NE is vital to fully exploit the opportunities provided by the LEP. Thus, greater emphasis is being given on improving connectivity through all possible modes by developing the necessary infrastructure. However there are severe geographical obstacles and political and security related challenges. The Act East policy is a step to address the issues by revitalising the LEP.

## SAARC

During the same period, the idea of forming a regional organisation of South Asian nations - on the model of ASEAN - had been under discussion. However, Indo-Pak conflicts and lack of democracy in Pakistan prevented formation of any such organisation. In 1971 Bangladesh emerged as a new nation after the Indo-Pak war. For more than a decade thereafter, Pakistan as well as Bangladesh suffered political instability and army rule. 1985 marked a turning point in Pakistan when martial law was lifted and a democratic civilian government was formed. Bangladesh took the initiative to bring the other nations also together *"for cooperation among the countries of the area for preserving peace and stability"*. In order to avoid discords, it was also suggested that the organisation should refrain from any reference to security matters and only non-political and non-controversial issues to be on the agenda. Economic, social, and technical cooperation were to be its primary objectives.

Thus, the South Asian Association of Regional Cooperation was established in December 1985 with 7 members - Bangladesh, Bhutan, India, Maldives, Nepal,

Pakistan, and Sri Lanka.* It was an organisation for promoting cooperation for mutual benefit, collective self-reliance, and development of South Asia as an integrated region. SAARC also aimed to strengthen collaboration with other developing countries and with international and regional organisations with similar aims and purposes. It was based on the principles of sovereign equality, territorial integrity, and non-interference in the internal affairs of member nations. Collective cooperation was also meant to complement bilateral relations among the member states while bilateral contentious issues were to be excluded. Decisions were to be made on the basis of unanimity.

*Afghanistan was admitted as the 8th member in 2007. China, USA, Myanmar, Iran, Japan, South Korea, Australia, Mauritius and the European Union participated in the summit meetings as observers at different times.

SAARC was a major breakthrough in the region. At the time of its formation there was political stability within the concerned nations and there was a general desire for peace and cooperation. Hence SAARC was successful in the initial two decades in moving towards its objectives. To boost trade between its members, the "South Asian Free Trade Areas" (**SAFTA**) agreement came into being in December 1995 with the target of reducing customs duty of all goods to zero by the year 2016. (The goal however could never be reached.) In 2005, The SAARC Arbitration Council (SARCO) was established for settlement of disputes. In 2010, the "SAARC development Fund" (SDF) was formed. In 2011, the South Asian Regional Standards Organization (SARSO) was set up to deal with trade-related standards. SAARC even initiated steps to tackle terrorism.

However, despite taking several positive steps, the **success of SAARC was modest** at best and positives for India remained to be limited. Intra-regional trade continued to be low and cooperation among the nations in many areas was also not smooth. India was pivotal to the success of SAARC but many of the members, while taking advantage of India, did not fully reciprocate. This was due to domestic problems and electoral politics within certain nations, strategic as well as economic conflict of interests between the members, and Chinese endeavour to spread its hegemony in the region. As a consequence of lack of cohesion among the members, SAARC started going down the hill.

While political problems continued with the neighbours, India was gaining little from SAARC economically. India was not even getting cooperation on security related issues, that is, cross border terrorism. Finally, it was due Indo-Pak tensions that SAARC came to a standstill. The last SAARC summit was held in Nepal in 2014. Pakistan was scheduled to host the 19th summit of SAARC in Islamabad in November 2016. However, due to the 2016 Uri terror attack, India cancelled its participation because of Pakistan's involvement in the terror attack. Thereafter, Bangladesh, Bhutan and Afghanistan also withdrew. Since then, there has been no summit and SAARC seems to have come to a dead end and may even become defunct.

## INDIA AND SAARC

India is the largest nation of SAARC, with the highest GDP, and modern technology. While other nations have much to gain from India, India has much less, except security at the borders. If security itself is not assured, then India has nothing to gain. Without India, any such regional body has no meaning, but the politicians of some smaller countries, the Pakistan army, and China have ensured the demise of SAARC. India finds it better to have bilateral relations with countries with common interests, like Bangladesh, rather than waste time on such a fragmented organisation.

Besides the political issues, there has been little consensus among the members on other subjects also. The member nations compete more than cooperate and intra-regional trade has been low. This is also because the productivity of nations other than India and Bangladesh is very low. **Geographical barriers** - rivers, mountains, and forests - are also affecting connectivity and hence transportation of goods is cumbersome. India has supported infrastructure projects such as development of road and rail networks to improve connectivity with Bangladesh and Nepal, but there has been little success elsewhere because there are also issues of unsettled borders, maritime and fishery disputes, problems of terrorism, smuggling, narcotics trafficking and cross-border refugee migration.

India's interests in this region are undoubtedly very critical for establishing its position as a regional power but certain nations call it **'big brother'** attitude on part of India. Many of the leaders of the smaller nations suffer from inferiority complex and there has been a perceptible 'gang-up' syndrome of the neighbouring countries against India. Some have accused India of attempting to undermine the efforts of regional integration by pursuing bilateral agreements with individual member states. However, India's concerns are strategic more than economic.

India has little to gain from trading with these poor nations. India is pioneering in the services sector like IT, and is aspiring to enter the high tech economy. For this, relations with USA, EU, and other richer nations are more beneficial. As regards security, India finds it better to have bi-lateral dialogue with the concerned nations rather than jostle in such a heterogeneous group where members do not have much in common. While they need Indian resources, they resent India's dominance, which is obviously inevitable. Hence India is giving more importance to establishing bilateral relations with neighbours rather than wasting time and energy in trying for group activity.

India, as well as the other member nations, can benefit through SAARC cooperation because the region could be a thriving market for various goods and services. Synchronising economic policies can help trade while **improvement of regional connectivity** would help to provide investment opportunities. This is a window for job creation in the labour-intensive manufacturing sector. A liberal investment structure within SAARC can also help to attract foreign direct investment while cooperation would also facilitate transfer of technology among the members. Trade of agricultural products would provide food security as well. Regional cultural commonality may also promote tourism. However, containing extremism in the region through security cooperation is pivotal for the survival of SAARC and Pakistan is the biggest obstacle in this field.

China, in partnership with Pakistan, has played a major role in sabotaging SAARC. China's "Belt and Road Initiative" is an attempt to influence smaller SAARC members through heavy investments, which in turn antagonises India further. In fact, building a road through occupied Ladakh is open violation of India's territorial sovereignty. India does not have the means to outmanoeuvre China, and hence SAARC has lost meaning. SAARC was meant to make the region stable and integrated. The fact is that it has done neither. Many nations are constantly having domestic political and economic problems and have unstable governments. In case of Afghanistan and Pakistan, it is not even clear as to who runs the government. Hence, despite all the potential that such cooperation has in store, the future looks very dim.

**India too shares a part of the blame** and many of the factors have been common in straining relations with the immediate neighbours. There have been policy mistakes in the past due to ideology based dealing of international relations. One of these has been trying to support democracy in other countries. Democracy is no guaranty of friendliness. Sri Lanka, Nepal and Maldives are democracies but each has problems with India, primarily because of democracy. The other is making morality an issue. Matters like violation of human rights and suppression of women in certain countries cannot become factors in the equation to decide upon international relations. Morality means mortality in politics and relations should be based on the self interest of the nation, and not on moral values.

There are also many problems in India's dealing with bilateral and multilateral international and regional issues. Some of these are:

* Non-fulfilment of commitments due to bureaucratic procedures and interministerial discoordination.
* Inadequate and inappropriate staffing of the Ministry of External Affairs, and consequently of the personnel in the foreign embassies who are often out of sync with the needs of the modern times.

- Neglect due low priority given to smaller nations for several decades.
- Disregard of strengthening people-to-people's relations, especially in democratic neighbouring nations.
- Domestic eco-political pressures on the ruling governments.
- Compulsions of regional/provincial politics of the border states of India.
- While helping the less developed nations, India's approach was also condescending at times reinforcing the sentiment of 'big brother' bullying.

We also need to examine India's bilateral relations with each of India's neighbours to understand why SAARC as an organisation has reached this dismal point.

## NEPAL

India and Nepal share a unique relationship due to shared culture, religion, transnational kinship and 1700 kilometres of open borders. While the geo-strategic position of Nepal makes it critical for India's security, its land locked situation makes Nepal significantly dependent on India. Further, while Nepal is a much less developed tiny nation, India is a regional power. These very factors have made Indo-Nepalese relations one of a love-hate brotherhood.

The beginning of India-Nepal relations was cordial. In **1950, the Treaty of Peace and Friendship** was signed. This enabled India to establish army posts on the northern borders of Nepal to counter intrusion from Tibet. Recruitment of Gorkhas in Indian army was also permitted. During the same time, India helped restoration of the rule of Maharaja Tribhuvan. India's influence over Nepal was perceptible at this time and this was to be the beginning of the sentiment that India was interfering in the internal affairs of Nepal. It was also to be the beginning of rudimentary democracy in Nepal.

In 1954, Nehru signed the Panchsheel agreement with China. Soon after, Nepal also entered into a peace treaty with China, and thereafter, China began spreading its influence in Nepal. Nepal declared itself a 'zone of peace' and during the Indo-China war of 1962, Nepal adopted a stance of complete neutrality. Nepal also remained neutral during the Indo-Pak war of 1965. In 1969, Nepal asked India to call back army officers deputed on the Nepal-China border. During the same period, Nepal started to raise objections about the Treaty of 1950 calling it as one sided.

In 1970, two trade related treaties were signed between both the countries. In 1972 King Birendra became the Maharaja of Nepal. Thereafter began a period of cooperation and India took the responsibility of development in Nepal. Stress was given to economic issues and customs duty was removed on a large number of goods made in Nepal. Nepal was also given exemption to take goods by road to Bangladesh. However, differences again cropped up the 1980s due disputes on the issues of **import of weapons by Nepal from China**, the subject of citizenship, and differences about the trade and transit treaty.

Nepal restricted the numbers of Indians working in Nepal while the Nepalese had full freedom to work in India. Nepal also imposed high taxes on Indian goods while other countries were given concessions. The trade and transit treaties were finally cancelled in March 1989. Thereafter, India imposed tax on all goods exported to Nepal. India also demanded international prices for coal, iron, cement, etc., exported to Nepal. This increased the prices of goods in Nepal and caused severe problems for the masses.

During this period **domestic politics** had started creating its own problems in Nepal. In 1960, King Mahendra had dissolved the parliament and banned all political parties. There were many political parties in Nepal and these kept struggling for restoration of democracy. India, while maintained relations with the Maharaja, but also kept supporting the democratic leanings in Nepal. This ambivalence created its own problems in the relations. Finally, constitutional reforms were accepted by King Birendra and parliamentary elections were held in 1991. Meanwhile, many factions of communist parties also came up. In 1996, the China sponsored **Maoist groups began a civil war** to end the monarchy.

The situation took an unexpected turn for the worse in 2001 when King Birendra and family were massacred. At the same time, the Maoist groups escalated the civil war which culminated with the abolishment of monarchy in 2008. Thereafter Nepal entered the era of electoral turmoil with different factions of communist parties and the non-communist parties vying for power. This has led to formation of successive unstable coalition governments. While the communist leaders of Nepal were guided by China to adopt an anti-India stand, the other parties remained ambivalent. The Nepalese politicians used the China card as a bargaining chip for leveraging and anti-India stand as an electoral plank.

Nepal is politically divided not only on ideological grounds but also **geographically divided** on ethnicity based demographic factors. The northern Nepal is hilly and peoples of that area are racially different from the peoples of the southern terai region, called as the Madhesis. The Madhesis form about 30% of Nepal's population and are more akin to the peoples of the border states of Bihar and U.P. This has further complicated Nepalese politics.

In 2015, a new constitution was formed in Nepal. The Madhesis felt that they have been politically undermined in the constitution and began an agitation. The agitation took the form of blockade of goods coming from India. The Nepalese government blamed India, alleging that India was deliberately blocking the goods in support of the Madhesis, and that India was interfering in Nepalese affairs. The blockage caused lot of hardship to Nepalese peoples and relations of the two nations have never come back to normal. The Nepalese governments now keep raising contentious issues that continue to strain the relations.

The issue of settling **boundaries** has become a serious issue in the last couple of years. It has to be understood that India's borders with Nepal, Bhutan, China, and Burma (Myanmar) are a legacy of British Raj. The root of the dispute lies in the fact that India-Nepal borders at a few points were not clearly demarcated when the British ruled India. When India became independent, all territories under British rule were taken as part of India. However, from the 1980s, Nepal started claiming certain areas as part of Nepal. The issue was never escalated, nor resolved. In May 2020, Nepal, unilaterally out of the blue, released a new political map that not only claimed **Kalapani** in its entirety but also Limpiyadhura and Lipulekh areas of Uttarakhand. These territories had been a part of India for the last over 75 years and this sudden move is simply a China prompted provocation which also has electoral purpose. While Nepal has not backed down from its position, it has agreed for a peaceful resolution through dialogue.

The recently introduced 'Agnipath scheme' has become another cause of discontent. Under this scheme, soldiers are to be recruited for a fixed four-year term on contract basis in the Indian army. The scheme applies to Nepali Gorkhas as well. Nepal has rejected the scheme and has stopped Nepalese citizens from joining Indian army in this system. This is causing resentment among the Gorkhas.

India has its own issues with Nepal. India alleges that Nepal is misusing the concessions given in the trade treaties and dumping Indian markets with the goods imported from other countries, mainly China.

China's involvement in Nepal's infrastructure projects through its **Belt and Road Initiative** is seen as a security issue as it undermines Nepal's role as a buffer state between India and China.

The **open and porous borders** with Uttarakhand, Uttar Pradesh, West Bengal, Sikkim and Bihar are unmonitored and poorly guarded and are a security problem for India. India suspects that a large number of ISI sponsored terrorist groups have established bases in the terai region of Nepal and they cross the borders at will while Nepal is not taking any action to check their activities. Smuggling, and arms and narcotic trafficking are also rampant.

India's souring relations with Nepal is the most unfortunate chapter of Indian diplomacy. Nepal is the only other Hindu majority nation with extremely close cultural ties. It is also one neighbour which has received the most help from India. Yet it is most hostile. It is futile to argue who is at fault that things have come to such a pass.

The question is: **what can and should India do now**?

Firstly, India has to accept that Nepal is an independent and sovereign nation, and not an extension or appendage of India. Further, having commonality of religion and culture has limitations in the modern age. There has to be something material to cement the ties. Economic bonds are more powerful than cultural bonds.

India has also to acknowledge that China is a compulsion for Nepal, that Chinese presence in Nepal is very real, and that it is not likely to vanish any time soon. Instead of trying to compete with China for political influence, India should compete on the economic front and concentrate on the bilateral aspect. In this field, India has decisive advantages over China due to proximity and accessibility. Because of the formidable Himalayas, China can never provide the sort of connectivity for transit of goods and peoples as India can do. Language is another barrier for China and the Chinese can never establish the sort of people-to-peoples rapport as Indians can do. Lastly, Nepal is a Hindu nation, and religious commonality does matter. Hence, China has unbreakable limitations. India should capitalise on these strengths.

The most important factor in this equation hence becomes the **citizenry of Nepal**. Since Nepal is a democracy, only popular support of the peoples can help India regain its leverage. Their support has to be earned and not to be assumed or taken for granted just because they are Hindus. For this, the Indian government should expedite execution of promised/proposed plans for infrastructure and connectivity development like roads, oil pipelines, railways, etc. India should also increase investments - government as well as private - on joint ventures that benefit the local people as it will help create a positive image of India. Supporting economic growth at grassroots level will also promote people-to-people linkages and build trust.

India should also help development of tourist centres in Nepal and promote **Nepal's tourism** - particularly religious tourism - in India. If even a fraction of those who visit Vaishno Devi or Tirupati start going to Pashupatinath Temple of Kathmandu, the tables would turn in favour of India. Since going to Nepal is easy and does not have the hassle of visa, Indians will throng to hill stations and Hindu shrines of Nepal while hardly any Chinese would come to Nepal for tourism. China has no way to stop this. It will increase people-to-peoples contact and increase trust besides bringing revenue for Nepal.

India and Nepal are members of several multilateral forums like BBIN (Bangladesh, Bhutan, India, and Nepal), BIMSTEC, SAARC, etc. These should be used to let

Nepal be helped by other members also. Once the involved businesses, like the local contractors, hoteliers, etc., develop a vested interest in such projects, and the masses get employment, the peoples will compel the governments to be more committed to maintain good relationship with India.

Many of the projects, like the development of hydropower, would be economically beneficial to India as well. In fact, Nepal's economic growth and development is in India's own overall interest. Prosperity is the best antidote to communism and a domestically peaceful and stable Nepal is the best security assurance for India.

Lastly, and perhaps most importantly, India has to be **sensitive towards the Nepalese**. Peoples of small and underdeveloped states always suffer from inferiority complex and are touchy about humiliation. They should never to be made to feel that they are being demeaned because they belong to a less developed state. The peoples have to be given respect, not just the high dignitaries of the government, and India should not be seen to be patronising. India has always provided humanitarian help to Nepal. When a massive earthquake hit Nepal in April 2015, India was the first responder and helped in rescue, relief and restoration. Such help should not only continue but should also to be seen as help without strings attached. There has to be no room for quid pro quo in such endeavours.

As regards politics is concerned, irrespective of what good India does for Nepal, there will always be the element of anti-India factor in the volatile Nepalese domestic electoral competition. With another change in the government in July 2024, Nepal has had 13 Prime Ministers in the last 16 years. Nepal will continue to have unstable coalition governments. Hence, contentious issues will continue to linger, and newer issues will keep cropping up, and many would have no amicable solution. India needs to take such negativities in due stride and should never retaliate, or ever be ***seen*** to be interfering by taking sides. India need not exert influence: It should have influence by deeds.

Many of the aforesaid points are to an extent also applicable to India's relations with other neighbours also, and hence need no repetition in the successive sub-chapters.

## SRI LANKA

Sri Lanka became independent in February 1948 and had historically close cultural ties with India. Both were also under the British rule. However, Lankan domestic electoral politics and the Sinhala-Tamil conflict have always affected Sri Lanka's political relations with India. Nehru's condescending approach towards smaller nations also affected the relationship. In order to assert its position, Sri Lanka began raising maritime boundary issues soon after independence and claimed the island of **Katchatheevu**. It is a tiny and uninhabited island in the middle of the Palk Straits. The island had come under the jurisdiction of Madras Presidency during the British rule, and as such, had become a part of India with the transfer of power in 1947. However, unable to comprehend the implications of territorial sovereignty, Nehru declared that he had no interest in retaining the barren island. In 1974, Indira Gandhi formally ceded the island to Sri Lanka to appease the neighbour.

It must be understood that an island may be small and worthless in terms of landmass but sovereignty over an island gives a nation extensive area in terms maritime boundary. This includes control over transit, exploitation of seabed resources and fishing rights. As a result of this naïve decision, India lost control over a large sea area in the Palk Straits and the Gulf of Mannar. All the problems that small fishermen of Kerala and Tamil Nadu face today are because of this decision. It frequently also leads to arrest of Indian fisherman by the Lankan navy and is a constant cause of dispute with Sri Lanka. Hence, instead of improving relations by appeasement, it has only led to more bitterness as well as problem of livelihood for Indian fishermen.

In 1987, Indian army (**Indian Peace Keeping Force**) was sent to Sri Lanka at the request of Lankan government to settle the civil war between the Lankan government and the Tamil rebels (LTTE). The whole operation was a fiasco and only ended up in souring India's relations with Sri Lanka. Soon after the withdrawal of IPKF, the civil war escalated thereby destabilising Sri Lanka. Political parties blamed India for interfering in Lankan affairs, for the failure of IPKF, as well as for helping the Tamils. The sordid episode also resulted in the assassination of ex-Prime Minister Rajiv Gandhi which further spoiled India's relationship.

The **Tamil issue** continues to haunt India's relationship with Sri Lanka. For one thing, India cannot abandon the Lankan Tamils for domestic reasons. Further, India also understands that a peaceful resolution of the issue is in Lanka's own interest. However, the Lankan government considers it as interference on part of India and is more inclined to suppress the Tamils rather than integrate them. The hiatus between the majority Sinhalese, predominantly Buddhists, and the Hindu Tamils is irreconcilable. The Lankan Tamils are also no less to be blamed for using violence for years which led to a full scale civil war.

India's **economic relations** with Sri Lanka are very strong and Sri Lanka depends on India for a very large number of goods. India has also consistently helped Sri Lanka materially as well as financially, whether it was the Tsunami of 2004 or Covid 19. However, in recent years China has established a strong presence in Sri Lanka. It has made extensive investments which have also put Sri Lanka into a severe debt crisis. Domestic electoral politics has further complicated the situation in Sri Lanka. The Lankan leaders understand that their nation cannot do without India, but at the same time they use the China card for leveraging their bargaining position with India.

India cannot afford to let China establish a base in Sri Lanka, nor can it use strong arm tactics which will only drive Sri Lanka further into the Chinese arms. Hence, India is tactfully playing a delicate balancing act. So far it has worked and the relationship will continue to be kaleidoscopic and ambivalent in the foreseeable future.

## MALDIVES

Maldives is a Muslim majority island nation, but fairly liberal and cosmopolitan because tourism is its pillar of economy. Maldives stood as a very stable state for long because Maumoon Abdul Gayoom remained the president from 1978 till 2008. He was also a reliable friend of India and India frequently came to his help. Being a close neighbour with deep resources, India always acted as the **first responder** in times of crisis. India was the first nation to help Maldives during the 2004 tsunami in which nearly 100 people were killed. In 2009, Mohammad Nashid became the President of Maldives. He further strengthened ties with India and signed a security agreement which permitted Indian military presence in Maldives. However, since then, every election has brought a change in the government and relations have swung from one of close friendship to that of extreme hostility, all because of domestic politics of Maldives.

In 2013 Abdulla Yameen became the President and started the **'India Out' campaign**. As India-Maldives relations came under stress, China started aligning with Maldives to lessen India's influence. Chinese investments through the Belt and Road Initiative and overall trade increased and so did the number of Chinese tourists. Yameen's pro-China policies also led to high indebtedness. Despite Yameen's attempts to engage with China and Pakistan, India continued to fulfil most of Maldives' defence related needs. India also helped during the Male water crisis of 2014.

In 2018 Ibu Solih became the President and Maldivian foreign policy shifted again to 'India First' policy. India's strategic position was restored with extremely close relations with Maldives.

In September 2023 Mohamed Muizzu was elected the President on 'India Out' campaign and Maldivian foreign policy has again taken a U-Turn. Since coming to office, President Muizzu has left no opportunity to demonstrate his anti-India and pro-China stand. He has forced withdrawal of Indian army personnel from Maldives declaring that he is taking these steps to ensure national sovereignty and to step outside overreliance on India. Religion is also now becoming a factor in Maldivian politics and Muizzu is joining hands with nations like Türkiye and Pakistan.

How his policies are going to play out remains to be seen. Quite like what has happened to Sri Lanka and Pakistan, Maldives may get into a debt trap and lose its sovereignty to China. Increasing Islamic radicalism in Maldives is a threat to the nation itself. It may also affect its tourism industry, and hence its economy.

From the Indian perspective, China's entry into Maldives is a cause of concern for **geopolitical reasons**. Maldives is of strategic importance due to its position on the main east-west shipping route. Maldives also has a role in the initiatives like 'SAGAR' (Security and Growth for All in the Region). China, or any other nation, is not in a position to help Maldives in times of crisis as India can do. However, India can do little for the present. Hence, India is just swallowing Muizzu's surly behaviour with equanimity and waiting for time. For all that Muizzu is trying to do, hobnobbing too much with China, and other Islamic nations, and disregarding India may in the long run prove to be damaging to Muizzu as well as to Maldives. In the end, Muizzu may lose the next election and things may return back to square one.

## BHUTAN

India and Bhutan have sustained a relationship of unwavering and unstinted friendship based on mutual respect, trust, and spirit of cooperation for long. The two nations signed the Treaty of Friendship and Cooperation in 1949 and diplomatic relations between the two were established in 1968.

India has closely worked with Bhutan for its **socio-economic development** in practically every conceivable field, e.g., infrastructure and connectivity development, agriculture, urban development, health, education, energy, human resource development, etc., and community development projects of drinking water supply, irrigation canals, farm roads, health units, etc. India has constructed major hydro-electric power projects in Bhutan and more are planned. The two sides collaborated on the first satellite jointly developed by India and Bhutan thereby helping Bhutan in natural resources' management through high resolution images. RuPay Card was launched in Bhutan in 2019 to enable cashless payments and thereby ease travellers from either side. While the Reserve Bank of India ensures that Bhutan does not have problems of liquidity or foreign exchange, the Government of India also provides direct budgetary support to the Government of Bhutan.

India is Bhutan's top trading partner as well as the biggest investor. The **India-Bhutan Agreement 2016** on Trade, Commerce and Transit, provides a free trade regime between the two countries and also provides Bhutan duty free transit of goods to/from third countries. The two nations are also working to enhance cross-border connectivity by establishment of rail-links.

The relations have consistently been recharged by highest level visits. Prime Minister Modi visited Bhutan on his first overseas tour after winning the election in 2014. He undertook a State visit to Bhutan in August 2019, after assuming office for the second term. The King of Bhutan conferred the Order of the Druk Gyalpo, Bhutan's highest civilian honour, on Shri Modi in December 2021. The King of Bhutan has also visited India several times. Such high-profile visits have played a vital role in reinforcing mutual trust and understanding.

The reasons for enduring relations with Bhutan rest more on the unique national culture of Bhutan rather than on Indian diplomacy. Bhutan remained a very close country for centuries and is still rather restrictive for outsiders. Bhutan has never been conquered and tolerates no interference. Bhutan is a constitutional monarchy but its politics are very different from any other nation. Hence India has no reason or room to meddle and there is no scope for anti-India sentiment to grow. Best of all, Bhutan is distrustful about China as China claims a part of Bhutanese territories and has unresolved boundary disputes with Bhutan. Hence, Bhutan has no diplomatic relations with China, although there are official exchanges and dialogue between the two.

There are no border issues between India and Bhutan. However, China-Bhutan border dispute has brought India also into the scene. In June 2017, China began construction of a road in the **Doklam** plateau which Bhutan claims as its land. Bhutan protested about the Chinese construction of a road in its territory. This is a tri-junction point with India. India has no claim over Doklam but cannot permit Chinese control in the area as it can give access to China over India's strategically vulnerable "chicken's neck" - the Siliguri Corridor. Hence, India supported the Bhutanese claim and Indian troops intervened and stopped further construction. The standoff continued for over two months. Thereafter, India and China mutually agreed to disengage and the military face-off came to an end.

During the standoff, Bhutan took a firm stand against China. However, in recent years, Bhutan's stand on Doklam seems to be wavering as it is negotiating with China. This is causing concern in India as Indian stand is that since Doklam is a tri-junction point, India has to be a party to any settlement. If China increases its influence in Bhutan, it may undermine India's position in the region, and the strategic partnership between Bhutan and India may be at risk. India is keeping a close watch on the developments in Thimphu and Beijing as well as at the borders. However, whatever direction Bhutan takes, India should not let it reflect on the bilateral relations. India has to take care of its own security, and not depend on Bhutan.

## BANGLADESH

Bangladesh emerged as an independent nation out of the Indo-Pak war of 1971. It was considered as a war of liberation by the Bangladeshis and relations between the two nations started with extreme cordiality and goodwill for India. Tagore's poem became the national anthem of Bangladesh. However, in 1975 there was a military coup in which President Sheikh Mujibur Rahman was assassinated and his family took asylum in India. For the next two years there was political turmoil in Bangladesh and finally in

1977, General Zia-ur-Rehman came to power as the elected President. Zia-ur-Rahman lifted martial law, reinstated multi-party politics, (he was the founder of the Bangladesh Nationalist Party - the BNP) and allowed Sheikh Hasina, the exiled daughter of Sheikh Mujibur Rahman, to return to Bangladesh. At the same time, he emphasised upon the Muslim identity of Bangladesh rather than on Bengali nationalism and Islam was declared as the state religion.

As a Pak army officer, Zia-ur-Rahman had fought against India during the 1965 war. Hence he adopted the policy of keeping India at a distance and established close relations with Islamic nations including Pakistan, as well as with USA, China, and other western powers. India's position was thus undermined.

Soon, the **Farakka Barrage** became as issue of controversy. It is a dam on the river Ganga in Farakka, West Bengal. India maintained that it needed the barrage to keep the Hooghly River free from silt while Bangladesh demanded a fair share of the Ganga waters. The issue could not be resolved for long.

In 1981, another coup took place in which Zia-ur-Rehman was assassinated and General Ershad became the president. Thereafter, Bangladesh started engaging with India which led to the formation of SAARC in 1985. At the same time, Gen. Ershad maintained Islam as the pillar of his policy and engagement with Islamic nations and China increased. During the period, several radical outfits infiltrated and established their bases inside Bangladesh. These included ISI sponsored radical Islamic terror groups as well as banned outfits of India's Northeastern states like ULFA, and Maoist insurgents. Bangladesh's domestic politics was already churning due to conflicts between the political parties and the army. The emergence of subversive groups only complicated the scenario further and Bangladesh remained in political chaos.

**In 1991, Bangladesh returned to a multi-party democracy**. Thereafter, India-Bangladesh relations began to swing depending upon the party in power. There are two major parties in Bangladesh: The Bangladesh Nationalist Party (BNP) and the Awami League. The BNP is headed by Begum Khaleda Zia, the widow of Zia-ur-Rehman. She follows the policy of Islamic identity and is not favourably inclined towards India. On the other hand, Sheikh Hasina who leads the Awami League is more pragmatic and has a benign disposition towards India. During 1996-2001, the Awami League remained in power and the Farakka dispute regarding water sharing was resolved. India also gave tariff concessions to Bangladesh. During 2001-2006, a coalition government - led by BNP - remained in power. Consequently, the relations deteriorated during this period

The Awami League won the elections of 2008 by an overwhelming majority and Sheikh Hasina became the PM in January 2009. Thereafter, there was a consistent improvement in Indo-Bangladesh relations and both sides cooperated to resolve a large number of issues. The relations were based on the compulsions of pragmatism, and not on any ideology. Both needed each other and accepted that cooperation was better than conflict. In fact, conflict was disastrous for both. Prime Minister Modi also took very proactive steps to keep up the momentum and Sheikh Hasina responded positively.

The **Land Boundary Agreement of 2015** was a milestone in this direction. This agreement resolved the contentious issue of borders which was a legacy of the strange decision of the Radcliff Commission at the time of partition. India owned 111 enclaves inside Bangladesh (15,000 hectare) while Bangladesh owned 55 on the Indian side (7,000 hectare). The issue was settled by 100th Constitutional Amendment 2015. The enclaves on either side were exchanged and the citizens were given the choice to retain their nationality or acquire a new one. This largely resolved the border issue. Only a stretch of about 6.5 kilometres bordering Tripura remained to be demarcated.

Bangladesh became India's biggest trading partner in South Asia while India the second largest trading partner of Bangladesh. India provided duty free access to Bangladesh under SAFTA after 2011. India and Bangladesh also became partners in several regional multilateral organisations such as SAARC, BIMSTEC and IORA. The BBIN (Bangladesh, Bhutan, India, and Nepal) Motor Vehicles Agreement provided a multinational corridor for connectivity to the eastern states of South Asia. This agreement permits the member states to ply their vehicles in each other's territory for transportation of cargo and passengers, including of other countries.

Bangladesh is geopolitically important for India not only because of India's 'Neighbourhood First policy' but also for the 'Act East Policy'. However, cooperation with Bangladesh is most critical for the peace and security in the volatile **North East region of India.** The whole area is imploding with ethnic and religious conflicts which have domestic political implications and are a threat to India's national integrity and sovereignty.

The NE states are basically tribe centric, although conversion of certain tribes into Christianity during the British rule also added the factor of religion. As a result of gross underdevelopment and long festering ethnic conflicts, many rebel and separatist groups came to be formed shortly after Independence. During the 1960s, the Naxalite insurgency led to formation of Maoist groups as well. The problem got severely aggravated, and complicated, due to mass migration of refugees from East Pakistan during Bangladesh's war of liberation 1971. This began changing the demography of many of the states and the local populace did not want the outsiders to settle, whether Hindu or Muslim. However, certain political parties and the ruling governments - of the states as well as of the centre - facilitated the influx and cultivated migrants only to use them as vote banks for electoral purposes.

During the same period, concentration of Muslim migrants led to formation of **radical Islamic groups** supported by the various regimes of Bangladesh and by the ISI. The civil strife in Myanmar added to the problem as a large number of Rohingya Muslims took refuge in Bangladesh. Thousands were permitted to infiltrate into India by the Congress government during 2012-14. The TMC government of West Bengal openly supported these intruders. Many criminal groups also came to be formed that indulge in narco and arms trafficking. Infiltration continues unabated also because of the unguarded borders and corruption at the local level.

The problem is largely domestic, and of India's own making. However, many of these insurgent groups have bases in Bangladesh (as well as in Myanmar). It is also suspected that some extremist groups run income-generating ventures in Bangladesh and use the money to fund insurgent operations in India. Hence, cooperation with Bangladesh is necessary. The Hasina government understood that Islamic radicalism is a threat not only to her government but to Bangladesh as well. Hence, Bangladesh joined hands with India in dealing with security issues and in tackling the terrorist groups. Many militant leaders were arrested by Bangladesh and some deported to India. Beyond that, India has to set its own house in order and take care of its domestic problems.

There are other challenges as well. There is a huge trade asymmetry and contentious issues of non-tariff barriers between the two nations. Lack of proper infrastructure for smooth flow of goods across the borders also hinders trade. Connectivity is vital for both the nations and steps are being taken to increase rail links. India is now using Bangladeshi ports for transportation of goods to the Northeast. Bangladesh also benefits financially by providing transit facilities.

Water sharing issue has been partly resolved but **Teesta Water dispute** is one of the major impediments. While Bangladesh has sought distribution of waters on the lines of the 1996 Ganga Water Treaty, the agreement has not been reached due to objections from the West Bengal government. In fact, Mamata Bannerjee, the leader of TMC, wants to be a party to the agreement. Hence early resolution to the dispute is unlikely in near future.

As everywhere else, **China** is also a factor of concern. All parties of Bangladesh favour good relations with China. Bangladesh has a formal defence agreement with China while India does not. In 2016, Chinese President Xi Jinping made a visit to Bangladesh where the Bangladesh-China relationship was elevated to that of being strategic partners. Bangladesh is an active member of the Belt and Road Initiative and China is investing heavily in Bangladesh. It is a part of its 'string of pearls' strategy whereby China aims to encircle India by building strategic posts in India's neighbourhood. Bangladesh wants have a free trade agreement with India and is also considering joining the China sponsored Regional Comprehensive Economic Partnership (RCEP). This dual approach has raised concerns in India.

While Sheikh Hasina won the elections of 2014, 2018 and of 2024, she was increasingly accused of being authoritarian and for suppressing democracy. Agitations against her started in July 2024 and in a dramatic turn of events, she had to flee from the country on 5th August 2024. This has put the country into turmoil and the situation at present is not clear as to who is in control. Ultimately, India-Bangladesh relations will depend more on the domestic politics of the two nations rather than on the regional or global factors. As of now, there is considerable anti-India sentiment in Bangladesh due to Hasina's good relations with India. There has also been much violence against the Hindus. How long can any new government of Bangladesh sustain this stand remains to be seem. India on its part has to remain prepared for any change and not align with any political party of a neighbour.

## PAKISTAN

India has fought four wars with Pakistan and faced innumerable terror attacks sponsored by Pakistan. The border areas of Jammu and Kashmir also suffer from frequent shelling. Pakistan continues to occupy a sizeable part of Kashmir and describes it as a disputed territory. It has also interfered in India's internal affairs by way of disputing and internationalising laws passed by the Indian Parliament, like the abolition of Article 370. Despite all the personal efforts of the various Indian Prime Ministers, there has been no change in Pakistan's approach. The relations with Pakistan are unlikely to improve in foreseeable future for the simple reason that Pakistan is basically ruled by the army. Even when there is democracy in Pakistan, the Pak PM is more like the municipal commissioner of Islamabad rather than the real centre of power. The Pak army controls not only defence and foreign affairs but the businesses as well and this has made the generals extremely rich.

The biggest danger to nation states is that when **militarism** becomes the creed of a government, an army clique takes control over the entire system. The army, and its commanders, have an inherent interest in expanding the role of the army in all matters because it provides them with bigger budgets, better pay scales, perks and promotions, and above all, a sense of superiority in the social hierarchy. The army grows in power, not so much to subdue other nations, but to subdue the civilian majority of its own nation.

The situation becomes worse when the democratic civilian segment is unable to act as a counter-weight to the army faction. In such a situation, it is the army that takes all the decisions, which are not always conducive for peace, because an army needs a war from time to time, or else, it would lose its very reason of existence. To serve that end, the army top brass indulges in war mongering and creates an atmosphere of panicky combat readiness. In any case, the generals sitting in the safety of army headquarters do not get killed in wars. They have a stake in keeping the bogey of threat of India alive for their own power. And hence, whenever any democratically elected leader of Pakistan tries to respond to India's peace overtures, the army scuttles the efforts by staging some terror attack or some other type of provocation. Or they simply upstage the leader. Pak army generals are also well taken care of by China to ensure that relations with India remain on an edge.

At the same time, **religion** continues to be a factor in Indo-Pak relations. Pakistan was created out of communal strife and there are radical Islamists who profit by spreading communal hatred and inciting violence against the Indian state, from outside as well as from within. Many a times, the ISI plays the role of a facilitator in such activities. These non-state actors are serious impediments in improving relations. India understands that neither China nor the generals will give up their position of power. The jihadi elements will also not stop their activities. USA plays a double game in this Chinese checkers. For long it was a close ally of Pakistan, and even though China has replaced USA as the chief associate of Pakistan, USA is not willing to totally cede its position. Hence it also continues to help Pakistan by funding it. Thus Pakistan government is under no pressure to improve relations.

For another thing, it is not very clear as to who is running the government of Pakistan. On the other hand, Pakistan today is so deeply involved in its own economic and political problems that it is in no position to do anything. The monster of terrorism is now threatening the state of Pakistan itself and there is tension at its Afghan and Iranian borders. India has nothing to gain economically from improving relations. Security is the only issue for India. Since both are nuclear powers, there is no military solution to the problem. And the prevailing environment is not conducive for a diplomatic solution. India, now it seems, has given up. It is a futile and tiresome exercise trying to humour an obstinate neighbour who in any case cannot do anything.

Pakistan will not undertake another direct military adventure against India but would keep hurting India by other means wherever and whenever it can. All that India can do is to keep vigil inside as well as at the borders. And wait for things to unravel.

## AFGHANISTAN

On 15th August 2021, while the US personnel were fleeing Kabul for their life by planes, the Taliban retook control over the capital of Afghanistan. Since then, India-Afghan relations have been in a flux and history has ceased to matter.

When the Taliban first took control over Kabul in 1996, it was considered as takeover of Afghanistan by a Pakistan sponsored terrorist group. Hence, India did not recognise the new regime, closed its embassy and severed all diplomatic relations with Kabul. When the Taliban were ousted by the US led invasion in 2001, India promptly recognised the new regime and reopened its embassy. For the next two decades, India was one of the largest providers of humanitarian aid to Afghanistan. However, the government of Afghanistan, despite all the support of USA, was unable gain loyalty of the peoples and could not stand on its own feet.

Meanwhile, the Taliban regrouped and intensified attacks on the US backed government in Kabul. USA found itself sustaining a failed enterprise and decided to cut losses by withdrawing. While USA was negotiating a peace deal with the Taliban, India was worried about the return of Taliban as it had multifaceted implications for India, especially in view of Pakistan's supposed close proximity with the Taliban, and Taliban's involvement with radical Islamic groups that believe in cross border terrorism.

**Taliban's return to power in 2021** has created a major dilemma for India. India, like most of the other nations, has not yet recognised the Taliban government and the Indian Ambassador has been recalled.* While India has not formally established diplomatic ties with the Taliban, India needs to be present in Afghanistan and not leave the field empty for its rivals to play. China has already entered Afghanistan and has recognised the Taliban government. Hence, India has also reopened its embassy in Kabul in June 2022 by sending a team of "technical experts" to run the mission. Taliban officials have welcomed India's 'diplomatic upgrade' in Kabul, requested India to complete its development projects, and have offered security to its mission. These developments indicate a revision of the relations.

*The Afghan embassy in New Delhi was closed in November 2023 because the diplomats had been appointed by the erstwhile government. The Afghan diplomats have left India since then. India is yet to accept Taliban appointed diplomats because India does not officially recognise the Taliban government. (Pakistan, China, Russia and Iran are among the handful of countries that have allowed the appointment of Taliban approved diplomats.)

**New Delhi has avoided alienating the Taliban** and has also started engaging with the regime. This is because India wants to hold on to its presence in Afghanistan and retain its goodwill among the Afghans who see India as a provider of vital humanitarian aid. India has renewed shipment of food and medicines to Afghanistan. India has also continued the scholarship scheme for Afghan students and about 10,000 Afghan students are studying in India. Afghan cricketers practice and play in India including in the IPL. It was primarily because of this that the Afghan team reached the semi-finals of the ICC T20 World Cup held in June 2024.

India invested heavily in a very large number of development projects before the Taliban took over and India wants to renew work on the same. Giving up on Taliban would mean all the money and effort going down the drain. This revision in India's position is not due to any change in the character of Taliban but is driven by the position of Taliban's opponents in Afghanistan and India's security interest in the overall political matrix of the region. The centre of this game lies in Pakistan's relations with the Taliban.

When the Taliban gained power in 2021, Pakistan was happy and thought that it would have influence over Kabul. However, Afghanistan has long standing border disputes with Pakistan as it does not recognise the Durand Line. On the other hand, Taliban itself is deeply divided into pro-Pak and anti-Pak factions and one is not sure as to who is running the government. The entry of **Tehreek-e-Taliban Pakistan** (TTP) in the scene has complicated the situation for Pakistan as well as for Afghanistan. It must be understood here that Taliban was a joint venture of Afghans and the Pakistani government (ISI). However, TTP emerged as a separate group in 2007 and is today attacking Pakistan at the Afghan borders. Pakistan wants Kabul to rein in TTP but TTP is closely linked with the Afghan Taliban. As a result, Pak-Afghan relations are deteriorating by the day. Another issue of acrimony between the two nations is that Pakistan is expelling the Afghan refugees from its border areas. This is a healthy diversion of Pakistan's attention and resources as far as India is concerned. It may even help contain cross border terrorism sponsored by Pakistan. However, if the situation explodes, terrorism might spill over into India also.

While the Taliban regime is desperate to get recognition of its legitimacy in the international arena, India should not entertain high hopes of having good relations with the Taliban ruled Afghanistan any time in future. Taliban's ultra ideology, nefarious aims, and heinous methods, are so antithetical to those of India that the two nations can never come close. All India can do is to use subtle diplomacy to keep Pakistan involved in its own problems with the Afghans and monitor the situation closely.

## MYANMAR

India and Myanmar share the legacy of colonial rule as Burma was a province of British India till 1937. As such, there was considerable presence of Indians - workers and businessmen - in Burma. Burma became independent in 1948 and its relations with India were very cordial during the first decade. Both signed a Treaty of Friendship in 1951 and both were also members of the Non-Aligned Movement.

A military coup in 1962 brought army rule in Burma and this was the beginning of strained and uncertain relationship between the two nations. The ruling junta closed its doors to the outside world and curtailed democratic freedoms of the peoples. It also targeted the minorities and expelled the foreigners, including Indians. Hence, India distanced itself from the junta. While India maintained diplomatic relations with the regime, it also stood in support of the democratic forces. It was at this juncture that China entered Burma by giving full support to the military regime.

During the 1980s, there were pro-democracy uprisings in Burma. India criticised the junta, sided with the movements, and offered sanctuary to Burmese dissidents. Western nations also were critical of the junta. In retaliation, Burma came even closer to China. In 1989, it also changed the name of the country from **Burma to Myanmar**.

From 2011 to 2021, there was a semi-democratic rule in Myanmar. This provided India with a brief window of opportunity to renew relations. India provided assistance for humanitarian relief and rehabilitation in the areas affected by cyclones and earthquake.

However, **in 2021, the army again seized power** and revived the repressive policies. This has led to a multipronged civil war in Myanmar. In response, Myanmar has become even more insular and deaf to world opinion. As a result China has come even closer to the military regime. China and Myanmar share a 2,000 km border, and China is Myanmar's top trading partner and foreign investor. China is Myanmar's largest supplier of weapons and provides technical training to the Myanmar army. Beijing has repeatedly vetoed resolutions against the junta in the UNO.

India's options with Myanmar are rather limited. It cannot do anything about democracy and violations of human rights in Myanmar because the nation is not open to suggestions. It has also not bowed down to economic sanctions imposed by the western nations because it cares little about the welfare of its own peoples. India should also not try to venture into these areas, irrespective of the moral issues involved. Further, although India is actively involved in over a dozen projects in Myanmar, both in infrastructure and non-infrastructure sectors, it can do nothing about the Chinese influence over Myanmar. The ruling regime is aware of the strategic competition between India and China and plays one against the other to obtain benefits from both.

However, India has its own compulsions to engage with Myanmar. It shares a **1600 km long land border** and maritime boundary in the Bay of Bengal. While it was thought that this would provide India connectivity with South East Asia, Myanmar being the only ASEAN country which shares a land border with India, not much headway is possible in this field because of the ongoing civil war in Myanmar. Trade with Myanmar also has little promise because of problems on both the sides, and because Myanmar has little to offer and also has no interest. The regime is too preoccupied with its internal problems.

Hence, India's relations with Myanmar get reduced to India's security concerns in the North East. Certain of the rebel groups of NE have ethnic links inside Myanmar and have established camps on the other side of the border. Some even have ties with Myanmar's military. On the other hand, a large number of refugees and rebel groups from Myanmar have crossed over into India. This has led to increase of ethnic conflict in the NE states. Further, there has been an increase of arms and narcotic trafficking across the border which is porous and poorly guarded. The region is also an opium producing area.

One reason for this problem has been the **Free Movement Regime (FMR)** agreement with Myanmar implemented in 2018 as a part of India's Act East Policy. The FMR is a mutually agreed arrangement between Myanmar and India that permits tribes living along the border on either side to travel freely up to 16 km inside the other country without visa. While this was meant to help the tribes divided by the national borders to intermingle freely, it has made it easy for all types of hostile and criminal groups to cross the borders at will. India is now considering termination of FMR and fencing of the border. This may have adverse effect on the bilateral ties between the two nations as well as ethnic problems in the border areas.

The **influx of Rohingyas** due to repression of minorities in Myanmar is another problem. The Rohingyas were settled in various parts of India by the Congress (UPA) government. They are however a security concern because of their links with radical Islamic groups and a danger to social harmony in India. They are a burden on national resources in any case. While there is no solution to the Rohingya problem, India is engaging with the military junta to put a check on the insurgents. There has been some success in this field and the rest remains to be seen.

## CHINA

Spreading hegemony in south has been a centuries' old policy of China and led to the Indo-China war of 1962. India's relations with China remained tense thereafter and in September 1967, China again attacked the Indian posts at Nathu La and Cho La. However, this time Indian army retaliated with vengeance and the Chinese suffered severe losses. The Chinese army retreated in humiliation and that was to be the last direct armed confrontation between the two nations.

Other developments also took place in China after the **death of Mao Zedong** that moderated the Indo-Chinese relations. In 1978 Deng Xiaoping opened the doors to foreign firms and investments and China's rapprochement with the West began. In 1979, diplomatic relations with China were restored and the two nations also decided to initiate a regular process of bilateral dialogue to address the border issue and to improve trade relations. In 1991, the Cold War ended and this further facilitated Chinese engagement with the western economy. In thirty years, largely with western technology and finance, China transformed from a backward and insular nation to an economic giant. During the same period, China also became a major military power. The policy of hegemony had only been frozen for some time, not abandoned. After **Xi Jinping became the dictator of China in 2012**, the policy of hegemony was revived, and with renewed vigour.

India being a regional power has been the major roadblock in China's ambition to increase its influence in the South East Asia. China also understands that it cannot bulldoze India through military means any more. The lessons of Nathu La and Cho La are not to be forgotten. China may develop as many roads and military facilities in the Tibet region as it wants but the Himalayas are too formidable to be neutralised as a factor. China knows that it can never win a conventional war against India, and a nuclear war is not an option. In fact, China does not even want a direct military confrontation with India. Wars have very unpredictable outcomes, and in view of the US, Western, and regional opposition against the Chinese, China would not risk a war with India. It may well end up in domestic upheaval and end the dictatorial control of the Communist party.

Hence, China has adopted a four-pronged strategy against India. The first is to **keep the tensions at the borders alive** and escalate these from time to time as seen during the Doklam faceoff in June 2017 and during the Galwan showdown of June 2020. On both the occasions, when India took a firm stand, the Chinese backed down. China also uses its client state Pakistan to keep tension alive at the Indo-Pak border and to sponsor terrorism. The threat on both the sides of the border and terrorism within is basically to exhaust Indian resources and thus drain India economically. This is a war of attrition. As there is neither a diplomatic nor a military solution to it, these tensions will continue and India has to live with this situation for long.

The second is age old Chinese stratagem to tire the adversary by irritating it and keeping it on tenterhooks. Thus, China **challenges India diplomatically** wherever it can. China keeps releasing maps showing Indian territories as part of China and has even given Chinese names to Indian areas. Whenever a dignitary visits Arunachal Pradesh, China raises objection as it claims the state as a part of China. China also refuses visa to peoples of Arunachal Pradesh on the pretext that these are Chinese citizens and hence do not need a visa. At the international forum, China opposes India's entry into UNSC, NSG, etc. This strategy is not working much because India has its own good relations in the international arena while China is increasingly being seen with suspicion by the world community. Strangely, India remains rather subdued in this respect. India should not remain muted on this front and should not feel shy of similarly stepping up its diplomatic offensive against China. It should keep raising issues like Tibet, Taiwan, suppression of human rights, Uyghur Muslims, security, IPR theft, etc., at the international level.

That third strategy is to **colonise India economically**. In this approach, China has been largely successful, primarily due to UPA government's collusion with the Chinese during their rule 2004-2014. China has flooded Indian markets with cheap but substandard goods, made huge investments in strategic sectors, and infiltrated every branch of Indian apparatus - business as well as politics. This is a security threat as well as an economic problem. The Chinese have dug their heels so deeply in India that unless concerted efforts are made to reverse the situation, India will never be able to come out of the Chinese trap. This would require fundamental reforms and changes in India's policies and government working. It would also need informing the peoples of the situation so that the reforms get popular political support. Not much is being done on this front as of now.

The fourth tactic is to isolate and encircle India by what has been described as the '**String of Pearls**' policy. As a part of this policy, China is establishing its foothold in all of India's neighbours and encouraging them to take an anti-India stand. China also does not want any regional unity to develop in Asia that could counterbalance China, especially where India has any role. Thus, China has been able to sabotage the SAARC from inside. How India can deal with this tactics has been discussed in the earlier sub-chapters.

## ACT EAST POLICY

Although India had adopted the Look East policy in 1991, its success in the region was rather modest for the first two decades. During the period, China continued spreading its influence which was a cause of concern for USA. USA wanted India to play a more affirmative role in the region. In 2011, US Secretary of State Hillary Clinton, on a visit to India, emphasised the need for India to be more proactive in the Asia-Pacific zone. She appealed that India should "act east" instead of just "looking east." The expression was appealing and in 2014 the Ministry of External Affairs declared that India was now ready to "Act East". Prime Minister Narendra Modi reaffirmed this as a policy of India.

The Act East policy entails not mere political cooperation but also **strategic relationship** with nations in the Asia Pacific region. To a large extent, this is to counterbalance the China factor. During the 2022 ASEAN-India Summit, the relationship has been elevated to the level of Comprehensive Strategic Partnership. This has been followed by the first ever ASEAN-India Maritime Exercise held off the coast of Singapore. There is an increasing emphasis on infrastructure projects and collaboration in maritime security. ASEAN nations are forming bilateral defence relations and also acquiring Indian defence equipments.

The Act East policy also means that India's regional engagement should transcend the ASEAN framework through bilateral, trilateral and multilateral initiatives. The

**Quad** (Quadrilateral Security Dialogue), comprising Australia, India, Japan, and the United States, which was revitalised in 2017 after its short-lived initiation in 2007, is one of such moves. Besides maritime issues of the Indo-Pacific region, it also aims towards diversifying supply chains and thus to reduce dependence on China in strategically important sectors. In fact, USA now calls the Asia-Pacific zone as Indo-Pacific, which means that the strategic importance of Indian Ocean for its contiguity with the Pacific has finally been realised. At the centre of this shift is the increasing US-China strategic rivalry, which is redefining the regional and global structure. It has also meant the end of APEC. *

*The **Asia-Pacific Economic Cooperation** APEC was established in 1989 as a regional economic forum to promote sustainable growth and better economic relations among the member countries. With diverse nations as USA, China, Russia and Taiwan as members, not much could be expected out of it and not much has been achieved.

The Act East policy has a strong strategic dimension from the **maritime point** of view. While commercial shipping is vital for trade, naval prowess is critical for national security. Naval presence is also needed for checking piracy, smuggling, illegal fishing, and preventing terrorists from entering. (The Pakistani terrorists entered Mumbai in 2008 by boats). Hence, India is giving more emphasis to step up its naval capabilities. This includes coastal patrolling and aerial surveillance.

The need of naval power is not limited to the Bay of Bengal and the Arabian Sea. India has to secure the Indian Ocean as well and its connectivity to the Pacific. This is where the Malacca Straits and the South China Sea become important for India. The South China Sea is the 'maritime gateway' between the Indian Ocean and the Pacific. It has also brought USA, and other many other nations, on common grounds, and they want India to play a more proactive role to balance naval power which is increasingly tilting in China's favour. Recognising its significance, USA now describes the Asia-Pacific as Indo-Pacific. (The 'Indo' refers to the Indian Ocean and not to India!)

India has a major naval base on the Andaman and Nicobar Islands, and can play a crucial role in securing the **Malacca Straits**. However, India's capability to do much in the South China Sea is meagre. Nevertheless, India maintains a stand of cooperative partnership with the concerned nations, including ASEAN. While India is not a party to the maritime territorial disputes of the South China Sea, India has asserted its stand of maintaining the freedom of navigation in accordance with international laws. India has thus provided diplomatic support to an emerging alignment of USA and other nations in challenging China's aggressive actions in the region.

This is also reflected by the Modi government's **SAGAR** (Security and Growth for All in the Region) initiative of 2015. It entails strengthening maritime connectivity and developing the 'Blue Economy'*. This initiative has been extended to include the Pacific Ocean with the establishment of the India Pacific Oceans Initiative (IPOI) in 2019.

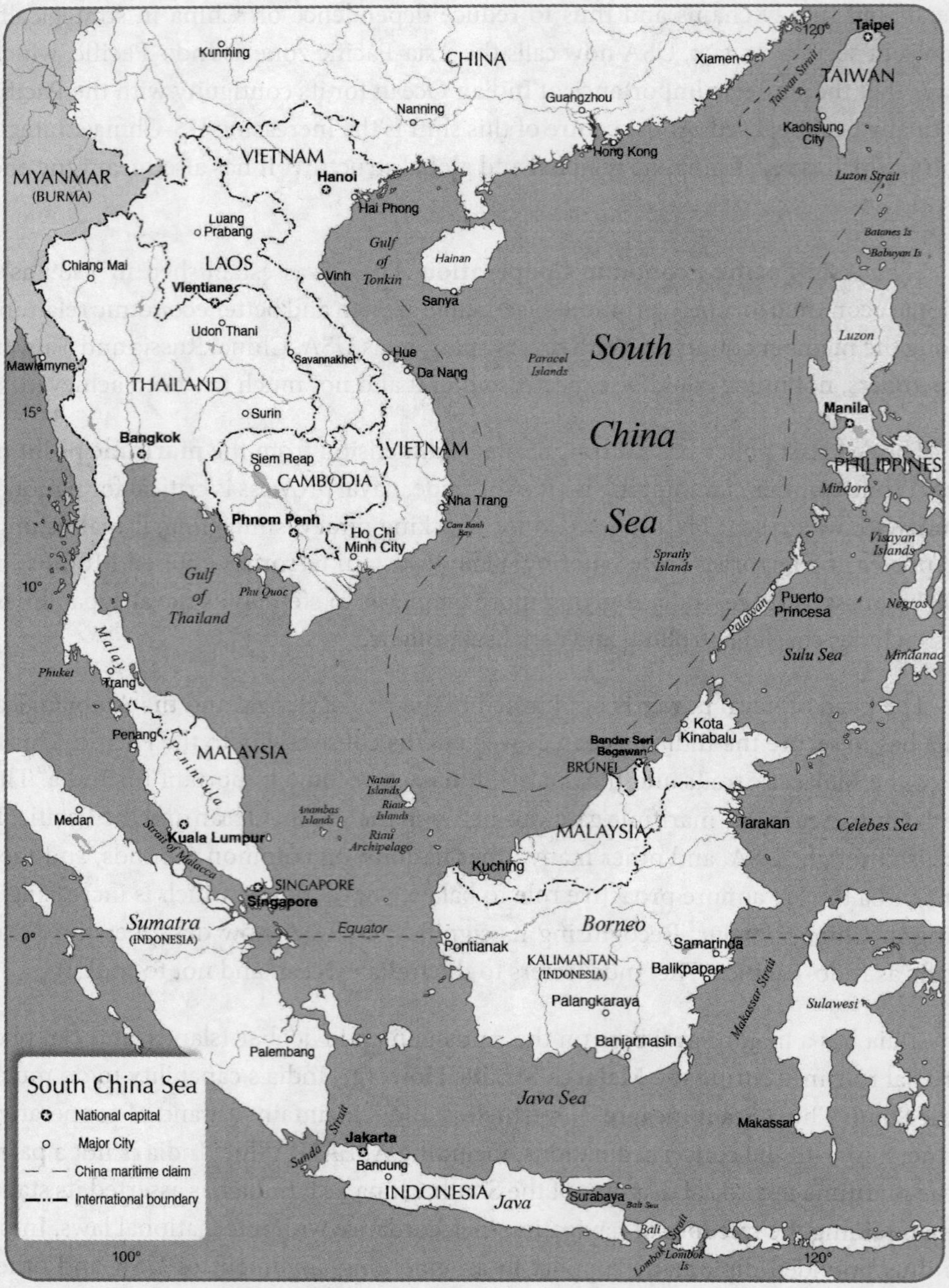


*'Blue economy' means development of fishing, seabed mining, offshore oil and gas exploration, environmental protection, maritime trade and tourism, and development of port infrastructure.

The Act East policy thus resonates well with the ASEAN because ASEAN also faces the Chinese challenge. China is aggressively pushing its influence to convert the region into its backyard. It has proclaimed the entire **South China Sea** as its own swimming pool and has also declared its aim to annex Taiwan. These threats affect all the nations of the region and this has also brought USA into the fray. With increasing rivalry between the world's two major powers, ASEAN is coming under growing pressure of a new international order.

However, ASEAN nations as a bloc are not unanimous in approach. The Philippines is the most affected and is building strategic partnership with USA. The Philippines has also purchased the Brahmos missiles recently from India as a protection from China. Vietnam and Indonesia are also very concerned but cautious in response. The others are silent on the issue because they feel that they are not affected and also do not want to confront China directly.

Division within ASEAN on the issue of Myanmar is another challenge. Myanmar is busy in a civil conflict and its military junta has made it an international outcast. While ASEAN as an organisation has banned Myanmar's military leaders from attending meetings, Indonesia and Thailand have differing views. India wants restoration of democracy in Myanmar but has avoided direct criticism of Myanmar's military rule. China is taking advantage of the situation and has embraced Myanmar.

Since ASEAN as a body lacks the ability and will to take any precipitate action on the issues, individual ASEAN members are building their own bilateral partnerships and coalitions. ASEAN members have and will inevitably continue to seek out alternative paths, whether bilaterally or multilaterally. They are also looking beyond ASEAN to have partnership with nations such as Australia, Japan, USA, UK and South Korea, and even India. India on its part has to keep strengthening its 'neighbourhood first' and 'Act East' policies.

## INDIA AND INDO-PACIFIC

Despite many efforts, India's influence in the region still remains rather limited. India and ASEAN have drawn up ambitious plans but little is coming up on ground. To an extent, this is due to India's own inconsistent internal policies, and also due to basic weakness of India in the regional and global situation. While other major powers have a more economically integrated relationship with Southeast Asia, India is yet to reach that level of compatibility.

A nation's strength rests primarily on its money power. However, **India's economic policies** continue to be a speed breaker in its growth and lack of economic reform has always been the weakest link of India's external engagement. Protectionist policies still remain well entrenched, bureaucratic inertia is as before, and procedural delays nullify the well intended initiatives. There is poor inter-ministerial coordination as reflected by the slow pace of trade negotiations with other nations. Key infrastructure projects connecting India and Southeast Asia fail to take off, or keep getting delayed. These factors prevent India from leveraging its geographic proximity and historical linkages with the Southeast Asia.

While ASEAN is India's fourth largest trading partner, the quantum of trade has been sluggish for reasons like origin rules, custom procedures, duty cuts, data sharing etc. As such, in comparison to other regional powers, India's level of economic integration with ASEAN remains modest. On the other hand, while China is India's largest trading partner, the ASEAN nations also have strong commercial links with China. Due to supply chain issues of critical high tech components, no nation can do without the other.

At the external front, India's critical challenge is from China. However, the fact is that India really cannot take the challenge head on and cannot go beyond a point. In comparison to powers as China, Japan and South Korea, India is relatively still a marginal power as regards the Far East is concerned. India needs to join hands with compatible partners in the region to meet the Chinese challenge.

**Japan** is the 4th largest economy and the most advanced Asian nation. While Japanese technology and investment has the potential to help India in upgrading its infrastructure and manufacturing sector, India's large consumer market presents opportunities to revitalise Japan's slowing economy. Japan has also helped India in building roads, bridges, Metros and industrial corridors. Japan is a major naval power and hence Indo-Japanese relationship is also strategically important. Japan has played a key role as a facilitator of India's eastward engagement. However, Japan and India are still relatively minor economic partners. Again, India's own economic policies come in way in building up this partnership to a higher level.

**Vietnam** is equally important for India, especially from the strategic point of view. Vietnam has tense relationship with China and its geostrategic position makes it a natural partner for India. However, Vietnam is also a commercial competitor of India in many sectors. As regards its issues in the South China Sea are concerned, India can do little with its limited naval power. India is more concerned about its immediate surroundings and cannot stretch its resources in the Far East. On the other hand, Vietnam has close ties with Russia and Putin visited Vietnam on 20th June 2024 and entered into a pact. This puts Vietnam in a very ambiguous position because Russia and China have become partners against the West.

**Indonesia** stands as a closer associate for India. Both are democracies with historical cultural links. Indonesia also stands out among the Muslim nations in the sense that it sees religion and culture separately. Hence, even while being a Muslim majority nation it is proud of its ancient culture which is predominantly Indian/Hindu. It was also the co-founder of the NAM. Besides being India's largest bilateral trading partner in the ASEAN, Indonesia has serious concerns about securing the Malacca and Sunda Straits. This is where India can play a role because Indian navy can resist Chinese encroachment in these waters. Closer ties with the world's largest Islamic nation would also help India internationally, especially among the Muslim nations, to build India's secular credentials and reduce concerns about the perceived Islamophobia in India.

**Australia** has encouraged India's eastward involvement and Australia-India relations are on an upward trajectory, in bilateral as well as multilateral structures. As Indian Ocean powers, it is natural for both to join hands on maritime security matters. Defence and security ties are developing and the Australia-India Civil Nuclear Cooperation Agreement of 2015 has been a milestone in this field. However, like all other white nations of the West, Australia also keeps commenting on the domestic issues of India and is also very soft on Khalistani separatists. Thus jarring notes keep emanating between the two nations.

The Russian invasion of Ukraine in 2022 has complicated the situation in Southeast Asia also. The renewed polarisation threatens to undermine the very idea of regional cooperation. The fact that rival states - USA, Russia, and China - are participants of several ASEAN initiatives is a strain on these forums. This places India in an unpleasant spot as it has ties with USA as well as Russia. As of now, India's stand of 'strategic autonomy' has played out well as both USA and Russia accept India's predicament - dependence on Russian oil and military hardware as well as the need of US investment and technology. However, how long can India maintain this position depends how the war moves forward.

## REGIONAL COMPREHENSIVE ECONOMIC COOPERATION

The RCEP was first proposed at the ASEAN summit of 2011 as a free trade deal agreement between nations within and outside ASEAN. India was also invited to join the group but opted-out. The RCEP formally came into being in 2020. The group has 15 members - Australia, Brunei, Cambodia, China, Indonesia, Japan, South Korea, Laos, Malaysia, Myanmar, New Zealand, the Philippines, Singapore, Thailand, and Vietnam. This has made RCEP the world's largest trade bloc with major Asian economies like China, Japan, and South Korea. The mandate of RCEP includes trade in goods and services, lowering of non-tariff barriers, protection of intellectual property rights, dispute settlement mechanisms, e-commerce, simplified service and investment requirements, and general economic cooperation.

After much debate, **India has decided not to join RCEP**. The given reason is that China would get a free hand in entering the Indian markets and would be the biggest gainer at India's cost. It would also be a security threat to India. Even if India tries to be selective, RCEP would give China back door entry through other member nations. Besides China, abolishing tariffs would enable other nations too to flood Indian markets affecting India's local manufacturers. India's agriculture, animal husbandry and dairy sectors may also be badly hit by cheap products from Australia and New Zealand.

While rejecting the RCEP, Modi government has declared '***Atmanirbhar Bharat***' as the national policy in all matters, including security and economy. The exact contours of the whole concept are not clear, and in the context of RCEP, the issues are debatable as well as controversial. There is no doubt that India needs to be self reliant, especially in the fields where security is at stake. Hence, the government is taking up steps to develop indigenous defence sector. India also needs to be safeguarded from threats of supply chain disruption of critical technological components and hence India has started developing the semi-conductor industry. While such measures of *Atmanirbhar Bharat* policy are vital, and should have been taken decades back, there is also an element of *swadeshi* thinking in the policy. ***Swadeshi*** could end up meaning closing doors to all outside goods, unless unavoidable. (India cannot stop importing crude oil!)

This may also end up meaning that the government has admitted that India is not in a position to compete with foreign goods and has no intention to enter into the competition. This would entail reversal of all reforms and return to the conservative insular policies of protectionism. This protection would basically be given to inefficient and low productivity low income sectors. This would be at the cost of the consumers. To take an example, free import of milk from New Zealand would reduce milk prices in India to one fifth. This would take away the livelihood of thousands of small cowherds. However, tens of millions of malnourished women and children would be able to afford milk. The options are clear, but decided by electoral politics. While the herdsmen can join hands and begin a political agitation, the malnourished masses do not even understand the issue.

Nevertheless, it is still too early to conclude how the notion of *Atmanirbhar Bharat* plays out. It can be a positive game changer as well a millstone. Non-participation in the RCEP has certainly put India at odds with many nations in general, and with Southeast Asia and Indo-Pacific in particular. They do not see India's stand as a safeguard against China - because most of the members have their own rivalry with China - but rather as a retrograde step towards protectionism. On the other hand, the government knows that isolation is detrimental and cannot be sustained in the globalised economy for long. As such, the government is negotiating free trade agreements with nations in a bilateral manner. Many of such deals have long been done and many more are under discussion. India is also negotiating FTA with the EU. This only shows the limitations of regionalism and multilateralism.

## REGIONALISM AND MULTILATERALISM

While regional cooperation provides multiple opportunities for all nations, it has rarely been successful except in the case of European Union. Even though Europe is much more homogeneous, EU also faces many problems and Britain left EU in 2020. The factors that afflicted - and still do affect - the South Asia and the Southeast Asia, and the various associations of the region are common, and as such we need to discuss the entire region in totality instead of discussing each of the body separately.

The members of the various associations in the region have a very complex relationship. Emergence from colonial rule and independence has also meant political reconfiguration and partitions. Its impact on national security perspective has shaped the concept of sovereignty in a way that is antithetical to the idea of supra nationality. Hence the spirit of regionalism has not been able to overcome that of nationalism. As such, it has not been easy to have a composite regional identity. Despite the need of trade and connectivity persisting, it has been difficult to transform the conflictual attitude of the members into that of collaboration. Political, ethnic and religious conflicts in the domestic affairs of many nations have also impacted internal stability and have been obstacles in regional cooperation.

In the present age of globalisation, **regional cooperation though unavoidable, has limitations**. Cooperation is possible only when there is scope for market driven integration. However, economic disparity among members and weak infrastructure are hurdles in economic cooperation. Further, globalisation and regionalism cannot go together very far. It's a paradox because the former means opening up while the later calls for contraction. Hence, the regional architecture is undergoing transition and regional initiatives are being challenged by newer, exclusive, and function driven initiatives like the QUAD and AUKUS (Australia-UK-USA) security pact.

Another challenge is that regional organisations are based on the principles of non-confrontation, non-intervention, and consensus. While such norms ensure longevity for bodies like ASEAN, they fail to settle disputes. Hence, nations have no other option but to resort to bilateral talks to resolve their problems. In any case, crowded platforms are not always conducive to constructive dialogue. Bilateral relations are more intimate and more confidence building because there are always issues which are better discussed in the privacy of closed doors than in open forums. Common grounds on specific issues of mutual interest can also be focussed upon more candidly in a one-to-one conversation while group discussions only lead to diluted generalisations. Hence, while regionalism and multilateralism can complement bilateralism, it can never be a substitute for it.

# Chapter IX

# India and the Middle East

The Middle East has been the hot spot of conflicts for over a century and still has the potential of being the flash point of an international crisis. In fact, after the 7th October 2023 attack by Hamas terrorists in Israel, a war is going on and what turn it would take is hard to predict. To understand the problems of the region, we need to go a bit into its history.

Most of the Middle East was a part of the vast Ottoman Empire before the outbreak of the First World War. The nations that exist today were vassal provinces of the Ottoman Empire ruled by the Turkish Sultan. These states were primarily Arab and had nothing in common with the Turks except religion. In order to sustain their loyalty, the Sultan of Turkey had anointed himself as the caliph, the supreme leader of Muslims. The peoples of the region were tribe centric and resented the rule of the non-Arab Turks. The 19th century saw rise of nationalism across Europe. It made a deep impact on the peoples of the Ottoman Empire also and the desire for self-determination and national sovereignty developed among these subjugated states.

## CREATION OF ISRAEL

When the First World War broke out, the Turkish Sultan decided to join the Central powers - Germany and Austria. Hence Britain, which had been the traditional supporter of the Ottomans, became an enemy and went about dismembering the Ottoman Empire from within. It instigated the subjugated provinces to revolt against the rule of Turkey and promised independence to the regional Arab chiefs. The Arab revolt contributed substantially to the defeat of Turkey in the war. However, the Arab states did not get independence after the war because Britain and France had decided through the secret **Sykes-Picot Agreement 1916** to partition the provinces of the

Ottoman Empire in their respective spheres of influence after the war. Neither the aspirations of the peoples for self determination, nor the promises made to the Arab leaders, were taken care of.

Having won the war, while France took control over Syria and Lebanon, the British divided the region under their control into the Emirate of Transjordan and Palestine. However, the Arabs resented the dominance of infidel powers over the predominantly Muslim Middle East and felt that Britain had gone back on its pledges to provide them independence.

During the war another development had taken place. In order to gain support of the Jews in the Middle East, as well as of the influential Jewish community in USA, the British foreign minister Arthur Balfour had issued a statement - the **Balfour Declaration** - in November 1917 in which the British government pledged for the creation of a Jewish homeland in Palestine. Jews were peoples without a nation and for long had suffered anti-Semitic pogroms and persecution in Europe. They had always dreamt of returning to the Biblical 'Promised Land' of Israel - the place of origin of the Jews - and had been seeking a state of their own. This had taken the shape of a Zionist movement in Europe. Soon after the end of the war, a large number of Jews of Europe began migrating to Palestine because they believed that the British would create a Jewish state in Palestine. They also began purchasing land from the locals for settlements.

While Palestine as a whole was largely an Arab Muslim province, for long there had been no conflict between the Jews and the Muslims. Islam and Judaism shared much in common and the handful of Jews in Palestine had lived in harmony with the Arab Muslims for centuries. However, arrival of a large number of Jews in Palestine started creating racial and religious tensions. Arrival of Jews increased significantly after Hitler took over power in Germany and Jewish settlements increased. This influx of Jews began altering the religious demography of the region. It led to increasing resistance by the Palestinian Arabs and there were violent clashes between the Arabs and the Jews. These clashes provoked the **Jews to form militant groups** and they began procuring arms from all over the world to fight the Arabs. All the while, the British administration in Palestine treated such conflicts as law and order problems and tried to remain neutral.

The Palestinians had always resented the British rule, and now resented it even more because the British administration seemed to be conniving with the Jews. This provoked a series of Arab revolts during 1936–1939. The revolts were however suppressed by the British forces, not because the British administration had any sympathy for the Jews, or antipathy towards the Arabs, but simply to maintain law and order.

However, since tension in the region was increasing because of immigration, Britain adopted a policy of **limiting Jewish immigration** and prohibited land purchases. Occupation of Palestine was also proving to be an unproductive headache for Britain, and as such, the government declared its intent to end its control over Palestine after ten years. Since this would have led to an Arab majority Palestinian state, the Jews opposed it. These decisions also contradicted the spirit of the Balfour Declaration. Thus, relations between the Zionists and British administrators in Palestine soured at this juncture. The Jews further strengthened their militant organisations as they realised that they were on their own now, and could expect no help from the British government anymore. It was to be a fight for their survival. The British administrators tried to curb Zionist militant activities and this led to direct clashes between the Jewish militant groups and the British forces.

Up till this stage there was little or no public sympathy for the Jewish cause in the western world. This dramatically changed after the Second World War. The horrid tales of **Jewish holocaust** that emerged after the end of the war created a general feeling of commiseration for the Zionist cause around the world. There was also a feeling of guilt that the world community had failed to protect the Jews. While the Jews in Palestine now vociferously demanded creation of a Jewish state, Britain - because of its own strategic and economic interests in the Middle East - did not want to antagonise the whole Arab world. As such, Britain refused to permit any further immigration of Jews. This led to eruption of even more clashes between the Arabs, the Jews, and the British forces. Britain increasingly found the situation untenable and wanted a way to somehow get out of the region.

The problem remained as to whom the British government should hand over the charge of Palestine. As such, Britain requested the United Nations to decide upon the fate of the region. On November 29, 1947, the UN General Assembly voted to **partition Palestine** into a Jewish state and an Arab state in such a way that each state would have a majority of its own population. The Holy cities of Jerusalem and Bethlehem were to be in an internationally administered zone.

While the Zionist leadership accepted the UN partition plan, the Palestinian Arabs and the neighbouring Arab states rejected the UN plan. These states - Egypt, Iraq, Transjordan, Lebanon, Saudi Arabia, and Syria - had formed an organisation called as the **Arab League** in March 1945. They questioned the very basis of formation of a Jewish nation in what for centuries had been an Arab territory. Thus clashes erupted between the Arabs and the Jews. By this time the Zionist militant groups had become very well armed and well trained, and the Arabs proved to be no match to the well organised and well equipped Jewish militia. In no time the Jewish forces took control over the territory allotted to the Jewish state in the UN plan, and even started extending their control on territories beyond the nominated borders. Unable and unwilling to control this anarchical situation, the British abruptly vacated Palestine in May 1948, and the Zionist leaders proclaimed independence of the State of Israel.

## ARAB-ISRAEL CONFLICTS

Immediately after the declaration of independence by Israel, the Arab League states attacked Israel. Not only the Israeli armed forces overwhelmed the invading Arab armies, it even conquered additional territories. The war was terminated by an **armistice in 1949** whereby Palestine was divided into three segments. While the State of Israel retained most of its territory, East Jerusalem and the West Bank were given to Jordan, and the Gaza Strip was given to Egypt. No independent Palestinian Arab state was recognised. While independence of Israel was recognised by United Nations, and also by most of the countries across the world, the Arab countries continued not to recognise the existence of Israel and tensions continued after the armistice of 1949. It was the period of escalating Cold War and thus the Middle East also got segmented into American and Soviet camps. While USA espoused the cause of Israel, Soviet Union developed close relations with the Arab nations.

In 1953, an army coup ended the monarchy in Egypt and **Gamal Abdel Nasser** became the President. In order to secure his position in Egypt, he tried to project himself as the champion of Arab cause, and asserted Egypt's leadership in the Arab world. For this it was necessary to reduce British influence in the Middle East. Thus he started an anti-imperialist campaign and developed close military relationship with USSR. To further strengthen his credentials in the Arab world, Nasser declared nationalisation of the Suez Canal Company in 1956 which was jointly owned by Britain and France. This led to a conflict as Britain and France, along with Israeli forces intervened.

While the Egyptian army was badly beaten at the war front, USA was apprehensive of an armed intervention by Soviet Union. USA had established extensive interests in oil in the region and did not want a conflict that would allow USSR to establish a foothold in the Middle East. In order to avoid the hostilities into escalating into a major war, USA made UNO to intervene. Britain and France were asked by the UNO to withdraw their forces. Despite having suffered serious military setbacks, this was considered as a great victory for Egypt in the Arab world, and Nasser appeared to be the leader of a pan-Arab coalition against western imperialism. This encouraged Nasser to take more drastic steps.

Since no definite peace treaty had been reached between Egypt and Israel, both the nations continued to be hostile to each other. Surging with over confidence after the Suez success, Nasser planned with Syria, Jordan, Lebanon and Iraq for a joint attack on Israel. However, in a surprise assault on 5th June 1967, the Israeli air force destroyed the entire Egyptian air force on ground. In the **Six-day War** that followed, the Egyptian,

Syrian and Jordanian armies were conclusively beaten back. Israel captured the West Bank from Jordan, Gaza Strip and the Sinai Peninsula from Egypt, and the Golan Heights from Syria. Thus Israel expanded from its original size by almost two times and the military prowess of Israel was clearly established.

After another inconclusive war in 1973, Egypt made peace with Israel in March 1979. By this treaty, Israel agreed to withdraw its armed forces from the Sinai Peninsula, while Egypt agreed to keep the peninsula as a demilitarised zone. Jordan renounced its claim over the West Bank in 1988. Thus the Palestinian cause seemed to have been given up

## THE PALESTINIAN PROBLEM

While the Arab nations had made an uneasy peace with Israel, the issue of Palestinians remained unresolved. As a result of the wars, a large number of Palestinians became refugees. They were scattered in Jordan, Lebanon, Syria, Saudi Arabia and the Gulf states, and lived in refugee camps. Except for Jordan no other Arab state accepted them as citizens. This was ostensibly so because giving them citizenship would dilute their right to an independent Palestine. The truth was that the entire Arab world was so sharply divided on tribal and racial lines that no Arab state wanted to have the Palestinians. They were treated as a problem, and cause of wars that had inflicted heavy losses to the Arab states. The presence of Palestinian refugees in Lebanon also caused a prolonged civil war during 1975–1991 which led to the formation of a terrorist group Hezbollah which started running a parallel government in Lebanon.

Palestine was no more a nation, but only a notion, a state with a long history but **without a political geography**. While Israel was a healthy reality, the idea of an independent Arab Palestine had become a non-issue for the world community. The Arab world had given up on Palestine, except for occasional ceremonial and symbolic pledges of support. No one wanted another war with Israel for the sake of Palestinians. There were enough wars to fight within the Arab world, and enough of internal problems for the states to confront.

During the period, the **Palestinian Liberation Organisation** - a body formed by the Arab League in 1964 - became the sole champion of the Palestinian cause. Led by Yasser Arafat, the PLO indulged a series of terrorist attacks on the Israelis. The Arab nations were divided but wanted peace and an end to the violence as PLO activities were affecting them as well. This led to a series of secret peace talks in Oslo, Norway, between the concerned nations as well as the PLO. In August 1993, the Israeli and PLO negotiators came to certain agreements, known as the **Oslo Accords**, which were signed in Washington. By these accords, the PLO recognised the state of Israel and gave up violence. Israel in turn recognised PLO as the legitimate and sole representative of the Palestinian people. It also accepted Palestinian self-rule in the occupied West Bank and committed to withdraw from the Gaza Strip. In a way, it was intended to pave the way for establishment of an independent Palestinian state on the 1967 borders, with East Jerusalem as its capital.

The PLO reorganised itself and took the shape of the **Palestinian National Authority** for the purpose of self governance of the Palestinian territories in the West Bank and the Gaza Strip. The Israeli troops pulled out of Gaza in 2005 and the Gaza Strip was formally handed over to the Palestinian Authority.

Certain Palestinians were however not happy with this arrangement. Thus, another militant organisation came to be formed called as the **Hamas** in the Gaza Strip. It was a mix of an armed group and a political party. It aimed to destroy the state of Israel and create a Palestinian state governed by Islamic laws.

The Palestinian Authority (PA) was to be a democratically elected government. In the elections of 2006, the Hamas won in the Gaza Strip while the ruling party Fatah won in the West Bank. This led to a split by which while PA administered only the West Bank, Gaza virtually became a separate state ruled by the Hamas. While Hamas established a dictatorial Islamic regime in Gaza which was determined to annihilate Israel, the PA followed a policy of peacefully dealing with the government of Israel.

While Hamas kept attacking Israel from time to time, and Israel retaliated with severity, the Palestinian Authority could do nothing. The split between Hamas and the PA thus also broke the spirit of the Oslo Accords. While the foreign governments largely recognised the PA, most of the western nations declared Hamas as a terrorist organisation. Only a few nations kept relations with the Hamas and some secretly provided it with arms and funds. In order to check this, Israel imposed severe controls over Gaza. It restricted Gaza's airspace, borders, cellular frequencies, coastal waters, and electricity supply. Egypt collaborated with Israel in cordoning Gaza as it did not want Palestinians to infiltrate into its region. This hardened the Hamas stand to destroy Israel.

Meanwhile, the situation in the **West Bank** also was no better. The Palestinians lived in enclaves, rather in enclosures: They were residents inside Israel but not its citizens. The Palestinian Authority depended on Israel for everything as Israel controlled the movement of goods and peoples. Israel imposed stringent restrictions including military checkpoints and impregnable barrier walls. The Israelis also began establishing settlements in the West Bank which was something like annexation of the territory. Hence the very idea of a separate Palestinian state vaporised.

The Palestinian Authority cooperated with Israel in much of this as it was no more a democratic body. No elections were held after 2006 and the West Bank governance became one-party one-leader authoritarianism. The PA in fact used Israeli forces to curb its own citizens. It was also seen as a corrupt body that was not supporting the Palestinian cause of self-governance. In fact, the Palestinian Authority had lost authority over the Palestinians. This led to violence in the West Bank also.

## THE GAZA CRISIS

Meanwhile some more Arab nations worked for peace in the region. USA played a key role in facilitating the overtures which led to the signing of the **Abraham Accords** in 2020. The name 'Abraham' symbolised the shared territorial heritage and the common religious descent of Judaism, Islam, and Christianity. It was a series of agreements to normalise relations between Israel and some Arab states. This consisted of a general declaration and bilateral agreements between Israel, the United Arab Emirates, Bahrain, Sudan, and Morocco. The nations agreed to have diplomatic relations and collaborate in a diverse spectrum of sectors including security. The declaration spoke about the following ideals:

- Respect for human dignity and freedom, including religious freedom.
- Promotion of interfaith and intercultural dialogue to advance a culture of peace.
- Cooperation and dialogue for friendly relations among nations and lasting peace in the Middle East.
- Tolerance and respect for every person irrespective of race, faith or ethnicity.
- Support for science, art, medicine, and commerce to maximise human potential and bring nations closer.
- End of radicalisation and conflict to provide a better future for all.
- Pursue a vision of peace, security, and prosperity in the Middle East and around the world.

The ideals of the Abraham Accords were fundamental to Islam, Christianity and Judaism but were totally opposite of what the Hamas was pursuing. It felt that the Arab world has abandoned the Palestinian cause. Iran also did not want such a grouping to come up in the Arab world as it would be a challenge to its own power. Hence, Iran began providing arms and funds to the Hamas in a big way. Iran also brought the Hezbollah and Houthis to join hands with the Hamas. Emboldened thus by Iran's support, the Hamas made a surprise attack by land, sea, and air, on Israel on 7th October 2023. Over a thousand Israelis, mostly civilians, were killed while some 250 of them, including elderly women and children were abducted. In retaliation, Israel started a full scale war in Gaza.

**The attack by Hamas** holds the prospect to undo whatever little the Abraham Accords have achieved and has put the entire region into turmoil. Israel is determined to exterminate Hamas because it poses an existential threat to the Jewish state. Progressive Arab states like UAE, Saudi Arabia, and Egypt, do not want Hamas to gain power as radicalism is a threat to peace and prosperity of these nations. At the same time, they do not want to be seen to be sitting silent over Israel's decimation of a Muslim region, which has caused death of thousands of women and children. Egypt is particularly worried about the likely exodus of Gaza refugees into its territory. Iran wants to keep the region on boil for its own strategic ends. The Iranian regime is also facing opposition from its own peoples due its repressive religious policies and hence wants to divert national attention towards an Islamic cause.

While the western nations have no sympathy for Hamas, they also are disturbed by the killings of the civilians. More than that, these nations have sizeable Muslim population and they are demanding the government to act against Israel in order to stop the war. While they may not amount to much in terms of votes, western governments are afraid that inaction on their part would increase Islamic radicalisation and would lead to terrorism. Hence, many of the nations are also putting pressure on Israel to agree to a ceasefire. But Israel seeks a final solution.

The question is what is the solution? The Palestinian issue needs to be addressed to in totality. One way forward is the oft suggested '**Two state solution**'. However, since Hamas, Iran, a section of Palestinians, and certain terrorist groups, are not willing to accept the very idea of existence of the state of Israel, Israel also cannot agree to the creation of an independent state of Palestine which would be a constant threat to its own existence. In any case, Israel has occupied so much of territory in the West Bank through new settlements that there is no space left for creation of a Palestinian state.

Another issue is as to **who governs the Palestinian state**, especially the Gaza Strip? The Palestinian Authority has lost its grip in the West Bank and has no control in Gaza. It has become unpopular and is seen as a subcontractor to Israel in maintaining the military occupation. The Palestinians are so divided over the issue that they have made themselves incapable of self governance. The various factions and outside forces would also not let them join hands for self rule. An independent Palestinian state would neither be financially self sufficient, nor politically stable, nor militarily defensible.

One solution can be that a consortium of neighbouring states takes control of the region, and in collaboration with Israel, develops institutions for self governance, at least in Gaza. However, no nation wants to get too directly involved in administrating the region as it has multiple implications. It's too hot a potato to handle and the solution may be worse than the problem. In any case, much of Gaza has been reduced to rubble and no nation would like to take the onus of governing it because it has become ungovernable.

The other option is that the UNO takes this charge. But would this be acceptable to the involved parties? On the other hand, UNO's role in the whole affair has not been fair. Antonio Guterres, the current Secretary-General of UNO, has been critical of Israel but has not said a word about Hamas. In fact, several workers of UNRWA (The *United Nations Relief and Works Agency* for Palestine) participated in the terrorist attack!

## THE MIDDLE EAST TODAY

Peace still eludes the Middle East because of the multiple conflicts that plague the region. The Arab world is today at war with itself. This is a region that defies solution and remains in turmoil because of the policies initiated by the British and other European governments, because of its oil wealth, and because of religious radicalism.

US intervention in the region has only made the situation worse and the two Iraq wars have turned it into a virtual inferno. While the first invasion of Iraq by USA in 1991 was justified to some extent, because Iraq had invaded and annexed Kuwait, the second invasion of 2003 was falsely justified on the myth of 'Weapons of mass destruction' that Iraq was presumed to have developed. The stockpiles of WMDs were never discovered but Iraq got divided between Shia and Sunni segments, and the whole region has become a battle ground of conflicts between several players.

The loss of central authority of the government of Iraq has only helped entry of ISIS in the region. The Kurds have also taken advantage and have created their own autonomous state. This has brought Turkey also into the conflict because it has a sizeable Kurd population that wants independence from Turkey. USA has similarly destabilised Libya also by removing Gaddafi. Tyrants like Gaddafi and Saddam Hussein were at least keeping the states intact. The loss of central authority has only led to chaos.

The **Shia-Sunni conflict** that started since the inception of Islam continues to divide the region. Iran as the major Shia power is at loggerheads with Saudi Arabia, the bastion of Sunni Islam. Iran supports militant groups as Hezbollah that keeps Lebanon in turmoil, and supports the Houthis who have started a civil war in Yemen and are now entering the Gaza conflict. Iran also keeps threatening both Israel and USA and its desire to become a nuclear power has only added to the tensions.

Saudi Arabia has allied with USA since long, and although it still has not officially recognised Israel, it has maintained a policy of not getting involved in any conflict with Israel. As a worldwide promoter of Wahabi Islam, it funds militant groups outside but has to contain them inside. Syria wants to get back Golan Heights which it lost during the 1967 war, but the Syrian government is fighting for its own survival. The civil war and the ISIS have reduced much of Syria to rubble and what with USA and Russia fighting a proxy war on its land, its future is uncertain. Lebanon is besieged with the problematic Hezbollah, a militant anti-Israel Shia Islamist group funded by Iran. While Saudi Arabia dictates much of Lebanon's policy, it is in no position to do anything except to survive on oil and US armour. Jordan has made peace with Israel but has the problem of housing the largest concentration of Palestinians refugees.

While the millions sheltered in the refugee camps across the region present a humanitarian crisis of staggering proportions, people are finding their own solution by **immigrating to Europe**. This carries the seeds of a much bigger problem for future. These migrants carry with them the trauma of bloody conflicts as well as a strong dose of religious bigotry. Many of them may be fanatics too. With their numbers increasing, sympathy for the refugees is getting replaced by apprehension, even revulsion. Migration is being perceived as a reverse crusade, a peaceful and silent Islamic invasion for which the European nations are neither prepared, nor have an answer.

Coming from a deeply orthodox culture these migrants are unlikely to ever get assimilated into the liberal Christian Europe. In order to maintain their cultural identity, they would themselves make no effort to integrate with the western society. They would live in segregated groups and would continue to sustain a sense of injustice living in a nation in which they are not welcome, and hence would have no stake for peace in the society of their immigration. They are only likely to nurture more of fundamentalism, become radicals and take to extremism. This would be one of the most formidable challenges for Europe in the times to come. The victory of the far right parties in the EU elections of June 2024 indicates how Europe intends to deal with this challenge.

## RISE OF ISLAMIC FUNDAMENTALISM

The 20th century saw the rise and revival of Islamic fundamentalism in the Middle East. Breakup of the Ottoman Empire, the subsequent/consequent creation of Israel as a nation state, the autocratic structure of governance of the newly independent states, their oil-wealth, and hence, western interest and interventions in the region, and the influence of the entrenched Muslim clergy over the poor and uneducated masses, were the factors that contributed to this development.

When the First World War broke out, the British aroused Arab nationalism in order to defeat the Ottoman Empire, and provoked the Arabs to rise in revolt against the rule of Turkey. British interest was purely political and strategic, and not religious. Europeans had long given up on the idea of Crusades. However, the conservative clergy has a propensity to see and depict every issue from a religious angle. Hence, they portrayed the Arab revolt as a Christian ploy to subjugate the Muslim world by making the Muslims fight among themselves and kill each other, which is against the tenets of Islam. Nevertheless, nationalism and anti-Turkish feelings prevailed over religious sentiments because the Middle East provinces wanted to be free of Turkish yoke. However, after the war was over, the peoples realised that instead of getting independence, they had come under the **rule of infidels**. European control over the region during the inter-war period confirmed the view of the clerics and was resented alike by the moderate nationalists and the religious conservatives.

Shortly after the end of the Second World War, the entire Middle East became free of colonial rule. While it was a matter to be rejoiced by the Arabs, the simultaneous creation of a Jewish state in the middle of what was predominantly a Muslim region became a sore point for the Arab nationalists as well as the conservative Muslims. Successive victories of Israel over Arab nations and the unequivocal support of USA to Israel made things worse. Thus, the moderate nationalists as well as the conservative fundamentalists turned against the policies and presence of western nations in the region.

The newly independent nations of the Middle East adopted different policies as far as religion was concerned. While some tried to adopt a semblance of Sharia laws, especially where curbing freedom of women was concerned, many others went about modernising their countries, as Turkey had done. Such governments adopted secular ideals of nationalism and religion was left to the clerics who had no role in state matters.

However, despite the wide variations in policies regarding religion within this plethora of nations, there were a few features that were common to all. Except for Israel, none of the new states that came into being was liberal or democratic. These were ruled by kings, sheikhs and sultans, military generals or single-party political dictators. Most of them had been put in place by western powers and depended on them for survival. Another common feature was that independence of these states was accompanied with **oil wealth**, and many of these nations became extremely rich. However, wealth remained concentrated in a few hands. As such, money and power were shared among a coterie of leaders, largely the family members of the ruling dispensations. They lived in opulent style in luxurious palaces, bought prime properties and yachts in Europe and America where they also spent a considerable time enjoying all the pleasures that the West has to offer.

**Exploration and export of oil** needed technical expertise, logistic support, and commercial infrastructure. Since the Arab states had neither of these, it was left in the hands of European and American private corporations as well as governments. The rulers of these states had no choice but to work in close collaboration with the western governments and private oil companies to exploit oil wealth. While this enriched the states and also helped in development of these nations on western pattern, it also added to corruption at the apex level. Since USA had a crucial economic stake in the region, it supported many of these dictatorial regimes. It was also easier to do business with corrupt autocrats than with unstable democracies. In 1953, Britain and USA conspired to overthrow the democratic government of Iran because the elected prime minister wanted to nationalise a private British oil company. After the coup, the nominal Shah of Iran became a dictatorial king.

While democracy was not adopted by any of the nations, the rulers appeased the poor and uneducated masses by adopting a policy of heavily subsiding everything with the money they had. Even though the people had no voice in governance, millions of Arabs were kept satisfied that they could live comfortably without doing any work. This created a basic contradiction in the evolving socio-political structure of states like Iran. On one hand it was materially progressing and turning European in character. Hijab had been banned and women wore skirts. Basic goods were available at cheap prices. At the same time it was being ruled by a despot who controlled the press and used police to ruthlessly suppress all forms of dissent. Modernisation was thus being done under the supervision of a primitive model of governance.

**Subsidies also affected the work culture** in these nations as productivity, skill development and education got neglected. The states made little efforts in this direction because the locals were not even needed for creation of oil-wealth. While the high-tech work was being done by western corporations, the menial work was done by migrant labour, largely Muslims from countries like India, Pakistan, Bangladesh, etc. While these migrant workers lived in ghettos and bunkers, often kept as captives and paid low wages, the westerners were permitted to establish exclusive enclaves where they lived with their families in an artificially created western environment. Presence of a very large number of western experts - technicians, engineers and related personnel - brought western culture also into the Middle East. To the conservatives it appeared as if western governments and oil giants, in connivance with the corrupt rulers have again taken over their country. While retaining political sovereignty was the issue for the nationalists, retaining cultural identity was the issue for the conservatives.

A section among the Muslims saw the spread of western way of life with alarm, as corruption of the pristine Islamic values. These conservatives perceived modernisation as western political hegemony and as a **cultural domination of Europeans over the Muslims** because culture and religion are synonymous for Muslim fundamentalists. They considered modernisation on western pattern as a deviation from the true spirit of Islam, and the cause of Muslim subjugation. Hence, they began opposing the socio-political changes that were leading to a cultural transformation of the Islamic society. These fundamentalists were particularly against the growing freedom among women. To preserve Islamic identity, they wanted the states to adopt Islamic laws and to force the Muslims to return to the traditional tenets of Islam. They were also opposed to the idea of parochial nationalism because it only divided the Muslim community and was contrary to the Islamic concept of fraternal internationalism, that all Muslims formed one nation.

The Islamic world thus underwent through a phase of re-awakening and organisations like the **Muslim Brotherhood** came up in Egypt to educate people how westernisation was corrupting the Muslim society. The leaders of Muslim Brotherhood propagated that western culture and Islam were incompatible. They also held that Muslims were again being colonised by the West and were being corrupted by its permissive and promiscuous culture. They rejected western institutions and held democracy in contempt because in their view only Allah was sovereign, not the peoples' representatives on earth. They adopted an anti-establishment, anti-western, and anti-American stand. Israel was portrayed as an enemy of Islam and liberation of Palestine was made a duty for all Muslims to fight and die for. The ruling regimes were seen as corrupt and immoral and became the first targets of these non-state actors.

The ruling regimes saw this rise of fundamentalism with apprehension. Thus, in 1969 some fifty odd countries established the **Organisation of Islamic Cooperation** with the aim of protecting the interests of Muslims. Their declared goal was to promote international peace and harmony through inter-faith dialogue. However, the real purpose was to control and channelize radicalism at home. While rulers like those of Saudi Arabia co-opted Islamic fundamentalists and used Islam as a source of legitimacy, many others tried to curb fundamentalism. What was common to all nations was that the rulers wanted to retain political power and maintain stability at all costs. Since all the regimes were essentially **police states**, they used the power of the state to suppress freedom and muzzle dissent, alike of the fundamentalists who wanted implementation of Sharia as well as of the moderates who wanted democracy. They used the army, the secret services, the police, and the bureaucracy as instruments of repression through which opposition could be silenced. This made the masses vulnerable to the teachings of radical leaders who exploited their poverty and lack of education to further their agenda. Thus the ruling regimes unwittingly undermined the forces of moderation and strengthened fundamentalism.

In January 1979, the oppressive **regime of Shah of Iran was overthrown** because he was seen as a stooge of USA who was corrupting the Islamic society through westernisation. Thereafter, a deeply theocratic anti-American regime led by conservative orthodox clerics took charge of Iran. However, being deeply religious and sternly opposed to modernisation, the new regime was equally intolerant on political, social or religious matters. As a result, instead of liberating the Iranian peoples, the revolution deprived them of their basic human rights. Women were the worst sufferers as they lost all their freedom, and to the outside world it seemed as if the entire revolution was aimed only at enslaving the women. To win the loyalty of the people, the regime declared Iran as an Islamic Republic. This encouraged the fundamentalists the world over, and in order to placate them, many otherwise secular democratic governments of Muslim majority nations - like Bangladesh - adopted the tag of 'Islamic' republic.

## RADICALISM TO TERRORISM

The Islamic revolution of Iran was a major setback for USA. The subsequent siege of US embassy in Teheran, during which the US staff personnel were held hostage for 444 days made USA a prime target of the fundamentalists. Subsequent US actions in the region only triggered more reaction, more hostility towards USA, and fundamentalism took the shape of radicalism.

In December 1979, the Soviet army invaded Afghanistan to rescue the pro-Soviet regime in power. In order to check Soviet control over Afghanistan, USA helped in the formation an Afghan militia force called as the Mujahideen. Muslims of many nations joined the Mujahideen and USA provided weapons and money. The war against the Soviets contributed to the emergence of **al Qaida** in Saudi Arabia, an extremist group led by Osama bin Laden. The Saudi regime proscribed the group because Osama was a staunch critic of the Saudi monarchy. Hence, Osama shifted to Afghanistan. The war in Afghanistan continued for years and ultimately in 1989, the Afghan Mujahidin, in collaboration with al Qaida, forced the Soviet army to retreat. During the same period, Pakistan also intervened and with active US help created an extremist group known as the Taliban. This led to a civil war in Afghanistan and by 1996 the Taliban had taken total control over Afghanistan.

Meanwhile, in August 1990 Iraq invaded and occupied Kuwait. This was not acceptable to many of the Arab nations, particularly Saudi Arabia. Thus USA, being an ally of Saudi Arabia, intervened and led a multi-national invasion of Iraq in January 1991 and Kuwait was liberated. The First Gulf War and subsequent imposition of economic sanctions on Iraq led to widespread poverty and deaths. Even though Muslim nations like Saudi Arabia were a part of the coalition, the fundamentalists saw this as yet another attempt by USA to subjugate a Muslim nation. While USA was entirely guided by economic strategy, the radicals saw and portrayed it from a purely religious point of view.

Since the Saudi regime was a close ally of USA, and Osama was hostile to the Saudi ruling family, **USA also became a target** for Osama. He wanted USA to get out of the region. To send his message to USA, Osama organised bombings of US embassies in Tanzania and Kenya in 1998. This made al Qaeda, and especially Osama bin Laden, a prime target for USA. Since bin Laden was at that time a guest of the Taliban in Afghanistan, USA demanded Kabul that Osama be handed over to USA for trial. While the Taliban refused to accept the demand, Osama plotted the attack on Twin Towers of the World Trade Centre on 11th September 2001. This made USA to invade Afghanistan in October. By December 2001, the Taliban had been overthrown and a US supported Afghan government was installed.

USA made '**war on terror**' a policy matter and on the same pretext invaded and occupied Iraq in 2003. This only made the radicals to turn more hostile to USA and acts of terrorism against USA, as well as against all nations and societies considered as allies of USA increased. At the same time, extremist organisations like ISIS came up. These radical groups used terror within the Muslim nations to force the governments - and the peoples at large - to adopt strict Islamic laws and practices. As a result, most of those killed by Muslim terrorists were Muslims. In order to prevent radicalism at home, a number of Muslim regimes began to court the conservatives. This was also to make them act as a countervailing force against the moderate nationalists who wanted democracy and accompanied freedom of speech, liberation of women, and respect for human rights.

The **tussle between the moderate liberals and conservative fundamentalists** continues to haunt the Muslim world today. While the liberals talk about development and prosperity, these appear to be vague and unfulfilled promises to the masses. On the other hand, the radicals manipulate the poor and the uneducated. They do not promise anything in the present life but assure people of pleasures of heaven in the afterlife. To achieve the same, they preach that a true Muslim must obey the orders of the religious leaders, fight and kill the infidels, and if necessary, die. They also want their governments to join in this holy cause. However, the ruling regimes are unable to decide the way forward. They can neither join the radicals nor can they support the moderates beyond a point.

Hence, radicalism is the grumpy elephant in the room of these rulers. Since they cannot remove it by force, they have given it a comfortable sofa to sit. They occasionally feed it as well so that it remains quiet. But the elephant wants more space to move about and throw its weight around and raise its voice. And it has plenty to weight to throw around. The rulers will pretend to ignore it, and even deny that it is really there as long as they can.

Radicalism is on the rise in many parts of the world wherever there is a sizeable Muslim population. Where they are in a minority, the fundamentalists become great champions of democracy. They demand all types of freedoms: freedom to practice their religious laws in personal matters, freedom to have separate schools - madrassas - for children, freedom to propagate religion, and even freedom to preach separatism and subversion. They also resist the ordinary Muslim from getting integrated with the majority mainstream. However, where they are able to capture power, as in Afghanistan, they impose draconian restrictions and implement strict Sharia laws.

Radicalism can be checked only by the Muslim world, not by outsiders, and certainly not by 'war on terror'. This **needs empowerment of the moderates**. And of the women too! However, without the freedom that a liberal democracy provides, the moderates can never gain the strength to check radicalism. Lack of freedom prevents the moderates from even entering into a constructive dialogue with the masses. Liberal democracy however is as much a threat to the ruling regimes as the extremism of the radicals. It is a dilemma for these regimes as they want to curb radicalism but do not want to give power to the people.

The Arab nations are also realising that total dependence on oil money is not sustainable. With climate change becoming a major issue, fossil fuels are getting replaced by renewable sources of energy. With better technology they are also becoming cheaper. At the same time, autocracy is also not sustainable indefinitely. Nor is perpetual enslavement of women. Certainly not in this age of Internet and mass media! Conservative theocracy cannot go along with modern scientific thought and technology, and without technology, nations cannot survive. Rather, the people will not permit such governments to survive. A handful of fundamentalists cannot hold the entire community hostage to their imaginary ideals and the Muslim world cannot remain insulated from rest of the world. Globalisation has made it imperative for nations and societies to integrate. Agitations against the regime have started in Iran, led by women. Ultimately, the Arab world will have to decide its own course of action.

## INDIA AND THE MIDDLE EAST

India's trade relations with the Middle East go back to several centuries. People to people contacts continued during the British rule as Britain had colonised Egypt. After Independence, Nehru's approach towards the region was one of benign neglect. The newly independent nations of the Middle East were underdeveloped small nations and in constant conflict. Nehru stood for anti-colonialism and socialism and hence was at odds with the western nations which had developed deep inroads into the region because of their oil wealth. As regards the Arab-Israel conflict was concerned, Nehru took the cause of Palestine and opposed Israel at every forum. This was primarily to gain Muslim votes in the domestic electoral politics. However, that did not earn India the confidence of the Muslim nations and they consistently supported Pakistan against India.

India's ideological espousal for democracy was another hurdle because except for Israel - with which Nehru decided not to have diplomatic relations - no other state of the region was democratic. The states were ruled by autocratic monarchs and military dictators. The ideology of non-alignment also did not matter because no nation was truly non-aligned. Hence, for decades India had no political or economic presence in the Middle East and the region was merely a source of crude oil for India.

However, the situation had started to change from the early 1970s. Since Syria, Jordan, and Lebanon were poorer states and involved in their own problems, 6 nations of the Persian Gulf - Bahrain, Kuwait, Oman, Qatar, Saudi Arabia, and the United Arab Emirates (UAE) - formed their own body called as the **Gulf Cooperation Council** (GCC) in 1981. These were oil rich and progressive states and more concerned about economic development than about regional and religious conflicts. These states started infrastructure modernisation with the immense Petro-dollars they were earning. [Egypt was not a GCC member but closely associated with the GCC.]

While western companies were managing the development projects, they needed workforce that could toil in extreme heat on low wages. It was at this juncture that unskilled as well as semi-skilled Indians began working in the GCC States in a big way. Their remittances helped India in terms of foreign currency and hence the Gulf began to gain importance for India. More and more Indians went to the Gulf for earning good money. Soon, the Indian workforce was not merely of blue collar labourers but also of high tech skilled professionals in the construction and services sectors like transport, finance, general management, medicals, education, etc. Thus Indian presence in the Gulf States swelled many times. Since these nations could not have done without Indian workers and professionals, their perception about India began to change.

Having been beaten repeatedly by Israel in wars, the Middle East nations had realised the futility of armed confrontation. They had lost the appetite for wars with Israel which could not be won. USA was a prime player in the region. On one hand, USA gave unstinted support to Israel as far as security was concerned, and on the other hand, USA was deeply involved in the economic development in the region - not by aid, but by using the petrodollars of these very nations. The **Gulf States needed peace for economic development** and USA facilitated scaling down of the conflict in a phased manner through various bilateral treaties and the Oslo Accords. There thus came about an ideological shift in the Gulf States - from religion and regionalism to that of prosperity and nationalism. They were also getting concerned about the growing radicalisation within their states which could only be countered by improving the material quality of life of the people.

Meanwhile, P.V. Narsimha Rao had become the Prime Minister of India in 1991. He changed the direction of domestic economic policies and India became open to the western world. Since the conflict with Israel had abated, the Palestinian cause began losing relevance in India. This helped the Rao government in establishing full **diplomatic relations with Israel** in 1992. Nevertheless, even though Indians were increasing in numbers and importance in every field in the Gulf, India's diplomatic ties and trade relations remained tepid at best. Risk aversion continued to overshadow India's approach in the Middle East and the governments could not de-hyphenate bilateral political relations with nations from Pakistan. Relations with Israel improved during the NDA government 1998-2004 and Israeli Prime Minister Ariel Sharon visited India in 2003. However, after the Congress came back to power in 2004, the relations were again put on a back burner for domestic Muslim vote bank politics.

## MODI DIPLOMACY

It was only after Narendra Modi became the Prime Minister in 2014 that India's relations with the Middle East went through a paradigm shift. Thus, was done by Modi by establishing personal relations with the heads of the governments, especially with the rulers of the Gulf States, and one-to-one personal relations matter a lot for the autocrats, especially for the Arabs. While Manmohan Singh, as the PM of the UPA government (2004-14), visited the Middle East merely four times during his ten year tenure, Modi has made countless visits to the Middle East as a part of his 'extended neighbourhood' policy.

Modi's most significant achievement has been to **delink India's bilateral relations** with the individual nations from the Middle East politics, especially from the Arab-

Israel relations. Modi visited Israel in July 2017 and was the first Indian PM do so. In February 2018 he went to Ramallah and became the first Indian PM to visit Palestine. It was to declare that while India would have good relations with Israel, it also stood for Palestine, and that the two were not mutually exclusive. President Mahmoud Abbas of Palestine paid a return visit to India the same year affirming India's commitment to Palestine. Modi thus exposed the irrelevance of the belief that a neutral nation like India cannot be friendly with Israel and the Arab nations at the same time. Strategic partnerships do not necessitate India to commit to support partners in their own conflicts. It offers India the flexibility to continue economic and political cooperation with competing rivals in the Middle East at the same time. This position has now been accepted by the Middle East nations.

Fortunately, this stand coincided with the gradual easing of relations between the UAE and Israel, which ultimately culminated in the signing of the Abraham Accords 2020. This helped India strengthen its ties with Israel as well as with Arab nations. Today, **Israel** is India's second-largest supplier of sophisticated military hardware, software, and defence technology systems. The relationship has also moved beyond defence and security. Israel has provided technologies in many fields like agriculture. Indian tech companies find Israel's high-tech economy and culture of innovation suitable for investments. There is also extensive co-operation in counter terrorism, intelligence sharing, and cyber security.

**Modi has given special attention to the GCC nations**. Modi's visit to UAE in August 2015 was the first by an Indian PM in 34 years and his visit to Bahrain in August 2019 was the first ever made by an Indian PM. The bilateral relationship between Israel and India is no longer an issue of concern for the Gulf nations and they also associate closely with USA. Hence, the Gulf States also have responded positively considering India's economic growth, potential market for trade and investment, political influence as a major regional military power, and commitment to neutrality and non-interference. The deepening of India-Gulf relations is thus as much an outcome of India extending a friendly hand towards the Gulf as it is about the Gulf States too reaching out towards India. As a result, the relationship is becoming mutually beneficial and extending into new fields beyond economics.

Modi's diplomacy has strengthened political relationships and developed trust and willingness to work together on sensitive issues of strategic dimensions. Modi has thus transformed India's relationship with the Gulf States from one that focused on oil to that which includes trade, investment, defence and security cooperation, including counter-terrorism, and maritime security through naval cooperation in the Arabian Sea and the Gulf. Of course, it has to be said that Modi's success has been backed by India's growing economy. India's standing in the Gulf is best reflected by the fact that Modi has been decorated with the highest civilian honours from many Gulf countries. In a unique and unprecedented instance of diplomatic success, Qatar freed eight Indian nationals in February 2024 who had been sentenced to death allegedly for spying.

## INDIA-GCC RELATIONS

India and the GCC States are critically important for each other in several fields. Both have multiple opportunities as well as challenges ahead.

**Energy security** is among the foremost of these. The Gulf countries are major oil and gas producers and India is heavily dependent on imports. Although India's dependence on the Gulf for oil has marginally decreased following Russia's invasion of Ukraine in 2022 as India began importing discounted Russian oil, the Gulf still supplies more than half of India's total crude oil demand. Oil imports from Russia are uncertain and dependency on the Gulf would continue, or may even increase in future. India also needs liquefied natural gas from Qatar.

On the other hand, India is a major exporter of petroleum products due to its surplus refining capacity. Much of India's crude refining capacity has been developed to process crude oil that meets Arabian specifications. Logistically, there is a clear advantage in terms of distance and proximity, especially for the refineries located on the west coast of India. Thus, oil trade with the Gulf will continue for long.

However, the Gulf States realise that with pressure mounting about climate change, total dependency on oil money may not be sustainable in the long run. Fossil fuels would in any case not last till eternity. Hence, transition of the economy away from reliance on hydrocarbons is necessary. India is pioneering in the field of renewal energy and cooperation in this field would be mutually beneficial for all. Saudi Arabia has launched "Vision 2030", which seeks to reduce the Kingdom's reliance on oil production, Bahrain has emerged as a regional hub for banking, and the UAE has diversified into multiple fields.

**Economic Cooperation** hence becomes very important for both. The GCC is India's largest regional-bloc trading partner and trade is significantly more than that with the EU. India seeks to diversify commercial relations and boost bilateral non-oil trade with the Gulf nations. Indian businesses have also entered various sectors such as construction, real estate, finance, education, and tourism. Indian companies have become competitive in securing infrastructure contracts in Arab nations and Arab companies have secured mutually beneficial energy deals in India. The Gulf has lucrative markets for Indian goods. With millions of Indian working there, the market is already available for Indian products. UAE and India have also agreed to conduct trade in their own currencies instead of the dollar. A Free Trade Agreement is also being negotiated with the GCC.

The Gulf nations are rich and thus have substantial **investment potential.** They have some of the largest sovereign wealth funds in the world and are now looking towards large and rapidly growing markets like India where they can make long-term investments which will provide the best returns. With India becoming an increasingly attractive economic market, Saudi Arabia, Qatar, and the UAE, have announced ambitious targets of foreign direct investment in India in strategic and non-oil sectors like renewable energy and AI for digital transformation.

The **India-Middle East-Europe Economic Corridor** (IMEEC) is an initiative unveiled by PM Modi at the G20 Leaders' Summit hosted by India in September 2023 as a part of the "Link West" policy. The proposed corridor is to connect India to Europe via the Middle East, including through the UAE, Saudi Arabia and Israel, by rail and by sea. The initiative is supported by France, Germany, Italy, the EU, and USA, and is considered as an alternative, or counter, to China's Belt and Road program. The project has also been supported by the G7 during the summit of June 2024. On the face of it, the project seems to be impractical and unviable, and may never see the light of the day due to regional conflicts and problems of transportation through multi-modal means involving multiple transhipments. Nevertheless, the very fact that Gulf nations have agreed to the notion shows the inclination towards collaboration.

India's improving relations in the Middle East is being viewed favourably by USA for securing its own shaky position in the Middle East. This has led to the formation of **I2U2** in 2021 that brought together India, Israel, UAE and USA on the same platform with a vision of a "New Middle East". The proposed India–Middle East–Europe Economic Corridor is a further step in the direction and many Western powers are facilitating the deepening of India's relationship with the Middle East.

The **Indian Diaspora** has played an important role in India-Gulf relations. The Gulf nations house millions of Indians who help in building infrastructure in the Gulf. Their remittances back home helps Indian economy in return. Strengthening ties with the Gulf nations benefits Indian workers by providing them state welfare and protection, and creates employment opportunities by easing labour migration. India's expatriate community has led to increased people-to-people contacts, cultural exchanges and tourism, which in turn has improved mutual understanding and goodwill between the nations. The new Hindu temple in UAE inaugurated by Modi in February 2024 is recognition of the role of Indian diaspora as much as a signal of Gulf's advance towards moderation.

India's developing relations with **Saudi Arabia** have special and multilayered implications. Saudi Arabia is India's fourth-largest trading partner due import of crude oil. Both nations also share intelligence regarding terrorism. Saudi Arabia's friendship has helped India in improving relations with other nations in the Middle

East. Domestically also, having good relations with this wealthy and influential centre of Islam is beneficial to India.

## CHALLENGES IN THE MIDDLE EAST

India needs to sustain strategic convergence and cooperation in the Middle East spanning political, economic and security interests. India stands to gain much by broadening its relations with the Gulf, but it faces challenges of a deteriorating security environment.

India's relations with **Iran** are becoming more and more complicated. Ever since the Islamic revolution of 1979, Iran has been in conflict with USA. In 2019, USA imposed economic sanctions against Iran due to its nuclear program. This compelled India to cease its crude oil imports from Iran. China did not care about the US sanctions. Hence China grabbed the opportunity and began importing oil in a big way from Iran. This brought Iran closer to China which is a cause of worry for India.

Iran nevertheless maintains good relations with India. It allows transit of Indian goods to Central Asia and Afghanistan. The two nations are also cooperating to develop the Chabahar Port for this traffic. However, Iran's Islamic extremism is creating problems for its own regime as well as for its international relations. In 2020, Iran made adverse comments regarding India's revocation of Article 370. Iran's alliance with terrorist organisations like the Hamas, Hezbollah, and the Houthis are also problematic. Iran's growing ties with China are another hurdle. India is also concerned about Iran developing an atom bomb.

The Islamic regime of Iran is itself sitting on a time bomb. With discontent mounting among the masses about the deteriorating economic conditions - a result of US economic sanctions - and repressive measures in the name of preserving the purity of Islam, the regime may take the gamble of entering into a major conflict with Israel so as to control the domestic situation. This will be globally destabilising and India can do little about it.

In July 2024, Masoud Pezeshkian has become the new President of Iran. He claims to be a reformist. While he may not be able to do much about moral policing due to the overarching command of the Ayatollahs, he may try to get waiver from US sanctions by relaxing its nuclear program because the economic conditions of Iran are in deep distress. How things progress remains to be seen.

The **Pakistan factor** and ISI sponsored terrorism remained an issue in the India-Middle East relations for long. However, the Gulf nations are as worried about terrorism as is India. Further, Pakistan's continuing economic and strategic decline, and domestic political instability, has made it a lot less relevant to the present Gulf geopolitics. Pakistan is today contemptuously looked down upon as a nation of beggars. While the Pak government keeps begging Saudi Arabia for money, the largest numbers of beggars in the Gulf States come from Pakistan. Pakistan is no more a factor in India-Gulf relations.

**China** is also trying to become an important player in the region. Iran's tense relationship with USA and US-China rivalry has made Iran and China natural partners. China has also played a role in bringing Iran and Saudi Arabia - adversaries for long - together. Yet, China has limitations in the Middle East. Firstly, it is nowhere near displacing USA as the lead actor in the Gulf: China is not a viable alternative to USA as far as the region is concerned. Secondly, Gulf nations are rich and do not need Chinese money like Pakistan and Maldives. Lastly, China's relationship with Iran makes it an uneasy partner for the Gulf nations. If Iran continues with its belligerent approach, China would lose its friends as well as its investments in the Gulf.

As regards India is concerned, howsoever deep inroads China tries to make in the Gulf region, it would not affect India's position. Chinese workers can never replace Indians in the region and the multifaceted relationship that has evolved between India and the Gulf can never be replicated by China. However, China would do its best to undermine India in every field. India has to be alert and smart to earn trust in dealing with the Gulf rulers as well as with the peoples.

**Religion** continues to be a sensitive issue in the Middle East. While Modi has successfully delinked religion and Arab-Israel disputes from bilateral relations, the ruling BJP is seen, and is also being purposefully depicted, as anti-Muslim by many, especially by India's opposition parties. But it serves the radical elements abroad well for their own jihadi agenda. Unfortunately, some members of the BJP also make anti-Muslim comments occasionally. This reinforces the perception that the ruling party, and hence India as a nation, is Islamophobic. While the opposition parties will continue with this negative tirade without realising what damage it does to India as a nation, the members of the ruling party have to understand that this is not in India's interest in any way and should take care.

## INDIA AND THE GAZA CRISIS

When the Hamas attacked Israel on 7th October 2023, India's first response was a strong condemnation of the terrorist attack by PM Modi and full support of Israel. This tweet met with severe criticism, not from the foreign governments, but from anti-BJP parties in India. They deplored that India has given up its traditional policy of supporting the Palestinian cause, and that BJP was anti-Muslim. The MEA immediately reacted and reiterated India's historical support of the Palestinians, and that India still held that the two-state solution is the only way out, but India was against terrorism in any form.

While the Hamas poses an existential threat to Israel, and Israel has every right to defend itself, its actions in Gaza are seen as disproportionately severe by the world community, including by its Western allies. They are calling for restraint in attacks on civilians and some way of stopping the war and release of hostages. As the war in Gaza continues, India is constantly assessing the situation and adjusting its stand accordingly by adopting a more nuanced and balanced approach. India has not opposed ceasefire resolutions in the UNO but has opposed resolutions that condemn Israel but remain silent about the Hamas. India has also offered material humanitarian aid for the Gazans. India has thus reasserted its foreign policy of strategic autonomy characterised by its commitment to non-interference and neutrality.

So far, the Gulf nations have accepted India's position. However, the attacks by the Houthis on merchant shipping in the Red Sea since the outbreak of the Hamas-Israel war has added a new dimension to the issue. While India is not an involved party in this conflict, disruption of maritime traffic affects India as much as other nations. This is so because the Gulf region has **geostrategic significance** due to its energy resources as well as due its location at the crossroads of major international trade sea route. Geopolitical rivalries and conflicts in the region and the rise of extremist groups have created challenges for regional stability. These issues can have spill-over effects on India's relations with Gulf countries and pose security threats for Indian citizens residing in the region as well as for India as a nation. It also directly impacts India's energy and security needs.

So far, India has remained silent on the problem as its ships have not been directly attacked. However, **international merchant shipping** has a very complex structure. The ships are owned by companies of one country, these are registered in some other country, carry cargo from a third country to several other countries. The ship's crew belongs to multiple nations, with a large number of Indians. As such, attack on shipping affects many nations. For the present, the companies are rerouting the vessels via the Cape of Good Hope. It has increased the transportation component of the cost of goods and affected the supply chains by delays. On the other hand, USA and Britain have formed a task force to take the Houthis head on.

India has a strong naval presence in the Arabian Sea. However, India has stayed away from the US naval coalition despite an invitation from Washington. Although India is party to IMEC and I2U2, it would avoid getting directly involved in the complex politics of the region. India would rather have its navy patrol in those waters independently and address distress calls when required. India's main aim is to ensure that sea routes remain open and that Indian sailors are protected. The Indian Navy has increased its deployment of warships and is also acting to check piracy and rescue the crew of the hijacked ships irrespective of nationality.

The Houthis will not be permitted to disrupt the maritime traffic through the Red Sea for too long as it affects all nations, especially the Gulf States. Egypt also loses transit revenue of the Suez Canal. To what extent these nations would tolerate what affects their lifeline, and to what limit of brinkmanship Iran would be able to go in this conflict is difficult to predict. So far India is doing a well calibrated balancing act, but if the conflict escalates - in Gaza as well as in the Red Sea - India's diplomatic success would come under serious stress.

❖❖❖❖

# Chapter X

# Vasudhaiva Kutumbakam

The matrix of International Relations is exceedingly complex and in a constant state of flux. While there are conflicts going on in certain parts, much of the world is at peace. While the optimists see a bright future ahead, the pessimists see the light at the end of the tunnel as the headlight of the train coming from the opposite direction. While there is much cooperation around the world, there is also rivalry and competition. Ultimately, people have to reconcile differences, and live with the differences. Because there is no other choice!

The human community of the planet has to live as one family, even if it takes a few more centuries to reach that level of collective maturity. That is where the ancient Indian thought of ***Vasudhaiva Kutumbakam*** becomes the most important objective that peoples across the world need to understand. The concept is being forcefully advocated by the Modi government and it was made the logo of G20 summit held in India in September 2023. It is time the Sanskrit verse of Maha Upanishad becomes the mantra of UNO!

*This one is of mine, that one is of other*
*So says the small minded*
*The magnanimous one says*
*Entire humanity is one family*

❖❖❖❖

# Appendix I

# Nations in the Geographical Regions

**The Balkans** includes Albania, Bosnia, Herzegovina, Bulgaria, Croatia, Kosovo, Montenegro, North Macedonia, Romania, Serbia, and Slovenia.

**Central Asia** stretches from the Caspian Sea in the west to China and Mongolia in the east and from Afghanistan and Iran in the south to Russia in the north. The region consists of the (former Soviet) republics of Kazakhstan, Kyrgyzstan, Tajikistan, Turkmenistan, and Uzbekistan.

**Caucasus** is the region between the Black and Caspian Seas. It consists of Southern Russia, Georgia, Armenia, and Azerbaijan.

**Southeast Asia** consists of the regions that are geographically south of China, east of the Indian subcontinent and north-west of Australia. It includes Brunei, Burma (Myanmar), Cambodia, Timor-Leste, Indonesia, Laos, Malaysia, the Philippines, Singapore, Thailand and Vietnam.

**South Asia** region consists of Afghanistan, Bangladesh, Bhutan, India, the Maldives, Nepal, Pakistan, and Sri Lanka.

**Indo-China** is the peninsular region south of China and comprises of modern day Cambodia, Laos, Malaysia, Myanmar, Thailand and Vietnam.

**Far East** region comprises of China, Japan, North Korea, South Korea, Mongolia, Taiwan, and the easternmost portion of Russian Siberia.

**Middle East** comprises 18 Arab countries including Bahrain, Egypt, Iraq, Jordan,

Kuwait, Lebanon, Libya, Mauritania, Morocco, Oman, Palestine, Qatar, Saudi Arabia, Sudan, Syria, Tunisia, United Arab Emirates and Yemen.

**Near East** basically meant the maximum extent of the Ottoman Empire from Turkey to Egypt.

**Asia Minor**, also referred to as Anatolia, is usually synonymous with Asian Turkey.

❖❖❖❖